Majoring
IN THE
Minors

PATRICK M. SULLIVAN

SAN DIEGO, CALIFORNIA

Published by
Montezuma Publishing
Aztec Shops Ltd.
San Diego State University
San Diego, California 92182-1701
619-594-7552
www.montezumapublishing.com

Copyright © 2020

All Rights Reserved.

ISBN: 978-1-7269-0282-3

Copyright © 2020 author Patrick M. Sullivan. The compilation, formatting, printing and binding of this work is the exclusive copyright of Montezuma Publishing and the author Patrick M. Sullivan. All rights reserved. No part of this work may be reproduced, stored in a retrieval system, or transmitted in any form or by any means, including digital, except as may be expressly permitted by the applicable copyright statutes or with written permission of the Publisher or Author.

Publishing Manager: Lia Dearborn
Cover Design: Angelica Lopez
Design and Layout: Lia Dearborn and Angelica Lopez
Formatting: Angelica Lopez

Contents

1. The Edge of a Baseball 5
2. On the Inside Looking In 11
3. By the Book 15
4. A Minor Miracle 21
5. Minor League, Minor Cost, Major Fun 25
6. "How Many to Go?" 29
7. The Designs, the Names,
   the Nicknames, and the Zaniness 35
8. The Structure 39
9. What's Your Favorite? 51
10. Rickwood Field 53
11. *Gets*, *Go-Backs* and *Rebuilts* 57
12. The Ballparks/The Teams 63
13. Epilogue: Is a Quantum Shift Coming? 289

THE EDGE OF A BASEBALL

People who've only known me as an adult probably assume my pacifier was a baseball. People who've only known me since 1972 know me as both an umpire and a play-by-play announcer. People who've only known me since 2011 know of my project to see a game in every Minor League park. People who've only known me since 2015 know I have done that.

My introduction to *the* baseball was a little later than my pacifier days, playing Five Dollars with the neighbor kids in a vacant lot at the end of our street. It was a hard-knock introduction. A year or two later, when I was twelve, I played Little League.

See, I wasn't very good at either. I'm roughly as good with a bat or a ball as Ralphie, in the film *A Christmas Story*, is with a BB gun – and I don't mean in the dream sequence.

We played a lot of Five Dollars down there. A dozen kids or more at a time would crowd one end of that lot, awaiting the batter's fungo from the other end.

If you're not familiar with this national non-pastime, it's played with a bat and ball but no bases. (Maybe it should be called baseless-ball.) The people trying to catch the ball aren't teammates but competitors. The batter tosses the ball up and hits it toward this august group, and there are no rules about how they jostle for it. If the batter delivers a good high fly ball, it comes down to something resembling a rugby scrum. Because of the scoring system, this is less true once the ball grounds.

Catching the batted ball on the fly gets you a dollar. (I should say here no money actually changes hands; I don't want to send the police down that street looking for illegal activity.) A catch on one bounce earns seventy-five cents. Two bounces, four bits. Three or more, including rolling, is a quarter. Picking up a ball that has stopped, or as they say in the actual game of baseball "rolled dead," nets nothing. These also apply in the negative; a muff costs whatever would have been earned. Some kids stayed outside the scrum and went for the missed ones; two one-hoppers that way is worth more than one on-the-fly catch with a lot less risk to the body. Me, I was in the scrum.

As you – especially those of you who know the card game Blackjack – may have deduced, earning five dollars wins the round for the fielder, and with it the next turn at bat.

I don't remember ever earning such a turn. I do remember getting a head thumping once. I was directly under a sky-high fly; I couldn't have missed it if I tried. I'm getting jostled a bit but am holding my ground, glove high ahead of the catch, when another glove appears over my head from my right and momentarily blocks not just the ball but the whole blue sky. I lower my face – don't ask me why, but I'm glad I did – and the ball landed right on my skull. I don't know if the invader pulled back or just missed the reaching catch. I do know that hard knock hurt. For days. We also had a rousing shouting match about whether that ball hitting me on the head should have cost me a dollar. The way I learned the game, on that field with those kids, it had to be a failed catch – not just bouncing off of the body. Not all of us remembered it that way. Try to find a set of written rules – at least in those pre-Internet days!

OK, let's try a real game with real rules: Little League.

A word about "Little League" – I'm sure *official* Little League Baseball won't like what I'm about to say, and sexagenarian me respects that as a business matter, but the fact is my little hometown had an independent recreational youth league it called Little League. So sue … somebody.

How long ago was this? We heard the bat crack, not clang – but I think mine was the last season (our) league used wooden ones.

Of course, I was the kid they stuck in right field and batted once a game. I say that without bitterness. I couldn't field, I couldn't throw, and I couldn't hit; outside of that, I was a helluva ballplayer. Hitting, especially. Know how some people can't hit a fastball and some people can't hit a curveball? I couldn't hit a baseball.

I can't swear this is true, but I believe I struck out every time but one – and the exception was the only time I remember putting a bat on a ball that whole season. It was late in the year – it would be the last inning of the last game if this were Hollywood, but this isn't and it wasn't – and we had a runner on third with less than two out. I only remember that because of what happened. I don't remember the score or if there were any other runners or how many outs there were. I don't even remember the count. I do remember doing something very fundamentally sound in baseball – completely by accident, of course, I hit behind the runner. A pitch came in and I took my usual wildly undisciplined swing. There went the ball dribbling toward first base! I was so surprised I didn't run immediately; I only remember that because I remember becoming aware of voices screaming *"Run!"* and *"Go!"* Writing this today, I wonder for the first time if I cost myself an infield single. The first baseman fielded the ball inside the baseline and beat me to the bag by at least fifteen feet, but how long had I stood there?

Ah, well. The runner scored from third. Possibly before I left the home plate circle.

I made my way to the bench, dejectedly, and was greeted with "Way to go!" Eyes on the ground, I said, "Guys, I'm still hitting zero-zero-zero." That's when our coach said, "You drove in a run!" It is perhaps a measure of how bad I was that such was delivered for a weak infield out, even if it did score a run. It couldn't have been a big run, or I'd remember that.

Bless that coach. I never met him before baseball, but when one of my aunts heard who was coaching me she told me they were old friends. Coach only had one batting signal. At the time, I didn't know that was unusual; having since learned a bit about baseball, I can only guess he was trying to keep the game simple for us. His one sign was: "Look at me before you get in the box.

If my hand is on my belt buckle, I want you to bunt." I don't ever remember remembering to do that during that entire season. At one at-bat a game, of course, "the entire season" would be about a dozen plate appearances. It must have been forty to fifty pitches, though, and I don't think I remembered to look for a sign once. Coach never berated me for that, but he never even said a word about it to me. I'm sure I missed many a bunt sign; if he'd have bunted anybody, he'd have bunted me. Poor guy must have thought I was uncoachable. Probably correctly. I hope I've improved on that personality flaw since.

Over the years and writing now, I think I pretty much mentally blacked out every time I went to the plate. Good hitters say they block out, but they're talking about avoiding distractions. I'm talking about putting so much pressure on myself I couldn't think. That didn't seem to happen on defense, but I neither remember catching a ball on the fly or not catching one I could have. Of course, when I got to the rolling ball I often had no idea what to do with it.

I do remember Coach once saying he might put me on the mound. It was after we won the last game of the next-to-last week of the season. We had two games coming in the last week, and he said he might put me "out there" in the first of those. Now, I get that his point was the second game was so much more important than the first to our standings – but I actually started thinking maybe I could pitch. I couldn't hit a cutoff man from the outfield, but maybe I could hit the catcher's mitt from a lot closer. This is a product of too many TV shows and movies featuring a nobody who becomes a somebody just before the sun goes down and he rides off into it. (The films *The Man who Shot Liberty Valance* and *Unforgiven* together illustrate the difference very well. If you haven't seen them, I highly recommend both.)

We did win the league that season. I say that for the sake of historical accuracy, not because I had anything to do with it.

I even went out for the high school team when I got there. Crazy. And cut crazy fast.

I wasn't learning much about strategy from all this, but then our hometown's favorite Major League team had a big season that brought me two huge discoveries: Major League Baseball, and the fact that you could "see" it on the radio.

Despite having less talent than anyone else I ever saw pick up a bat or a glove, I had fallen hopelessly in love with the game. Our hometown was about two hours from the MLB club we all followed, and I listened to almost every contest – even the ones three time zones behind us, even (when I could get away with it) on school nights. That went on the next year, too, when I used up six C.S. Peterson scorebooks. (I would improve on its system – recording things the system doesn't, like the sequence of pitches toward the final count, pick-off attempts, and on which pitch a stolen base or balk happened. I could today reconstruct a complete play-by-play from one of my scoresheets. No, I've never done that…but I could.) I learned a lot of strategy seeing it on the radio, but in hindsight I learned precious little about execution.

Nevertheless, my life was now on an unalterable course. Well, two parallel courses: I was going to love baseball; I was going to make my living describing games to fans who couldn't be there.

If this were a Hollywood script, you would be about to read about my MLB play-by-play career. Well, it isn't a Hollywood script. A baseball may be round but it must have an edge – because from my pre-teens on I've lived my entire life on it.

On the Inside Looking In

Come spring, I came out when the city recreation department called for volunteer coaches.

As I mentioned, I had learned a lot about strategy, but execution was a whole 'nuther thing. Soon I was the field manager of a team with players aged ten to twelve. Perhaps remembering my own coach's belt buckle, I drew up an extremely rudimentary playbook. You're here; the ball is hit here; here's what you do. The whole thing ran two pages and one of those had a diagram of the defense on the field. There was some really good talent on that team, and I imagine the best of them thought they knew more about the game than their skipper. They probably did. If I had a do-over, I'd probably hold back less and listen more.

As manager, coaching third base fell to me. I had about as much skill judging throws against runners' footspeed as I'd had judging fly balls to right field. I don't remember any glaring mistakes that actually cost us anything, but I was as uncomfortable out there as I had been while trying to hit. There was a play when I held a runner at third because the outfielder was two steps from the ball when it landed, but then he uncorked a towering wild throw. Intended for home plate, it was actually heading toward our bench between home and first. Eye on the ball but being too careful, I didn't release the runner until everyone was screaming for me to do so. That throw had the insolence to hit the screen at least twenty feet above our cheering players. That's in play, though, so it's a good thing I (we) sent him.

I had a dark moment that season. We had only nine players show up to one game, barely missing a forfeit, and afterward I decided to sit the guys down and talk about that. I was unconsciously modeling myself on Sgt. Carter of TV's *Gomer Pyle*. One of the parents came to me afterward and said, "You don't seem to understand you were talking to the kids who *did* come." Good point!

After the season, I asked the Rec Director to move me up to the thirteen-to-fifteen league the next year. Today, I can't tell you why I asked for it. Looking back now, I know I did not have the makings of a coach. Then, I guess I was still thinking of Hollywood scripts. Nor do I know what the Rec Director was thinking when he gave it to me. I suppose he had exactly as many new volunteers as he had openings.

So now I'm coaching guys who are as little as a year younger than I, probably every one of whom could play the game better than I. About the only thing I remember worth noting of the rest of that season was defying baseball tradition: I coached first instead of third.

Maybe I do know why I went for it. Thinking back, I remember how much more I loved what many of us came to call "real" baseball. No offense meant, that's the term my generation used to differentiate leagues that allow leadoffs from those that don't. Perhaps the greatest rite of passage into a boy's teens was leading off.

For reasons that will soon become clear, let me mention here that at this point I had never seen a rule book. My rules knowledge was based solely on what I'd learned seeing games on radio and TV. Our league kept a rule book in the building that doubled as a league office and ballpark shed. I'm not sure I even knew that when I was coaching, so it was probably just there for umpires.

Speaking of umpires, let me also say I don't remember ever getting into an argument with an ump in either of those two seasons of coaching.

By the end of that second season, I knew I had no more business running a ball club than playing on one.

Luckily, the still-going big-league season soon put a different idea in my head. I was seeing a game on the radio when a catcher-interference call on an apparently unsuccessful attempt to steal home handed the game to my favorite team's arch-rival. Our broadcaster, whom I had perceived as very fair and also rules-knowledgeable, was absolutely confounded. As was I, until I thought: Wait a sec. As an umpire in the Majors, presumably as much at the pinnacle of his profession as a *player* in the Majors, how could he possibly have been that wrong?

No Internet in those days, nor did the local library have a rule book. To my surprise, not every sporting goods store carried them. I finally found one that did, and quickly thumbed through a copy. *Official Baseball Rules* being laid out well with a table of contents and an index, I found the rule quickly enough that no clerk suggested I buy the book or put it back.

While I hadn't literally seen the play, there was no room for doubt the call could have been correct. And my broadcaster friend would have had virtually no vantage point to decide even if he knew the rule. If the catcher's reach forward took away the batter's ability to hit, that was catcher interference.

That thought was quickly shoved aside by another. *Umpiring.* Maybe I could be an umpire.

I know many coaches think umpires get into umpiring because they like to control things. Anybody who saw me go Sgt. Carter on my kids would probably be sure of that. It wasn't that way at all. I saw it as a way to be a part of the game I loved and actually contribute to it.

I paid for the *OBR*, took it straight home and read it cover to cover.

BY THE BOOK

For more than forty years, that book and its successors were within my physical reach an alarming amount of the time. If I was driving, it was in the car. If I was working, it was in the car if it wasn't in the workplace. It accompanied me to that room we all use but try not to mention. I read it again and again and again.

While I liked to think this made me a student of the rules, it was in one way a negative. I had to learn the gray areas by talking with and observing other umpires, but before I could do that I had to accept that there *were* gray areas. I knew from seeing games on the radio and especially the TV that first basemen could cheat a bit in stepping off the bag while catching an infielder's throw to put the batter out, a tag had to be pretty obviously late to be called late, and more balks are not called than are called – but I was having none of that. Its beautiful rules were part of this beautiful game, and I wasn't going to trifle with them.

They *are* beautiful, but I will say they're a tough read. It's said that's because they were written by lawyers. While I have no evidence either way, I don't think they were written by lawyers. I think they were written by athletes trying to write like lawyers, and I think that's why they're such a tough read.

Digesting and re-digesting the *OBR* wasn't the only thing keeping me from graying up. From a variety of evidence with which I'll not bore you, I've accepted that I have one of the most black-and-white brains on the planet.

So, I learned to umpire by watching games, mostly on TV, in the remaining weeks of that big-league season and the post-season. I got the positioning down quickly and, if I say so myself well (not that it's hard), but it's harder to learn stance and other mechanics that way. I don't mean to belittle my hometown, but we had no training program at all. I went to the same rec guy who agreed to my coaching and said, "I'd like to be an umpire" and he pointed at me and said, "OK, you're an umpire." Literally.

I now realize it took me a few years to become even decent. One call in my very first game almost made me quit, when the batter took an oh-two pitch that was over the point of the plate right at the knees. I called it a ball, and I knew immediately I was wrong. I did learn a lesson, realizing that happened because I knew pitchers are taught to waste an oh-two pitch in the hope of a stupid-swing strikeout. My next thought was, "Call what you see and not what you expect" – a lesson thoroughly driven home when the batter homered on the next pitch. This still isn't Hollywood, but that was the only run of that game. *I* did that.

Not having had any control over what I was seeing on TV screens, I didn't get to see enough platework to learn much – not even where to set up, because at that time the two leagues did that differently. I chose the National League way, on the inside corner. Initially, I did my vertical alignment on the batter's belt but would later learn better from a partner who eventually worked in the Majors. I also remember that if a pitch was headed outside, I'd shift over so I could line up the ball's location with the outside corner. That might make sense to those who've never umpired, but it will make those who have cringe. I'm glad I caught sage advice from partners to correct those and other flaws.

Sometimes I had to learn from an arguing coach. Chief among these is when I missed a play at first that had the first baseman, the pitcher trying to cover and the batter-runner all arrive at nearly the same time; I got to hear a coach say in these exact words "You missed that one" and explain to me that you watch the feet and the bag and listen for the ball to hit the mitt. That said, and also saying you can't do something for decades without improving, I became – based on feedback and assignments – a pretty good ump. Still, that is not the way to learn.

I would also learn to gray up.

I don't recall anyone but me ever declining to award a base to a batter who'd been hit by a pitch for not trying to avoid it, but I did so probably a dozen times in my forty-plus years. That *is* a rule, but calling it *begs* controversy. Most umps say to call it only if the batter actually leans into the pitch – but even though they say that, I've never seen anyone but me call it at all. I had one batter argue with me by demonstrating that he twitched – "I went like that" – and I said, "If that's an effort to get out of the way I want to see your effort to hit the ball." I never could stop myself from calling it if a guy just stood stock still and took one, but if my colleagues were being literal they would not call even those. I did stop so closely calling a guy stepping a little out of the box on a swing. I learned to give the early step-off at first base, one of several such we call neighborhood calls, and not to call non-obvious balks. Only once did I try to expand the strike zone. This might have come with practice, but I was so inconsistent that day I decided I needed the visible references – the edges of the plate and the strike zone borders extended from the batter's body. On all but the last, I evolved because I grew to understand the need for consistency among umpires; on the last, I thought it more important to maintain consistency within myself.

All that said, for all my career and considering that my real work took me around the country for most of my life, fellow umpires and coaches would quickly assess my strength as rules guru and my weakness as too by the book on the field.

I never had any designs on becoming a professional umpire – well, while umpires of amateur games who are paid are professional umpires, you get my drift – but I did literally thousands of games from (actual) Little League up to college ball. My last few years were happily engaged in Men's Senior League Baseball, happily working with guys who were happily playing baseball not softball – some of whom *were* ex-Major Leaguers.

During my umpiring days, I got the idea of capturing some of the many conversations I'd had about rules and umpiring. I polished it for years and finally published it in 2017.

Most of my professional career was in radio. Although my day job was rarely sportscasting, I did manage to get in many years behind the microphone at high school and a few college games. In fact, I did my first baseball play-by-play at the age of fifteen; someone from the station actually had to drive me to the away games. I did more football and basketball than baseball, unfortunately, because those are the scholastic money sports.

Being an American male of my generation, my mindset was to emulate my dad, at least in non-job matters. (I never had his mechanical talent.) So, after a hitch in the military, toward the end of which I got married, followed by a hitch in college, toward the end of which we had a baby, I found myself working more for money than for passion.

There was a moment, though. When that marriage ended, I bore down on baseball. The next year I was doing play-by-play in the low Minors, but I may have the record for being the oldest debuting PBP announcer in pro baseball history. I would do two more seasons, and a couple of stadium PA, but simply could not earn enough of a living to keep at it.

In another odd confluence, the last of those years also saw Major League games canceled by strike for the last time. (Unless what's fermenting at this writing creates one in 2022.)

I love the game. Perhaps I haven't managed to convey how much I love the game. More than twenty years later, I remember the feeling in the pit of my stomach when I finally accepted there was going to be no World Series in *that* ugly struck season.

I decided – sometimes I say I swore, but to be accurate I didn't actually speak an oath or touch a Bible – never again to watch a Major League Baseball game.

I had a better idea.

A Minor Miracle

Soon after I discovered big-league ball, I learned of its feeder system from broadcasters' references to players "coming up from our farm club at such-and-such." In fact, I remember listening to my favorite big-league team play its Class Triple-A club in one of those infrequent exhibitions.

US professional baseball teams play in one of these kinds of leagues:

1. Major League Baseball – the National and American leagues

2. Minor League Baseball – the seventeen leagues whose teams develop players for MLB teams

    a. Affiliated baseball – the top fourteen of these leagues, most of whose teams are independent profit-seeking operations that contract with an MLB team to develop its prospects

    b. Complex leagues – the three entry-level Rookie leagues, whose teams are all owned and operated by their MLB parent, do not charge admission or sell concessions, and usually play not in a professional baseball stadium but on a side field of one

3. Organized baseball – 1) and 2) together

4. Independent baseball – leagues, some of them decommissioned MiLB circuits, whose teams sign and pay (so, yes, professional) players who may or may not have been drafted but are not currently signed by an MLB team

Everyone knows MLB as the acronym for Major League Baseball; another good one to know here is MiLB: Minor League Baseball. MiLB's business model has a different and very specific challenge: I knew they existed, but it never even occurred to me to go see such a game – even though there were three within ninety miles of my hometown and the nearest MLB club was 110 miles away. It's like the cola wars. I like the taste of the number three cola more than either of the big two, but their marketing (like on ballpark scoreboards!) keeps them so top-of-mind, I hardly ever think to grab the one I like best. (Yes, I can tell the difference, to my ex-wife's chagrin; insisting that wasn't possible, she once challenged me to a taste test, and I named all three of them.)

My ignoring MiLB wasn't the snobbery I would later hear from a fellow fan during my long boycott of MLB. I accidentally generated a debate by posting about this in one of the old online newsgroups, and part of the exchange went like this:

Him: You should watch the Majors.

Me: How about I watch what I want to watch, and you watch what you want to watch?

Him: It's better in the Majors.

Me: Do you love the game, or the players? I love the game.

Him: But you're not watching it at its best.

Me: Who cares? Watching *it* is the best.

Reading back over that now, I'm not too sure he didn't win the exchange, logically. I almost wrote "not too sure he wasn't right," but for me no logic supersedes personal preference. If I'd rather watch MiLB, for any reason from its cheaper cost to a lost World Series to just because, that's that. Same for him; I wasn't trying to get him to abandon the Majors, just telling him why I had and that I wasn't lost without it.

I took in my first Minor League game the year before I first worked in the Minors. It happened pretty much by accident. Using a multi-course golf card I'd bought from a charity, I played a round near Toledo. Being about as good at golf as I am at baseball, I got done much later than I expected and decided to stay the night. After

I checked into a motel, it hit me out of the blue that Toledo had a minor-league baseball team called the Mud Hens! It was too late to think about going that evening, but I pulled the phone book from the nightstand and dialed (yes, dialed) the phone. A live person (yes, live) answers, of whom I ask, "Are you home tomorrow?" "Yes, sir, playing the Syracuse Chiefs." "Got room for one more?" She actually chuckles before saying, "Yes, sir, come on out."

So, after I checked out of the Toledo motel that Sunday, I headed for its suburb of Maumee.

The Hens played there in those days, in a big boxlike ballpark that was normal for that level in that time. The bigs were still playing in what had come to be called cookie-cutter, flying-saucer or donut ballparks, and if I coined a similar term for these it would be cake-box ballparks. This was neither a positive or a negative, though. To crisscross Shakespeare and Doyle, "The game is the thing."

The place wasn't packed but was far from empty. It held well over 10,000, based on which I wouldn't be surprised if there were five or six thousand there that day. I remember being reminded of a county fair, from enough vendors along the concourse to make me think of a midway.

I made a beer and food run, bought a game program, and settled into my seat. I didn't have a scorebook with me, of course, and decided not to try to keep score on the much simpler scorecard in the program. I wish differently now. Wouldn't I love to have a scorecard of that game? I did buy a postcard that included a photo of the jam-packed stands at the first game played there – Lucas County Stadium at the time, and Ned Skeldon Stadium when I visited. I still have that postcard.

I wish I'd kept a scorecard not just as a souvenir but because I'd love to set up the wow finish for you. My memory says Syracuse broke to an early lead, the Mud Hens closed but didn't quite catch up, the Chiefs widened the gap, and Toledo finally tied it late. What I know for sure is they went to the bottom of the ninth tied at six. I don't remember how many outs the Chiefs managed to get, but I do remember the Hens loaded the bases and then got a game-ending (the term walk-off wasn't around yet) grand slam. I think their first baseman jacked it. It was a major thrill.

When I'm sitting in an oak-paneled study or around a hot stove talking baseball, I claim to be a purist who loves a good pitching duel with great defense. When I say that, I mean it. I think a difficult double-play is easily as beautiful as a monster home run, and a lot more dramatic. The trouble with slugfests is they're usually as one-sided as a ball you know is gone when it leaves the bat. Let me see a nip-and-tuck game any day.

That's the thing about me, though: I have also told people, quite honestly, that I have never found myself bored or unhappy at a baseball game. Now, a bad moment for my team of preference makes me unhappy, but not in the sense of wishing I weren't there. Just, I wish I hadn't seen that.

By the time the strike happened, I had seen Minor League games in twelve other ballparks – the first at which I worked, the ten I soon got doing play-by-play, and part of one nearby higher-level game our road crew took in when ours was rained out.

So, with a viable alternative, I could turn my back on the Majors without turning my back on the game I love.

MINOR LEAGUE, MINOR COST, MAJOR FUN

My live-game gap actually started in 1990, the last year I happened to go to a big-league game before the strike. After that, I didn't see a single MLB game in person – and if I saw one on TV, with a brief period of exceptions, it was because I wasn't in control of the set – until 2014.

(If you're wondering how such a big baseball fan could have gone even four years without seeing an MLB game, that was financially based. My team was, at that time in my life, more than two and a half hours away by car and not cheap.)

Based on the number of people who greeted learning of this quarter-century of self-denial with surprise, skepticism and even sadness, I understand I'm in a small minority versus normal (read: MLB) fans. First, I wonder how many of them have even tried the Minors option and, second, how many are so committed to the Majors for the same reason I was: marketing-driven top-of-mind awareness.

I am not trying to convince anyone to switch to the Minors. Conversely, I don't like it when people act as if I've made some concession. The highest-priced seat I've ever sat in that was in my favorite spot – to the right of behind the plate, where the third base line, if extended, would run right to me; great view of the right-handed hitter and the play at the plate – for a Minors game was $27. That was in Sacramento, CA – not only Triple-A ball (one step below the Majors) but one of the Minors' finest and top-drawing stadiums. In the low Minors, that ticket can be as little as $5. Since I finally did start going to the Majors again (we'll get to that) I paid nearly $50 for a seat in Oakland that was probably a quarter of the way toward first base from that spot, and I paid more than $150 for a seat in San Francisco that was right on that line but in an upper level. That was the high/low of the MLB games I've seen in this millennium.

I know this is going to make me sound like my own grandpa, but teen-aged me at big-league games paid eight bucks for my seat – even in today's money, that's less than $50 – and two bucks to park!

The price *should* be higher in the bigs, of course, but are the big guys really worth *that* differential? Your call; personally, I have more than enough fun at a Minor League game to enjoy not paying the big price – and that doesn't count the ancillaries. I could have spent $50 just to park at San Fran, but that lot was full; I paid $20 and walked almost a mile. I spent over $200 that day, without buying a souvenir and with some wondering if I could ever have taken the family of my married days to a game there.

I find the Minors to be every bit the same wonderful game but a better bargain. I can't honestly say I'd have ever dumped the bigs solely for those reasons, given that I didn't even think about that after the Toledo game, but I can say I never missed MLB in all the years I ignored it. The only exception I made was during the 1998 McGwire-Sosa home-run derby. I caught some of those games on TV – to see history, only to realize later I'd instead been watching scandal.

I don't mean to sound condescending, but I just love the game while many seem to love the players. It's the players I hear people buzzing about, not the game experience. While I do enjoy seeing the greats play great, it just doesn't seem possible for me not to enjoy any baseball game. On the other hand, I can see that if you like to follow specific players then the Minors – where the better a player is the sooner he gets promoted – isn't the place to do it.

My boycott did cause me to lose all track of the bigs. There was (of course) a time I could throw you the current standings, every World Series winner and loser since 1903, and a lot of individual stats about my team plus a good bit of the other teams in its league. By 2002, I had lost all that. I remember that because that summer, a co-worker and I had an exchange during which he seemed embarrassed for me while I felt nothing short of proud.

We were in the bar/restaurant atop a Minor League stadium when the starting eights were announced for the Major League All-Star Game. To my (pleasant) surprise, looking at that big-screen TV, I recognized one name on each side. I mentioned this to my colleague, a long-time Cardinal fan. I knew one because he had played at my favorite university, the other because he had transcended baseball into pop culture and become A-Rod. My friend, looking up and down the names, asked who I *did* know. I told him. I could see him taking another run through the lists as if to confirm something. Then he turned to me and said, "You don't know who Albert Pujols is?" I literally, but not maliciously, said, "Who?" "He was the National League Rookie of the Year last year!" I smiled, maybe slightly maliciously, and said, "And I've been ignoring the Majors for years." We not only managed to stay friends but kept going to games together. I've heard him tell this story on me, and he doesn't tell it with malice. At least, not when I'm around.

Reminding you that my work had me traveling and even moving a lot, it became natural for me to hit any nearby Minor League park in which I hadn't seen a game. There was no intent beyond that at the time, but it would give me a head start later.

After those first thirteen stadiums, I contented myself with umpiring four to seven days a week and didn't see another minor-league game until I took two side trips while umpiring a national tournament in upstate New York in 2002. Once I got the idea, though, I piled them up. At that time, the "idea" was just to see games at whatever Minor League parks were convenient to wherever my work travels might take me. The *other* idea was a while away.

In keeping with my idea of seeing whatever games I could get to from wherever I was laying my head at the time, I was settling in for a game at Hank Aaron Stadium in Hoover, AL, on Saturday evening, July 9, 2011. The idea *may* have been taking subconscious root; on the drive there from Birmingham an interstate mileage sign made me realize New Orleans was only a couple of hours beyond Mobile. I had intended to stay the night in Mobile, also see the Sunday game there, and then drive back to Birmingham. Now, my brain churned. *Are the Zephyrs home? If so, that'll make a five-hour drive back; this can only work if they're playing a day game.* Using my smartphone to ascertain both were so, I literally changed plans on the fly.

Short-term plans, that is. I wasn't looking for anything more than a game in another stadium. I wasn't looking for a project, either, but one was about to hand itself to me.

"How Many to Go?"

Because now we had ... social media.

I was completely ready for the originally planned game in Mobile before it was ready for me. Aiming to arrive early has its benefits. Of course, you have less chance of missing the first pitch. You also get closer parking and shorter if any concession lines. It's nice to eat without rushing before getting lineups and maybe exploring the new conquest. Er, ballpark.

In such down time does my brain provide the occasional eureka. *Gee*, I thought, *I've been in a lot of ballparks!*

That thought and having time on my hands led me to start counting. The figure at which I arrived startled even me: thirty-three different Minor League ballparks. I remember thinking, *That's more than the number of* Major *League ballparks!*

That was an especially sweet realization because I have a cousin who decided, when he was in his twenties, to see a game in every big-league ballpark. At the time, there were twenty-four. I believe he had three when he started his quest, and I knew he had since completed the rest, but I didn't know if he'd done the six later expansion teams' parks that had run the MLB total to thirty. Yet I had more even than that!

This might have set me up, subconsciously, for what happened next.

I was on social media by then, and this seemed like a worthy moment. All my friends knew not only that I loved baseball but that I only did the Minors. So I snapped a picture and posted it with the caption "Minor League baseball stadium #33!"

The next time I looked at my page, the first reply I saw was: "33 down, how many to go?"

My first reaction was to laugh. As I reckoned things at the time, there were nearly 190 – but given that some of my existing Gets no longer had a team, the answer was almost 150 to go!

Telling this story, I usually follow that with, "And I was off! One of these days I'm going to send [that social media friend] a bill. I musta spent [insert whatever quick estimate seemed reasonable at the time] ..." I don't think that figure has hit six digits yet, but it's deep into five.

In fact, the idea that friend planted took a few days to grow above the groundline. I had vacation time. I could manage the resources. Minor League ballparks are grouped much more closely than in the Majors, so I could get what I was already thinking of as Gets in gobs. Heck, I had picked up six ballparks that Birmingham summer just on weekends – as far north as Louisville, KY, as far east as Zebulon, NC, as far south as Mobile, AL, and as far west as New Orleans. Soon I would calculate that, within my limits, I could see a game in every remaining Minor League ballpark except the two entry-level rookie leagues in four or five more years. I kept a map with color-coded push-pins in my office, and here's how it looked at the end of the 2013 season.

Now, in case you're inspired to try this, here are some tips:

1. If you aren't retired, plan on it taking years. It took me more than four, from a large head start! (If you are retired, or otherwise not tied to a place-specific job, the four full-season levels can be done in a single season.)

2. Start planning as soon as you see schedules, and set Google alerts so you do. Scheduling these trips is much more complicated than just lining up the cities you want because each city's team is only home half the time. If I were better with computers, I'd write a program for this. I sometimes wonder if I should use a travel agent, but I envision any I'd approach running screaming into an Employees Only place.

3. Given the amount of time it takes to plan one of these trips, I hate to say this, but: Do not assume the first schedule that comes together within your parameters is the best. Try to put together at least two or three successful options and then pick the best one.

4. Do NOT skimp on your travel time! I'd rather listen to music in an air-conditioned car for an hour than miss action because of a seventy-minute traffic or I-got-lost delay.

5. You'll be in a different city almost every day – schedule carefully! If you do get to the park two hours ahead, you'll be there about five and a half hours; after you subtract that from the twenty-four-hour day, don't forget to build in that necessary time-waster we call sleep as well as travel to and from tonight's hotel.

6. I always try to get into the time zone of the game the night before and not the day of. That hour makes a lot more difference in the morning than at night. Or is that just because I'm not a morning person?

7. Triple-check the location. My two-hour rule is the only reason I didn't miss some of my game in Yakima, WA; the address I had turned out to be the team's administrative office several miles from the stadium.

8. Factor the time zones! If you plan from a master schedule, it will likely show all times Eastern. This is good for computing travel time, but take care not to show up at 1 Eastern for a noon game in Omaha. If you have your cell set to automatic time zones, and you put your schedule in it, make sure you enter so it will show the correct time when you're there. I hauled backside to get from Denver International Airport to the Colorado Springs ballpark, only to find the game started an hour later than I thought. And I would have missed by three minutes.

9. Double-check game time on game day! You've seen the words "subject to change" on schedules and even tickets. I missed some of a Williamsport game because it was scheduled to start at 7. I didn't double-check that, and it started at 6 because they had been rained out the day before and were playing a twin-bill. My fault, not theirs…

10. Seek opportunities to see two games in one day – Team A in a day game, nearby Team B in a night game. I've tried this seven times, successfully five – but one of the two failures was the Williamsport case I just mentioned. I would have made it if I had known the new game time.

11. Plan your lodging carefully! I like to get a head start by driving until about midnight, but sometimes I take the closest hotel. I like hotel breakfasts, am not a morning person, and don't stop for lunch on these trips. Your lifestyle may not match, so be sure to plan and follow a system that works for you. I suggest setting a maximum gap between games on consecutive days, a gap that will vary by whether you follow my two-hour arrival advice and by how much sleep you need. CAUTION: If you cut everything close every day, you'll likely have an ulcer competing with the great memories.

12. Pack as light as you can! If you're flying to start or end your trip, especially if you are a souvenir person, you'll be flying back with more than you had flying out.

13. If you don't like to carry cash, take some anyway. Most minor-league parks still don't take credit cards for parking, and many specialty concession stands are cash-only. This is an improvement; I remember when the only way to use a credit card in most minor-league parks was to use an ATM – if the place had one!

14. Even if you don't have to fly, rent a car with unlimited miles unless you have a beater you can absolutely trust. On my longest trip, I put nearly 20,000 miles on my rental!

The Designs, the Names, the Nicknames, and the Zaniness

More and more, I see the word "zany" applied to Minor League Baseball. It's entertainment gone wild, trying to find its own crazy identity. It's the weirdly amusing nickname. It's even the design of the stadium and the activities that have nothing to do with baseball. What's going on?

Designs: You'll read about stadiums downsizing their number of seats, glitzing up their ballparks, and generally not reflecting their parents' clubs in style.

That's because they're not Major League Baseball teams. MiLB teams as miniature MLB teams worked as a business model when the nation was baseball-crazy, the National Pastime for about seventy years, but times have changed. As a fan, I love the game exactly as is, but as a person with some understanding of business and marketing, I see the problem and respect the solution. As one owner has said: Think Disney meets baseball.

Ballparks that succeed these days have some combination of non-baseball attractions. Bouncy playpens for children. Open areas where there could be seats but instead people can congregate and stroll. Full bars instead of beer through concession windows, like the spacious Samuel Adams Brewhouse in New Hampshire and the game-laden Band Box in Nashville. More and more are going to 360-degree concourses.

In its early days, baseball was so popular people went to watch the game. Today, it's at least as much about family-friendly mixing, people-watching, and seeing and being seen.

Another difference between the Majors and the Minors is, you might say, a half of a difference. Except in trying to salvage the 1981 campaign after a mid-season strike, the Majors play one season from opening day to getaway day. Most affiliated leagues – at this writing, ten of the fourteen – play two half-seasons per year. This creates two pennant races per summer, with varying rules on who qualifies and what to do if one team qualifies twice.

Names: What's in a name? In Minor League baseball, not very much. You might think teams would only change names – i.e., what is variously called location identifier, geolocator, or locale name – when it moves from one place to another. In fact, they can change any time an owner wants to change it – with league approval, and the league will usually approve. Why change? You might change a city/county name to one with regional appeal, like "San Bernardino" to "Inland Empire" or "Prince William" to "Potomac" or "Pocatello" to "Gate City." Maybe things aren't going well and you just think a change will help, although that's more likely to cause a nickname change. Then there's the name of the ballpark; in this day of selling the rights to name a ballpark to a sponsor, those change a lot. The Buffalo Bisons' playpen donned its sixth name for its thirty-second season.

Nicknames: There are some really odd ones. In Amarillo, grown men call themselves Sod Poodles. The Toledo team's nickname is Mud Hens. Then there's the Batavia Muckdogs. I think the New Orleans Baby Cakes takes the you-know-what. I was in Louisiana when it was adopted and every local's opinion I heard was negative, but the general manager plucked it from fan suggestions for its marketability with the New Orleans King Cake tradition. It did sell a lot of merchandise, and while attendance went up a little the next year it then went down a lot. While there are more negative factors than just the nickname, most notably an aging suburban stadium, the owners jumped on Wichita's decision to build a new downtown ballpark in Kansas.

How did we get here? Gradually. The line between goofy and fun is thin, for one. For another, part of the sincerest form of flattery is pushing the imitation envelope. As trademarking has changed, fewer words are available – at least without a rights fee in a business that's not as loaded with money at this level as people think. One answer to that is, for instance, what the owners of the team they moved to Pensacola in 2012 did. They wanted to be

"Wahoos" but a college had trademarked the word for sports use, so they went with "Blue Wahoos." Another is to capture catch phrases that have passed into our social consciousness, like "Trash Pandas."

Speaking of names: There was a time when, perhaps quaintly, a circuit would change its name because it no longer fit geographically. The Pennsylvania-Ontario-New York League changed its name to New York-Pennsylvania League when its only Ontario team moved south (but didn't go back and forth as three different Ontario teams came and went between 1986 and 1999 – possibly because by then the NYPL also had teams in … New Jersey). The Illinois State League, the Missouri-Ohio Valley League, and the Midwest League are all the same circuit; the ISL changed names when it admitted a Kentucky team and the MOVL did the same when it moved into Iowa.

At some point, leagues stopped worrying about this. The last such change I've found is in 1963, when the Western Carolina League – whose members were all in North Carolina – added a South Carolina team and – yes – changed its name to the Western Carolina*s* League.

Today we have an International League whose teams are all in the United States of America (but that has had teams in Canada and the Caribbean), a Pacific Coast League that has thirteen teams in states with no Pacific coast (but whose charter members were all in the three that do), a Texas League that has four teams in Texas and four in three other states (but whose charter members were all in the Lone Star state), a Carolina League that has five teams in the two Carolinas and five in three other states (which even at its founding had two in Virginia, six in North Carolina, and none in South Carolina), and a South Atlantic League with teams in New Jersey, Delaware, Maryland, and Kentucky. Only the Eastern, Southern, California, Florida State, Midwest, Northwest and Appalachian leagues truly fit their names – and I would note that while the California League does now and did at its founding, it went four decades in between with a team in Reno, NV.

Zany: This, of course, is about the between-innings entertainment – some would say antics – with a subset of some weird food items.

I hope I've conveyed that my love of the game is for the game, but the breaks – the most frequent in sports – are necessary and I am not among the purists who gripe about using them to entertain. I think those promotions are fun and creative, and they kind of go back to the family-fun mentioned above. I just don't want any of them to run longer than two minutes and delay the next half-inning. Lighten up, purists! It's *fun* to watch two people race each other after spinning ten times with their foreheads on the nubs of grounded bats. Even if it is usually a little ... unbalanced. (I did this once, but I spun five times one way and then five times the other. I'm not sure my theory of equalizing the imbalance was the reason, but I did win!)

Ah, yes, the food. One of the best places to set yourself apart from the other entertainment-dollar seekers up and down Main Street, USA, is right there in that concession stand. Yeah, we've gone way past hot dogs and beer! The West Michigan Whitecaps, famously, used to sell the 4,500-calorie Fifth Third Burger. Watch for promotions in which teams change their name for a day (or more) and play as some food item – e.g., the Binghamton Spiedies or the Trenton Pork Rolls. As ball clubs grow more into the idea of selling "unique," these kinds of moves become inevitable – and sometimes phenomenal, as you'll see when you get to the Fresno Tacos – er, Grizzlies. Not just zany, a lot of these play to local tastes (pun intended) and give visitors a chance to. For instance, the first time I ever ate Maryland crab cakes was at an Aberdeen IronBirds game – and ditto for étouffée at the New Orleans Zephyrs. In fact, very often when I'm in a park for the first time I'll ask 'em: "Got any local specialties on the menu?"

THE STRUCTURE

Author's Note: *Literally two days after I submitted my draft to the publisher,* Baseball America *and* The New York Times *nearly simultaneously broke a radical reorganization plan for Minor League Baseball by Major League Baseball. It is a proposal in negotiations to renew the Professional Baseball Agreement, which expires in September 2020. As a first proposal in a process with nearly a year to go, what will come of this is very uncertain. However, I'm adding an epilogue to lay it out so you know what you might be looking at if you are reading this book after the 2020 season.*

Ever wonder who the first baseball team played against? When there was only one team, how were there leagues?

In those days, baseball was neither organized nor remotely league-based. It was a pastime for young men; today's cornhole might be a good analogy.

This will require some history. It will also take us beyond the surface of Minor League Baseball – peering into its very structure – and can be confusing. Feel free to skip this chapter, but if you get lost in words and phrases like affiliation; player development contracts, or PDCs; and owned-and-operated teams, or O&Os, feel just as free to come back.

Despite the commission report that "established" it, baseball's supposed 1839 invention in Cooperstown, NY, is a myth. It's my opinion that the game was not invented at all. Rather, like many things of which we have a history we assume reaches back to an origin, it evolved. Similar "bat-and-ball" games – rounders, townball, and cricket – were being played well before 1839 in the still most-populated area of the country, the Northeast.

From these, and even from different early forms of its own self, baseball emerged (or merged) in antebellum America. Even its name evolved – from base ball to base-ball to baseball. By any name, in my opinion, it wasn't baseball until "soaking" ended. My logic is that soaking – putting a runner out by hitting him with a thrown ball while he's off base – can hardly have been done with a baseball as hard as we now use. Today, the first baseball game is said to have been played in 1846 under rules Alexander Cartwright published in September 1845. There's some argument whether Cartwright composed the rules or merely wrote down existing verbal ones. These rules introduced tagging instead of soaking, but the ball wasn't "hard" for a while longer; I have a souvenir replica of the balls used in Nashville during the War for Southern Independence – and while I wouldn't want to be hit by a hard-thrown one, they were cloth-bound. Today's hard baseball arrived with the 1876 founding of the National League.

Cartwright's rules had some quaint terminology: What we call a "run" he called an "ace" or a "count"; our "strikeout" was his "hand-out"; our "inning" was his "hand"; our "batter" was his "striker," and our "pitcher" was his "thrower."

An 1858 set of rules is regarded by some as today's games first nationally published baseball rules – but they were not only labeled as Massachusetts-based Town Ball, they still recognized soaking.

The sport began to take off after the War, as Yankees went home and played or remained as occupiers and played, and Rebels stayed home and played – but it wasn't yet organized. "Barnstorming" – playing essentially challenge games while traveling around – was the norm then. Another comparison might be to prize-fighting, where there's no regular schedule – just guys challenging each other.

In 1869, the Cincinnati Red Stockings became the first openly professional team, winning their first fifty-seven games playing amateur (maybe some not *openly* pro) teams. This success generated the sincerest form of flattery: other pro teams, which soon led to leagues. The first professional league, the National Association of Base Ball Players, formed in 1871. If that makes you wonder who *were* the first two teams to play a professional league game, see **Fort Wayne TinCaps (CURRENT)**.

Much evolution followed.

The National League, considered the first major (as opposed to professional) league, was founded in 1876. As rivalries, proximity and the logic of set scheduling started to make leagues become the norm, scores of leagues and hundreds of teams sprang up – spreading west and south. The Texas League, for example, was founded in 1888. By the end of the century, problems ranged from saturation to roster-raiding.

In 1877, the baseball became the hard one Jim Bouton, et. al., would grip when the National League adopted it as the official baseball of Baseball.

As stable as we think a two-league MLB is, it simply was not so throughout the pre-expansion era.

At one time or another in the late nineteenth century, both the International League and the American Association were considered major leagues on par with the National League.

The biggest turning point to date started at the turn of the twentieth century. In 1900, the National League contracted four teams. Big mistake! The Western League promptly expanded into four cities including three of those and, in 1901, changed its name to the American League. The brief but intense war that followed put the two circuits on par.

While our purpose of looking at MLB/MiLB history stops here, with Minor League Baseball's 1903 founding, these encroachments were far from over:

1. Federal League, 1914-15, defeated by the MLB teams' collective and strategic use of every clean and dirty trick in the book

2. Mexican League, 1940s, which did not try to become a major league but certainly interfered by offering MLB (and Negro Leagues) stars more money

3. Pacific Coast League, 1950s, nearly gained Majors status – blocked only when the near-simultaneous development of coast-to-coast live TV and coast-to-coast air travel made manifest-destiny expansion possible

4. Continental League, 1957, New York attorney William Shea's *de facto* response to NYC losing both the Giants and Brooklyn Dodgers to California; Shea disbanded the league (without ever playing a game) only when MLB agreed both to expand *and* to return National League baseball to the Big Apple

Expansion seemed to have closed the window on these efforts – but there's some evidence the American Association was trying to become a third major league in 1990, which may well have led to MiLB's decommissioning it seven seasons later.

At the dawn of modern MLB history, though, two big leagues working within one system was about the only thing that *was* working – for them, not so much for all of pro baseball. Scores of other leagues had to find a way to co-exist with a couple of relative titans.

There is strength in unity, and yet more strength in making a friend of that which threatens you.

Turmoil aplenty accompanied baseball's first turn of a century. The National League's contraction opened the door and the Western League stepped through to parity, but the war reverberated across every level of the game. After the 1901 season, in Chicago, pretty much the rest of professional baseball formed the National Association of Professional Baseball Leagues (NAPBL) mostly to get the AL and NL to stop raiding their rosters. It did that, but it also helped settle the NL/AL feud; the 1902 National Agreement – signed by the NL, the AL, *and* the NAPBL – ushered in the system we know today (except, in a move that matters little to the common fan, the NL and AL in 2000 merged into one entity called Major League Baseball). The NAPBL continues, operating as Minor League Baseball (MiLB) and overseeing seventeen leagues.

Owners of, and sportswriters following, Major League teams had referred to all professional non-Majors clubs as Minor League teams. Even after 1903, separating the term "Minor League" to mean just the teams in the NAPBL didn't come into vogue until the 1930s, when St. Louis Cardinal legend Branch Rickey invented the farm system. The term comes from his saying he would grow players like corn down on the farm. Before Rickey, MLB teams signed or bought contracts of Minor League players as needed; now, each big-league team runs a string of feeder ("affiliated") clubs to which they send players who are under contract with but not playing for the big-league team. This system was solidified in 1965, when baseball became the last big-four sport to draft coming-of-age players.

Another thing that evolved, rather than being invented, was the team nickname. Although some appeared as early as the 1840s, they were extremely informal. No one held meetings to strategize the best nickname based on marketing. Many were coined by sportswriters to alleviate the repetition of the city name in their stories – in at least one case superseding what the owner wanted. When Jack Dunn moved his Baltimore Orioles to Richmond, VA, in 1915, he intended to call them the Virginians, but the *Richmond Times-Dispatch* dubbed them the Climbers after they came from behind not once but four times to win their debut game.

Evolution continues, and you'll read about some of it in Chapter 12, **The Ballparks/Their Teams**.

So how does this work?

The key is the player development contract, or PDC: the piece of paper that ties "parent" (MLB) and "affiliate" (MiLB) teams together. Each PDC provides that the parent club will pay the personnel costs of the players and team field staff it assigns to the farm club, including most of their travel costs, while the farm club ownership provides the business operation that creates a place for the team to play and attracts paying fans.

Today, not counting the three entry-level rookie leagues that are part of the MiLB system but operate quite differently, 160 teams in fourteen leagues participate. That's down – reduced first by television, but since then mostly intentionally for efficiency – from a peak of well over 400 teams in nearly sixty leagues.

In all, there are two Class Triple-A leagues, three Class Double-A leagues, three Class A-Advanced leagues (usually called high-A), two Class A leagues (usually called low-A or full-A), two Class A-Short Season leagues (usually called short-A), two Rookie-Advanced leagues (usually called advanced rookie), and the entry-level Rookie leagues. When I started my project, there were four Rookie leagues, but the Venezuelan League has since disbanded. Those leagues, with each's number of teams in parentheses, are:

- Triple-A: International League (14), Pacific Coast League (16)
- Double-A: Eastern League (12), Southern League (10), Texas League (8)
- Class A-Advanced (high-A): California League (8 – was 10 until 2017), Carolina League (10 – was 8 until 2017), Florida State League (12)
- Class A: Midwest League (16); South Atlantic League (14)
- Class A-Short Season: New York – Penn League (14); Northwest League (8)
- Rookie-Advanced: Appalachian League (10); Pioneer League (8)

MLB requires each of its teams to have one farm club in each of the top four levels – the full-season levels. No one has more, although that is allowed; while no one is required to have any teams below those everyone does. The difference in the size of the thirty farm systems is all in the number of short-A, advanced rookie, and rookie teams each chooses to field. The Yankees, of course, have the largest system; the only one with a farm team in every short-season level has *six*: one short-A, one advanced rookie, *four* entry-level rookie, and so ten teams overall.

Many people (including, based on copy I've read, some reporters) assume farm teams are owned by the big-league teams that provide their players. In affiliated baseball, that is true of only slightly more than one in five teams – a number that has grown considerably in recent years. Some even assume this is true of front-office staff – but while they may be hired up through the obvious networking possibilities, front-office staff of an affiliated Minor League team are employees of that farm team with no corporate relationship of their own with the big-league parent.

Ownerships are corporations, of course, so this goes beyond, say, the New York Mets owning the Syracuse team. There's no rule that even a wholly owned MiLB team must affiliate with its owner – we recently saw the one-season exception of the Mets and the then-Chiefs, but all knew from the start this would last only through the PDC that was in place when the Mets bought the Chiefs. The same is true of cross-ownership. The Pawtucket Red Sox, for example, are not wholly owned by the Boston Red Sox – but some of the same people are in both ownership groups and it's clear the PawSox – soon to be the Worcester Red Sox – are extremely unlikely to change parents. For our purpose – which is primarily whether a farm team is open to change parents in an affiliate shuffle – I regard Major-Minor partners with any common ownership as being in an O&O relationship.

The Florida State League is mostly O&O, for a very specific reason. This Class A-Advanced circuit, uniquely, has most of its teams sharing their stadium with their major-league club. The big-league team plays its home spring training games in February and March, and the FSL club then plays in the same ballpark from early April until the Sunday before Labor Day. This is obviously much simpler when the MiLB team is the big-league club's farm team ... but affiliations change. The only sure way to keep this partnership simple is for the farm team to become an O&O, so that became the FSL norm. Nine of its twelve teams are wholly or partly owned by their parent club ownership, and I would not be surprised if a tenth joins this group very soon.

Some teams like to own their farm teams for other reasons – more control than money. The Atlanta Braves own all of their farm teams except the erstwhile Florida Fire Frogs (q.v. **[CURRENT]**) – in the FSL, and yes that's the team I have in mind for number ten – while the New York Mets and Yankees and the St. Louis Cardinals each own all but two of theirs. The parent of an O&O

incurs more monetary risk by taking on costs that are normally the Minor League ownership's, but benefits from having more control of its farm system.

One benefit is the ability to address ballpark dissatisfaction directly, and this has directly driven two things: the rise of O&Os to more than twenty percent, and much of the movement of Minor League franchises. This being a zero-sum game, it's almost like musical chairs. Almost! No one gets booted from the game by losing the last seat, but someone does get stuck with that chair. The business calls this being "paired." No MLB club is going to get paired in a level in which it owns a team.

In one example, the Boston Red Sox bought the Salem Avalanche to get out of Lancaster, CA. Lancaster Municipal stadium, aka The Hangar, is one of three ballparks in the high-A California League that have been a problem. The others are what is now Adelanto Stadium in the Mojave Desert city of Adelanto and Sam Lynn Ballpark in Bakersfield. Sam Lynn is simply old, worn out, and so aligned that night games are delayed by sunset. Adelanto and Lancaster have windy, high-mountain, pitcher-killing ballparks. Of the three, only Lancaster remains in the Cali League, and its team is affiliated with the – you guessed it – Colorado Rockies.

The best example is the Texas Rangers' byzantine 2016 effort to move from plight to flight.

Plan A: The Rangers buy the Wilmington Blue Rocks, contingent on Rocks' ownership buying the Binghamton Mets. In 2017, the B-Mets would move to Delaware, the Blue Rocks to Kinston, NC, as well as into the Rangers' farm system, and some other big-league club would get stuck with Adelanto.

That deal fell apart when the B-Mets withdrew from it. The resulting breach of contract lawsuit ended in a sealed settlement reportedly spurred by inside-baseball politicking that left every team where it was. Kinston, spending tens of thousands to ready Grainger Stadium for a farm club after several years without, immediately told the city's worried baseball fans and citizens that the Rangers had told them to continue to expect a team to start the agreed seventeen-year lease in 2017. That turned out to be because the Rangers had a ...

Plan B: The Rangers had apparently already gotten MiLB to agree, if Plan A failed, to move two franchises from the Cali to the Caro. So, they bought the High Desert Mavericks and moved the club from Adelanto to Kinston in 2017. It being necessary to have even numbers of teams in those leagues, the Houston Astros did them a favor by buying the Bakersfield Blaze and moving that club to a temporary facility for a couple of years while Fayetteville, NC, planned and built a new stadium.

As you see, three California stadiums directly led three MLB teams to buy three MiLB teams.

For the most part, though, the model remains the PDC. The C stands for contract, you'll recall, but think "form letter" when I say it's a form contract. This piece of paper lays out the terms, and the business rules of baseball allow no changes or side agreements. I've seen enough apparent exceptions to wonder how much wink-wink goes on, but by the adopted rules teams can only affiliate for two or four years, can extend an existing PDC any time, and cannot negotiate or even talk about affiliating with anyone other than their existing parent except in the period proscribed by the rule: Sept. 16-30 of even-numbered years. Of course, if you're in an affiliation during that period – just signed, or in the middle of a four-year one – you can't talk to anyone else even then. The period to break a PDC is even shorter than the period to find a new one: from the last day of the regular season (most leagues end on Labor Day) of the farm team's league until Sept. 11.

Under this system, you might expect teams to change a lot – a subjective term, I know – but there are safeguards. Not being allowed to talk to anyone but your parent for 102 out of every 104 weeks is the most obvious. Also, it takes an action to end a PDC; either team can do so by notifying its baseball hierarchy, but if neither does so the PDC automatically renews. (This makes it tricky for those of us watching them; there being no requirement to make any public announcements about these, we sometimes must wait for them to become obvious over time.) It being a zero-sum game, every broken PDC creates another. In this universe, twenty changes in an affiliation cycle has been a large number. Out of the nearly 130 farm teams that are not owned or operated by their parent, that doesn't seem to me to be "a lot."

This shifting can complicate things. The best example I recall is when Nashville, TN, went from Double-A to Triple-A in 1985. Affiliated baseball teams do not move from one level to another except when the hierarchy reclassifies a league or the whole structure. What actually happens is an owner acquires a team in a different level and moves it. Larry Schmittou, then majority owner of the Double-A Nashville Sounds, made Nashville a Triple-A city by buying the Triple-A Evansville Triplets, moving them to Nashville, and changing their name. What happened to the Double-A Sounds, then a Cincinnati Reds' affiliate? Schmittou moved his Double-A team to Alabama and renamed it the Huntsville Stars. Why do many people think it went to Chattanooga, TN? Because Schmittou's shift coincidentally happened in the same off-season as an affiliation shuffle, and the Reds and Schmittou's Double-A team coincidentally parted company. His Huntsville-based team joined the Milwaukee Brewers, and the Reds began a long run with the Chattanooga Lookouts – whom Schmittou never ever owned. Got it?

Here's where we need to understand the actual meaning of the term "franchise." Following Major League Baseball made teen-aged me think the franchise is the legal entity that occasionally moves around, but that's because movement in the bigs is limited to within the bigs. In fact, the franchise is the legal right a league assigns a business entity to operate a team – just as stores in restaurant chains are franchised by the chain.

What you think of this quandary is a matter of perspective. It's a fact that the legal business entity d/b/a the Nashville Sounds of the Double-A Southern League moved to Huntsville, AL, in 1985. It's also a fact that the players people watched in Nashville in 1984 who didn't get promoted, demoted, traded, or released played 1985 in Chattanooga. It is another fact that the Southern League franchise that was in Nashville in 1984 was in Huntsville, not Chattanooga, in 1985. It is still another fact that Metro Nashville-Davidson County went from having Double-A to Triple-A baseball that off-season, but it is yet another fact that neither the Nashville

Sounds ball club nor its Southern League franchise "moved up" from Double-A to Triple-A.

Speaking of moving around geographically, remember the legal entity piece of the above. When a "team" or "franchise" moves from one location to another, the owner of the legal entity has moved it. If the move is from one market to another, it requires the approval of some specific-margin vote of the league's other team owners. Whatever confusion ensues is either because the franchise or the affiliation – but sometimes not both – goes with it. Sometimes an owner decides to move, sometimes an owner decides to sell and the buyer decides or has already decided to move, and on rare occasions the league takes over a floundering team and effectively becomes its owner. At the end of the day, where the legal entity operates its team and by what geo-locator name and nickname are up to its present owner, subject to the aforementioned vote of fellow league owners. That's why, for me, the business entity is what to watch.

All that said, I understand as a business matter why team owners want to combine their histories. The actual difference between the Nashville Sounds of 1978-84 and of 1985-now demands a technical explanation, while a Nashville Sounds operation that dates continuously to 1978 commands the respect given longevity – and allows impressive feats like announcing the attendance of the 15 millionth fan.

While we're on the business end of it, a word about attendance: There's no question some teams inflate theirs, but perhaps not as much as you may think – and maybe not as many teams. There are two ways to count fans: sold tickets or turnstile count. All the teams I worked for counted sold tickets. Neither way can be completely accurate or independently verified.

Many ball club advertising packages, especially the bigger ones like wall signs, include tickets – usually, *season* tickets. They not only don't have a precise price of their own, because they're "added-value" or "schmooze-your-customer bait" items, many go unused. Say an ad buyer gets four season tickets this way; the full-season Minor League team has just added 280 to its final attendance figure without collecting a dedicated dollar or warming a seat.

On the other hand, people with passes come through turnstiles unless the team has a pass gate or some such alternative. MLB teams may do that, but no one I worked with in the Minors did – so the turnstile counts merged freebies and paying customers.

I know of (but am not going to name) teams thought to inflate their numbers, but the only way to get true numbers would be personal observation: counting. Even that wouldn't be exact; how would you factor in concession/restroom runs? If I were evaluating advertising with a team, I'd rather have turnstile counts – an unsold ticket doesn't have any eyes or ears to impress, while a scout or a player's girlfriend does – but we pretty much have to live with what the teams report.

Finally, there is one exception to the affiliation part of this system: the Appalachian League, a Rookie-Advanced short-season circuit. All ten of its teams are, technically, owned by their parent club. However, some are operated by their parent clubs and others are operated by a contractor or by the city. I count the former as O&Os and either of the others as affiliated. Also, while their teams traditionally honor the two-year affiliation cycle, they don't have to.

It's complicated … but it works.

WHAT'S YOUR FAVORITE?

This will be the shortest chapter, but I want to address it outside the realm of the individual ballparks because everyone asks it sooner or later. Usually sooner. Often immediately.

I'm willing to say it's Louisville Slugger Field, home of the Class Triple-A Louisville Bats.

Why am I so balky about saying *anything*?

Because this subject is entirely too subjective for my opinion to matter. I especially feel this way about trying to *rank* the 159 baseball stadiums, which some magazines and websites do.

As a lover of baseball, I believe its history matters. I can't look at old cake-boxes like McCoy Stadium in Pawtucket, arguably present-day MiLB's most historic, and not feel the history pushing my like-meter up. Yet people apply the word "dump" to them.

I've seen action in every ballpark, but I do have a hometown where I've seen hundreds of games. How do I fairly compare its ballpark with the scores of others where I've seen one?

Some people want to enjoy the game and never leave their seat unless nature demands intake or output. (That's me.) Others would rather walk around and take in the ballpark itself while watching the game to some personally preferred extent. (That's me, too – until the first pitch.) Whichever you prefer, there's no real comparing an old cake-box to a sleek new ballpark – not even a "downtown retro," which strives to incorporate both.

Then there's aesthetics. The scenery from a ballpark can steal your breath and float it away to become the only cloud in an azure sky. Does that make the ballpark itself more or less beautiful?

I don't see how. Does it make the ballpark experience more or less beautiful? *Of course.*

From the moment I saw AutoZone Park in Memphis, it was my favorite. That lasted until the first time I walked into Louisville Slugger Field. In my pantheon of greats, the Slug wobbled when I entered the spectacular stadium Pensacola opened in 2012 but Slugger held its favorite status – as, to my surprise, it also did after I saw my first game at brand-new, state-of-the-art and most-expensive-minor-league-stadium-ever Las Vegas Ballpark in 2019.

This is why even listing the best of the rest is futile. I could say which first comes to mind, but three and then four others follow before I can press the first key. As they say at the Oscars, it can't be done without forgetting someone.

In my opinion, "beautiful ballpark" is redundant. Ballparks, you see, are like people: Every single one is different, and every single one is beautiful in its own way.

I can't rank all those "own ways."

Rickwood Field

I can't overstate Birmingham's role in this quest. It's where I was working when the idea was planted.

Its saucer-style suburban stadium, Regions Park in Hoover, AL, was originally and then still colloquially called Hoover Metropolitan Stadium – affectionately, the Hoover Met. It was the home of the Birmingham Barons of the Class Double-A Southern League 1988-2012. Birmingham had three claims to baseball fame, two of which I knew at that time: (1) during National Basketball Association legend Michael Jordan's layoff from his game, he played baseball at the Hoover Met and drew ridiculous crowds; (2) the Met had hosted the collegiate Southeastern Conference baseball tournament so long it seemed permanent. I had to look it up to see the last time it hadn't.

Here's how I learned the third:

At a Barons game, I got into a conversation with an elderly fan about Minor League Baseball.

"Do you know," he asked me, "about Rickwood?"

I didn't. I'd been in Birmingham only a couple of weeks and knew I wouldn't be there for more than a few months. I had seen a video on the hotel tourism channel about Birmingham's post-bellum founding. For as young as it is, Birmingham has a lot of history. Yet that video overlooked Rickwood.

"Rickwood Field is the oldest ballpark that's still standing and ever had professional baseball," the gentleman said. Not that he didn't have me already, he went on: "It's a museum now, but once a year the Barons play a regular-season game there. It's called The Rickwood Classic."

I would later learn Willie Mays played his first professional game there, at least with a signed contract – for, of course, the Birmingham Black Barons. That's a fourth Birmingham claim to baseball fame.

The Rickwood Classic is always a Wednesday day game, and I couldn't make it that season. (I did visit it on a non-game day: Aug. 6, 2011.) With a year to plan, though, I did get to the 2012 Classic.

Rickwood, opened in August 1910, is the classic wooden ballpark of early last century. It isn't downtown, but it isn't exactly in the suburbs either. The area is known as West Birmingham, and it isn't all that far from downtown. The ballpark arises from a large lot – including ample but unpaved parking – in an otherwise residential area. It's wooden, it's old, and it's green. I couldn't forget it if I tried, and I mean that in the best possible way. I'd live in it if I could.

I've done a lot of baseball games in a lot of different places, but I've never been as awed as that day. During each classic, the players – even the umpires – are garbed as if it were a specific year between 1910 and 1988. The old manual scoreboard operates as in days of old. It truly feels as if one has been transported back in time.

The incredibleness of that experience is why only this ballpark gets its own chapter – but it still gets a vignette in the section on individual ballparks.

I have experienced it once since. I'll go whenever I can, but 2013 was irresistible: Birmingham had lured the Barons back into the city by building an incredible new downtown ballpark, and that afforded a one-time opportunity to see games on consecutive days in Organized Baseball's newest and oldest ballparks! Add that my daughter, her boyfriend, one of my best friends, and his wife joined me – what a couple of days that was!

GETS, GO-BACKS AND REBUILTS

The original idea, to see a game in every Minor League stadium in the country, would evolve as I learned things.

From the beginning, I was thinking only of Minor League Baseball – MLB's feeder system: those teams in Organized Baseball, atop which Major League Baseball sits. I never intended to tackle the independent leagues, even though they are professional in that the players are paid. It would have added forty percent to an already mammoth project. Many people still consider "minor-league baseball" to be any professional baseball that isn't Major League Baseball, but I had to be somewhat practical. In 2019, there were twelve independent leagues totaling sixty-three clubs.

Next, I had to decide how far down this hierarchy to go. I wanted to do all of them, of course, but the cost and logistics of the Dominican and the Venezuelan made me decide to keep it domestic. That left sixteen leagues totaling around 240 teams, all but one of which was in the United States.

The two domestic Rookie leagues seemed relatively easy because they're so compact. Their teams, which don't start play until mid-to-late June and end before Labor Day, are mostly where their parent team plays spring training, so the Arizona League was in a very compact radius of Phoenix while the Gulf Coast League was within the southern half of Florida.

In fact, they proved impossible. My first Rookie effort was in the GCL. Although even half of Florida is hugely bigger than Greater Phoenix, GCL teams play day (sometimes *morning*) games so I envisioned a lot of two-*Get* days with Florida State League night games. My first GCL game was in Sarasota, at Ed Smith

Stadium. While asking where to park, I mentioned my project and was greeted with, "You're really lucky. They *are* playing here today." I didn't realize what this meant, but soon would: My next *two* GCL games were not in the main stadium but on a side-field. Think high-school practice field. When this happened on the second straight day, I asked a staffer about it. "None of us play many games in the big stadium. It's because of the rent." That made sense; as I had learned at Ed Smith, they don't even charge admission or sell concessions. Reluctantly, I accepted the obvious truth that being in the complex was not the same as being in the stadium and that it would take years, luck, money and tremendous effort to catch them all in their "big stadium" – if it could even be done.

There's also the fluidity of the Rookie level. Teams take a year off for one reason or another, parent teams split their entry-level rookie teams in two, teams occasionally even go up or down a level while a stadium is being renovated (see **Kingsport Mets [CURRENT]**).

So, I reduced the project to Class Triple-A through Rookie-Advanced, which total 160. There are thirty teams in each of the four full-season levels, one for each MLB team, but there are forty in the four short-season leagues still on my list: twenty-two in short-A and eighteen in advanced Rookie.

Of course, I already had a good number. I don't remember the exact figure now, but it wasn't just a matter of subtracting what I had counted in Mobile; admittedly, I missed a few in that impromptu count, and several of those I had counted had since lost their team. I had already decided I was not going to subtract those from my total; whether Minor League ball was *still* being played in a ballpark or not, any Minor League park in which I had seen Minor League action would remain a *Get*. I didn't invent this to pad, but what with throwback games like the Rickwood Classic and roughly two teams a year changing ballparks, I now have 187 playpens even though there are only 160 teams.

By the way, there are only 159 Minor League stadiums in those fourteen leagues. Given that everybody plays almost every day, how can there be an odd number? Because two Florida State League teams share their park! How did I handle that? We'll see when we get there. I will say now I caught a lucky break there that really helped out.

This made me modify something else: I thought I'd been trying to see a game in every park, but I realized what I was *really* trying to do was to see a home game by every team. This would evolve into by every team by its current name in its current stadium. That created a complication: whether to count a stadium twice if I saw different teams in it because of franchise movements. Originally, I did – and for a long time I counted several twice, calling each a franchise-stadium (think foot-pound). For whatever reason, though, that always felt like cheating. Now, I separately count the number of home games by a current franchise – which at the end of every season has been (and will hopefully always be) 160 – and the number of affiliated stadiums in which I've turned the stile – which at the end of 2019 was 187.

This little project would get very complicated. First, I once missed a scheduled game time; you'll read that story when we get to that ballpark. I wouldn't say it was my fault, but I did learn a lesson and successfully compensated. The question was, should I count that park? Making rules for your own game is tough, or at least ethically demanding. I had driven over six hours one-way, but if I were going to do this right shouldn't I require myself to see a whole game? While I knew no one else was counting or vetting, could I honestly claim a ballpark in which I'd only seen part of a game? Thus was born the *Go-Back*. If I'm not present for every pitch and play, I count the stadium in my total of *Get*s, but I take the next feasible opportunity to go back. This would come up many times, usually because of weather.

Would I count a game that wasn't complete? Yes, but if the game didn't become official (five innings) it also became a *Go-Back*. The most frustrating thing – and it happened *three* times – was arriving after an all-day drive, turning the stile, being in my seat ready to go, and then the heavens opening up without a pitch being thrown. Three times! Another time, the right-field lights went out during play. The game was long enough to be official, seven innings, but it was tied and the rules required it be suspended rather than called. They finished it later in the week – when I was, of course, somewhere else. I didn't count that as a *Go-Back*, since I did see all the action played the day I was there, but I did get back when I could because I didn't see that whole game.

The other side of the *Go-Back* coin is the *Rebuilt*. I pulled up to a ballpark where I'd worked during the 1990s. From outside it was literally unrecognizable, even moreso once inside – I stood in a concrete-and-steel ballpark remembering a wooden one. When I hear of a renovation whose cost rivals that of building a new stadium, or a ballpark that missed a whole season for renovations or was torn down to the seating bowl, I hit it again to see if it's been renovated beyond recognition. My rule of thumb is: If I'm walking up to it or walking around inside and wouldn't know where I am just from what I'm seeing, it's a different ballpark. Lest you think I milk my total with this, I've made four such stops and Princeton, WV, is the *only* one I've so far counted the second time.

I consider my first *Get* of the project to be then-Zephyr Field in New Orleans, July 10, 2011. That was the next game I saw after the intent and planning started the night before in Mobile. It was a game to remember, as the then-Zephyrs edged the Iowa Cubs 2-1. I considered the project complete, knowing I'd be re-completing it every year, after seeing the Quad Cities River Bandits defeat the Clinton LumberKings 7-2 in Davenport, IA, April 12, 2015 – the first weekend of that season. Under my rules, that was the official finish – but I had a handful of *Go-Backs*. I used weekends and my summer vacation to get all of those plus that year's two new Minor League ballparks, and I was surprised at how much more final it felt when I got the last *Go-Back* in Williamsport, PA, July 12 – another squeaker as the Crosscutters beat the Connecticut Tigers 3-2.

Those were the last *Gets* and *Go-Backs* of the project, that is. I'm still filling up summer vacations staying current. Teams move and/or change their nicknames every year. They rarely line up geographically, so I fill in gaps with games in between. Sometimes I even do something else, like a museum or other tourist attraction. On the day of a Lynchburg Hillcats game, for instance, I took in Appomattox Courthouse. That's also how I saw Niagara Falls, Mount Rushmore, the Little Bighorn battlefield, and museums to Mark Twain, *The Music Man*, and the 1947 Roswell UFO incident.

Long before I got the last ballpark, a friend asked what I'd do when I had them all. All I managed to say, with a shrug, was "Keep seeing games." Remember, I'd been seeing games whenever and wherever possible for many years before this became a thing. If the Majors follow through on expansion talk each new big-league club will create around five new Minor League teams. Assuming I keep life and health, I may yet hit 200 MiLB ballparks.

Perhaps I can provide a more thoughtful answer now, though. I would like to do the Rickwood Classic every year, although my work makes that tough – but spending my career all over the country seriously eased the overall project. On non-work days, if there's a game within three or four hours' drive (yes, sometimes more) I'll probably go.

My rules also create some opportunities:

1. New stadium: if an MiLB franchise moves in, becomes a *Get* target

2. Team nickname change (permanent): stadium still a *Get*, but goes on *Go-Back* list

3. Stadium renovations

    a. if a *Get* undergoes an extensive renovation (this is subjective and has a terrible success rate, 25%), it remains a *Get* but becomes a possible *Rebuilt* and if so a new *Get*

    b. if a team plays elsewhere for some reason, and the "elsewhere" was ever the regular home of an MiLB team, this becomes a *Get* target (that started with the Rickwood Classic, but I don't see other throwback games as any different)

You may wonder why stadium names aren't in this mix. Well, I'll show my age again when I say if I had done this in my youth they would be. A stadium name in those days honored some person or place. While it can be argued no stadium was ever named for a poor person, such names were nevertheless an honor and not a business deal. Secondarily, naming rights contracts expire and thus can change more often than I think going back is worth.

At the end of the 2015, 2016, 2017, 2018 and 2019 seasons, I had all 160 current Minor League teams in levels Triple-A through Rookie-Advanced in their current playpen with their current franchise by their current nickname – even though between one and three new stadiums opened every one of those years. At the end of 2019, the actual number of different ballparks in which I've seen at least one Minor League game was 187. Counting professional rather than just Minors, as the 2019 Minor League season ended, my thirteen Majors took that number to a nice round 200. I also did all ten stadiums of the Cape Cod League in 2015, which I want to mention despite the fact that the players are collegiate amateurs because it is the oldest and very best of the wood-bat collegiate leagues. Also, I plan to go see games in each of the eight stadiums of the Australian Baseball League.

I had three Minor League *Get*s in 2019 and stand to have at least that many in 2020. I've never meant to try to *Get* the rest of the Majors, but now that I'm almost halfway there I'm slipping into it.

Oh, I promised to "get to" going back to big-league parks. As I mentioned, my regular work has taken me all over the country. Some of those trips had me in or near big-league cities, and as people realized what a baseball fan I was many looked askance when I wouldn't go see their big-league team. After one too many such conversations, I said: "All right, all right – when the last pair of cheeks that was running around a diamond in 1994 has retired, I'll *think* about going to a Major League game." While Alex Rodriguez was serving a long suspension from which I thought he'd never return, the last other player who dated to '94 retired. In 2014, I broke the boycott with the game in Oakland. Danged if A-Rod didn't return; what's worse, I would see a Yankee game in Boston in 2015 and danged if he didn't get a hit that day. Funny how life works out.

To borrow from, and slightly edit, Rod Stewart:

Every ballpark has a story ... don't it?

The Ballparks · The Teams

When I started collecting ballparks, which as you've read was quite by accident, I had no idea I'd ever write a book about it. So, I didn't take notes or even start an organized log until I realized one would help prioritize what remained. I do have all my scorebooks since 2012, though, so I've put in what first-visit dates and scores I could glean from them, the log and my social media account.

As you've also read, the first Minor League game I saw was in – or rather near – Toledo, OH, in 1989. The last *Get* – my first game at the last ballpark – was in Davenport, IA, at the Quad Cities River Bandits' 2015 home opener. Once this project was underway, I had found it necessary to develop the pesky concept of the *Go-Back* – a *Get* I have to get again for one of several reasons; I got the last of those in Williamsport, PA, later in 2015. I don't always buy souvenirs, but that time I had to. I mentioned the completion to the sales clerk, who rewarded me with, "Well, I'm just sorry we were the last one." Gee, thanks. I didn't want to be mean then but sometimes I regret not countering with the fact that it was my *third* try at that elusive ballpark.

I'm not going to attempt a personal chronology. Instead, I'll thumbnail each ballpark/team – first, of the current ones as of the 2019 season, then those that no longer host professional baseball but where I saw pro action, and finally of former Minor League ballparks that I've visited without seeing action. The game date and score listed for each stadium (I have all since 2012 and most before) reflects only my first game there. For those stadiums in which I've seen home games of two different franchises – the only exception, not locale name or nickname changes or incomplete games – I'll list the first of each.

Arranging them is tough because stadium names are bought and sold and thus change and teams don't always go by their city's name. I'm going with three sections:

CURRENT: Stadiums currently (as of the end of the 2019 season) with a team, alphabetically by whatever location identifier they currently use. This is usually but not always the city, and to help you avoid chasing wild geese I'll start with a list to disambiguate: (1) teams not using their city name; (2) cities you may think have a team that's actually elsewhere; (3) potential confusion over same-locale names in different states.

LEGACY: Stadiums that have hosted an MiLB team, but currently do not, where I *have* seen MiLB play: alphabetically by city

VISITED: Stadiums (in some cases, sites) that have had an MiLB team, but currently do not, where I have *been* but have *not* seen MiLB action: alphabetically by city

If you're looking for a current Minor League team in …, then you're looking for the …

Aberdeen, MD	Aberdeen IronBirds	Asheville, NC	Asheville Tourists
Akron, OH	Akron RubberDucks	Auburn, NY	Auburn Doubledays
Albany, NY	Tri-City Dust Devils	Augusta, GA	Augusta GreenJackets
Albuquerque, NM	Albuquerque Isotopes	Austin, TX	Round Rock Express
Allentown, PA	Lehigh Valley IronPigs	Batavia, NY	Batavia Muckdogs
Altoona, PA	Altoona Curve	Beloit, WI	Beloit Snappers
Amarillo, TX	Amarillo Sod Poodles	Bettendorf, IA	Quad Cities River Bandits
Appleton, WI	Wisconsin Timber Rattlers	Billings, MT	Billings Mustangs

MAJORING IN THE MINORS

Location	Team	Location	Team
Biloxi, MS	Biloxi Shuckers	Charleston, WV	West Virginia Power
Binghamton, NY	Binghamton Rumble Ponies	Charlotte, NC	Charlotte Knights (the team in Port Charlotte, FL, also goes by Charlotte)
Birmingham, AL	Birmingham Barons		
Bluefield, VA	Bluefield Blue Jays	Chattanooga, TN	Chattanooga Lookouts
Bluefield, WV	Bluefield Blue Jays	Clearwater, FL	Clearwater Threshers
Boise, ID	Boise Hawks		
Bowie, MD	Bowie Baysox	Clinton, IA	Clinton LumberKings
Bowling Green, KY	Bowling Green Hot Rods	Columbia, SC	Columbia Fireflies
Bradenton, FL	Bradenton Marauders	Columbus, OH	Columbus Clippers
		Colorado Springs, CO	Rocky Mountain Vibes
Brick, NJ	Lakewood BlueClaws (Lakewood is the name of the township)	Comstock Park, MI	West Michigan Whitecaps
Bristol, TN	Bristol Pirates	Corpus Christi, TX	Corpus Christi Hooks
Bristol, VA	Bristol Pirates	Danville, VA	Danville Braves
Brooklyn, NY	Brooklyn Cyclones	Dayton, OH	Dayton Dragons
Buffalo, NY	Buffalo Bisons	Daytona Beach, FL	Daytona Tortugas
Buford, GA	Gwinnett Stripers	Davenport, IA	Quad Cities River Bandits
Burlington, IA	Burlington Bees		
Burlington, NC	Burlington Royals	Des Moines, IA	Iowa Cubs
Burlington, VT	Vermont Lake Monsters	Dunedin, FL	Dunedin Blue Jays
		Durham, NC	Durham Bulls
Cedar Rapids, IA	Cedar Rapids Kernels	East Moline, IL	Quad Cities River Bandits
Charleston, SC	Charleston RiverDogs	Eastlake, OH	Lake County Captains

65

El Paso, TX	El Paso Chihuahuas	Granville, WV	West Virginia Black Bears
Elizabethton, TN	Elizabethton Twins	Great Falls, MT	Great Falls Voyagers
Erie, PA	Erie SeaWolves	Greeneville, TN	Greeneville Reds
Eugene, OR	Eugene Emeralds	Greensboro, NC	Greensboro Grasshoppers
Everett, WA	Everett AquaSox		
Fayetteville, AR	Northwest Arkansas Naturals	Greenville, SC	Greenville Drive
		Gulfport, MS	Biloxi Shuckers
Fayetteville, NC	Fayetteville Woodpeckers	Hagerstown, MD	Hagerstown Suns
Fishkill, NY	Hudson Valley Renegades	Hartford, CT	Hartford Yard Goats
		Hickory, NC	Hickory Crawdads
Fort Myers, FL	Fort Myers Mighty Mussels	Hillsboro, OR	Hillsboro Hops
Fort Wayne, IN	Fort Wayne TinCaps	Huntsville, AL	Rocket City Trash Pandas (expected debut 2020)
Fort Smith, AR	Northwest Arkansas Naturals		
Frederick, MD	Frederick Keys	Idaho Falls, ID	Idaho Falls Chukars
		Indianapolis, IN	Indianapolis Indians
Fredericksburg, VA	Fredericksburg Nationals (expected debut 2020)	Jackson, MS	Mississippi Braves
Fresno, CA	Fresno Grizzlies	Jackson, TN	Jackson Generals
Frisco, TX	Frisco RoughRiders	Jacksonville, FL	Jacksonville Jumbo Shrimp
Garden City, ID	Boise Hawks	Johnson City, TN	Johnson City Cardinals
Geneva, IL	Kane County Cougars		
Grand Chute, WI	Wisconsin Timber Rattlers	Jupiter, FL	shared by Jupiter Hammerheads and Palm Beach Cardinals
Grand Junction, CO	Grand Junction Rockies	Kannapolis, NC	Kannapolis Cannon Ballers (formerly Intimidators; field debuts in 2020)
Grand Rapids, MI	West Michigan Whitecaps		

MAJORING IN THE MINORS

Keizer, OR	Salem-Keizer Volcanoes	Madison, AL	Rocket City Trash Pandas (expected debut 2020)
Kennewick, WA	Tri-City Dust Devils	Manchester, NH	New Hampshire Fisher Cats
Kingsport, TN	Kingsport Mets	Memphis, TN	Memphis Redbirds
Kinston, NC	Down East Wood Ducks	Metairie, LA	New Orleans Baby Cakes (expected to move to Wichita, KS, 2020)
Kissimmee, FL	Florida Fire Frogs (moving 2020; where & brand TBD)	Midland, MI	Great Lakes Loons
Knoxville, TN	Tennessee Smokies	Midland, TX	Midland RockHounds
Kodak, TN	Tennessee Smokies		
Lake Elsinore, CA	Lake Elsinore Storm	Missoula, MT	Missoula PaddleHeads
Lakeland, FL	Lakeland Flying Tigers	Mobile, AL	Mobile BayBears (expected to move to Madison, AL, 2020)
Lakewood (actually Lakewood Township), NJ	Lakewood BlueClaws	Modesto, CA	Modesto Nuts
		Moline, IL	Quad Cities River Bandits
Lancaster, CA	Lancaster JetHawks	Montgomery, AL	Montgomery Biscuits
Lansing, MI	Lansing Lugnuts		
Las Vegas, NV	Las Vegas Aviators	Moosic, PA	Scranton/Wilkes-Barre RailRiders
Lawrenceville, GA	Gwinnett Stripers	Morgantown, WV	West Virginia Black Bears
Lexington, KY	Lexington Legends		
Little Rock, AR	Arkansas Travelers	Myrtle Beach, SC	Myrtle Beach Pelicans
Louisville, KY	Louisville Bats	Nashville, TN	Nashville Sounds
Lowell, MA	Lowell Spinners	New Orleans, LA	New Orleans Baby Cakes (expected to move to Wichita, KS, 2020)
Lynchburg, VA	Lynchburg Hillcats		

Niles, OH	Mahoning Valley Scrappers	Potomac, MD	no minor-league team (nearest is on other side of DC in Bowie) but sometimes confused with regional locale name used by Potomac Nationals of Woodbridge, VA (who are moving to Fredericksburg, VA)
Norfolk, VA	Norfolk Tides		
North Augusta, SC	Augusta GreenJackets		
Norwich, CT	Norwich Sea Unicorns		
Ogden, UT	Ogden Raptors	Princeton, WV	Princeton Rays
Omaha, NE	Omaha Storm Chasers	Pulaski, VA	Pulaski Yankees
Orem, UT	Orem Owlz	Rancho Cucamonga, CA	Rancho Cucamonga Quakes
Palm Beach County, FL	in Jupiter, shared by Palm Beach Cardinals and Jupiter Hammerheads	Reading, PA	Reading Fightin Phils
		Reno, NV	Reno Aces
Pasco, WA	Tri-City Dust Devils	Richland, WA	Tri-City Dust Devils
Pawtucket, RI	Pawtucket Red Sox (expected to move to Worcester, MA, 2021)	Richmond, VA	Richmond Flying Squirrels
		Rochester, NY	Rochester Red Wings
Pearl, MS	Mississippi Braves	Rock Island, IL	Quad Cities River Bandits
Pensacola, FL	Pensacola Blue Wahoos		
		Rome, GA	Rome Braves
Peoria, IL	Peoria Chiefs	Round Rock, TX	Round Rock Express
Port Charlotte, FL	Charlotte Stone Crabs	Sacramento, CA	Sacramento River Cats
Port St. Lucie, FL	St. Lucie Mets		
		Salem, OR	Salem-Keizer Volcanoes
Portland, OR	Portland Sea Dogs		
		Salem, VA	Salem Red Sox
		Salisbury, MD	Delmarva Shorebirds

MAJORING IN THE MINORS

Salt Lake City, UT	Salt Lake Bees	Toledo, OH	Toledo Mud Hens
San Antonio, TX	San Antonio Missions	Trenton, NJ	Trenton Thunder
San Bernardino, CA	Inland Empire 66ers of San Bernardino	Troy, NY	Tri-City ValleyCats
		Tulsa, OK	Tulsa Drillers
San Jose, CA	San Jose Giants	Vancouver, BC	Vancouver Canadians
Schenectady, NY	Tri-City Dust Devils	Visalia, CA	Visalia Rawhide
Scranton, PA	Scranton/Wilkes-Barre RailRiders	Wappingers Falls, NY	Hudson Valley Renegades
Sevierville, TN	Tennessee Smokies		
South Bend, IN	South Bend Cubs	Wichita, KS	Wichita Wind Surge (expected to debut 2020)
Spokane, OR	Spokane Indians	Wilkes-Barre, PA	Scranton/Wilkes-Barre RailRiders
Springdale, AR	Northwest Arkansas Naturals	Williamsport, PA	Williamsport Crosscutters
Springfield, MO	Springfield Cardinals	Wilmington, DE	Wilmington Blue Rocks
State College, PA	State College Spikes	Winston-Salem, NC	Winston-Salem Dash
Staten Island, NY	Staten Island Yankees		
Stockton, CA	Stockton Ports	Woodbridge, VA	Potomac Nationals (expected to move to Fredericksburg, MD, 2020)
Suwanee, GA	Gwinnett Stripers (Gwinnett is the name of the county; the ballpark is between Buford and Lawrenceville but closer to Suwanee than either!)	Worcester, MA	Worcester Red Sox (expected debut 2021)
		Youngstown, OH	Mahoning Valley Scrappers
Syracuse, NY	Syracuse Mets	Zebulon, NC	Carolina Mudcats
Tacoma, WA	Tacoma Rainiers		
Tampa, FL	Tampa Tarpons		

Even ballpark names get tricky. More and more have double names, with one or both sold, like something Field at something Stadium. Do we want the whole phrase? What about when the stadium owner (usually a political jurisdiction) calls it one name and the team calls it another? We could go by what most locals call it, what the media call it, how it appears in the box score, its official name in official documents, or we could make up an arbitrary rule like stadium name only. We could also become very confused. In the end, I believe what its owner calls it should govern. Specific to the double names, I let primary stadium signage determine whether to give both or which.

I. CURRENT (as of end of 2019 SEASON) MiLB TEAMS/STADIUMS:

Aberdeen IronBirds

Leidos Field at Ripken Stadium, Aberdeen, MD

Class A-Short Season New York-Pennsylvania League

Baltimore Orioles

Got: **July 2, 2012; Staten Island Yankees 7, Aberdeen IronBirds 5**

In 2002, Oriole great Cal "Iron Man" Ripken Jr. bought the Utica Blue Sox and moved them to his hometown's brand-new stadium bearing his family name.

The then-Florida Marlins' farm club had been unaffiliated in the early 1980s – a rarity in an MiLB league. *Boys of Summer* author Roger Kahn bought controlling interest for the 1983 season, but as a book project – he sold out after the season and published *Good Enough to Dream* in 1985.

The IronBirds eventually spelled the end of the longest affiliation in baseball history; the Appalachian League's Bluefield Orioles had been with Baltimore since 1958 but the big Birds dropped them after the 2009 season. The Appy is technically one level lower than the NYPL, but few big-league clubs have a team in both and the Orioles partnering with their home-grown legend was a no-brainer.

"IronBirds" simultaneously salutes Ripken's hitting streak and the O's. Ripken Stadium sold out every 'Birds game their first ten seasons. HOK Sport, already famous for Oriole Park at Camden Yards, designed the stately brick ballpark.

Ripken, declaring he wanted to own ten teams in ten leagues in ten years, bought other teams in 2005 and 2008 – but he sold those in 2012 and 2016. At this writing, he is peddling a majority interest in the 'Birds. His company also owns The Ripken Experience youth baseball camps in Pigeon Forge, TN, Myrtle Beach, SC, and Aberdeen.

Akron RubberDucks
Canal Park, Akron, OH
Class Double-A Eastern League
Cleveland Indians
Got: **July 3, 2012; Richmond Flying Squirrels 7, Akron Aeros 5**

In 1989, the Vermont Mariners moved into a brand-new ballpark in Canton, OH, joining the Indians' farm system – but they had only a short run as the Canton-Akron Indians. In 1997, a new "downtown retro" ballpark by architect HOK Sport (now Populous) drew them into the Rubber City – as the Aeros, for Ohio aviation figures from the Wright Brothers to John Glenn and Neil Armstrong.

Canal's opener drew 9,068, still the house baseball record. Their affiliation with the Indians is tied for ninth-longest among separately owned teams, but the nearby Tribe could veto any other.

In 2014, new ownership rebranded as RubberDucks – an also-ran from a 2009 rebrand trial balloon in which "Aeros" got two-thirds of a five-way vote – to salute the local rubber industry. Canal Park also does so, with a clock tower modeled on Goodyear's.

As beautiful on its own as to be expected from HOK, its tremendous view of downtown Akron is a real plus. Its name salutes the Ohio and Erie Canal, which passes just beyond left field and opened up the then-frontier state in 1825. The Soap Box Derby Parade of Champions rolls past the ballpark.

I've actually been here twice and missed it once. I got it when the team was Aeros but needed it again because of the change to RubberDucks. My 2014 try failed amid unbelievable traffic that defeated a marginally possible Maine-to-Ohio drive, but I got it on my 2015 trip.

Albuquerque Isotopes

Isotopes Park, Albuquerque, NM

Class Triple-A Pacific Coast League

Colorado Rockies

Got: **April 28, 2014; Albuquerque Isotopes 4, Salt Lake Bees 3, 12 inns.**

The Los Angeles Dodgers have a long history of affiliations with Albuquerque Double-A and Triple-A teams, most of them called Dukes, but they ended their most recent one partly because the Duke City's elevation makes it such a hitters' park. They did it dramatically, buying the Oklahoma City RedHawks after the 2016 season. What was a problem for the Dodgers, though, is perfect for the Rockies.

After Albuquerque Sports Stadium's condition cost the city its previous PCL franchise, what to do was put to voters. They chose renovation over replacement. HOK Sport (now Populous) then "renovated" it down to the seating bowl, and in 2003 the former Calgary Cannons moved in. The 'Topes say their playpen "opened" that year, but the websites of Populous and then co-tenant University of New Mexico Lobos baseball say it was "renovated." I never made it to the original, but given that story and photos I consider this a *Rebuilt*.

Playing as *Mariachis de Nuevo Mexico*, the 'Topes won the 2018 *Copa de la Diversion* (Fun Cup) Hispanic engagement event series – drawing a house baseball record for their May 5 *Copa* game.

While one might assume "Isotopes" is for nearby Los Alamos National Laboratory, the name was actually inspired by TV's *The Simpsons*. In the 2001 episode "Hungry, Hungry Homer," Homer – a safety inspector at the show's Springfield nuclear power plant – stages a hunger strike to keep the *Springfield* Isotopes from moving *to* Albuquerque. Colorful statues of the Simpsons populate the ballpark.

Altoona Curve
Peoples Natural Gas Field, Altoona, PA
Class Double-A Eastern League
Pittsburgh Pirates
Got: **July 4, 2013; Altoona Curve 15, Erie Sea Dogs 7**

This 1999 Eastern League expansion franchise was originally awarded to Springfield, MA, but after that city passed on building a ballpark it was redirected to Altoona. Ownership then topped that achievement by beating out EL expansion-mate Erie for the coveted Pirates' affiliation – despite the fact that Erie's previous New York-Pennsylvania League team was a Bucs' farm affiliate at the time.

Then-Blair County Ballpark drew a crowd of 6,171 to its 1999 debut and house baseball record 10,116 to a 2013 exhibition between the Curve and the Pirates. A 2012 naming-rights deal with Pittsburgh-based Peoples Natural Gas renamed it.

Its railroad roundhouse style salutes the industry that helped found, and remains a major presence in, the city of Altoona. In fact, "Curve"– one of only a handful of singular team nicknames in Minor League baseball – was inspired by the nearby 360-degree Horseshoe Curve. That 1854 railroad engineering marvel greatly lessened the incline for trains as they traveled the steep Allegheny mountainside. Horseshoe Curve joined the National Register of Historic Places in 1966.

The ballpark's double-deck design allows bigger concourses, which dilute crowd density. The Skyliner roller coaster in neighboring Lakemont Park is visible beyond right field, backdropped by the scenic ridges of the Alleghenies.

Amarillo Sod Poodles
Hodgetown, Amarillo, TX

Class Double-A Texas League
San Diego Padres
Got: **May 4, 2019; Arkansas Travelers 6, Amarillo Sod Poodles 4, spnd., 5 inns.**

The 2018-19 off-season saw four Minor League baseball teams change cities; three were commonly owned and simultaneously shifted. The San Antonio Missions, the latest franchise in the city's Texas League history that dated to 1888, went from the Alamo City to the Yellow Rose.

It nearly didn't happen. The Elmore Sports Group also wanted to shift the Triple-A Colorado Springs Sky Sox to San Antonio and the Rookie-Advanced Helena Brewers to the Springs, but San Antonio wouldn't replace Wolff Municipal Stadium. "The Wolff" has three Triple-A strikes against it – old, too small and not downtown – but Amarillo's willingness to build a ballpark convinced ESG to go ahead. The move was announced in June 2017 and ground broken Feb. 1, 2018. The Populous-designed ballpark's sand-colored brick exterior and false front-like main entrance create a western-movie feel.

Amarillo had forty-three seasons of affiliated ball 1922-82, the last twenty-two in the Texas League. That team, the Gold Sox, moved to Beaumont, TX, during the 1982-83 off-season and two moves later is now the Northwest Arkansas Naturals. This is the second time a franchise has moved from San Antonio to Amarillo. The first followed the 1964 season and, having since also moved twice, is now the Tulsa Drillers.

"Sod Poodles" is pioneer slang for prairie dogs. The stadium is named for former Mayor Jerry Hodge, who drove efforts to return affiliated baseball to Amarillo, with "town" a nod to prairie dog communities.

Arkansas Travelers
Dickey-Stephens Park, North Little Rock, AR
Class Double-A Texas League
Seattle Mariners
Got: **April 22, 2014; Tulsa Drillers 2, Arkansas Travelers 0; Tulsa Drillers 1, Arkansas Travelers 0, 11 inns.**

The Travs are among the Minors' more storied franchises, for several reasons. Little Rock hosted professional baseball as far back as 1887. "Travelers" comes from an 1840s story about a lost traveler meeting a squatter in the Ozark Mountains. Then there's the quintessential American personal success story: Ray Winder started as a ticket seller, ended up running the business, and saved baseball for the city so often they renamed the Travs' then-home for him. No later than 1957, he changed the location identifier from Little Rock to Arkansas – making the Travs, not the usually so credited Minnesota Twins, the first pro sports team to go by a state name. A rare franchise swap, with the Tulsa Oilers in 1966, took Little Rock from Triple-A to Double-A and finally brought stability.

Opened across the river in North Little Rock in 2007, the new ballpark also hosts the Arkansas Travelers Baseball Museum and further plays on history with its name. Hall of Famer Bill Dickey and his brother George were raised in Arkansas and played both Trav and big-league ball; brothers Jack and Witt Stephens were developers whose family donated the land.

The ballpark saw an unfortunate historical event in its first season, at this writing the last participant death in Organized Baseball, when a foul ball killed Tulsa Drillers hitting/first-base coach Mike Coolbaugh.

The University of Arkansas Razorbacks' annual game here has drawn more than 10,000 three times – something the Travs have never done.

Asheville Tourists
McCormick Field, Asheville, NC
Class A South Atlantic League
Colorado Rockies
Got: **Aug. 28, 2011; Asheville Tourists 15, Hagerstown Suns 5**

This beauty of a ballpark, built on a mountainside, can launch debate over its age. The original wooden facility opened in 1924, which would put it in the elite of still-open historical ballparks – but it was rebuilt in brick and concrete in 1992. The line between renovation and replacement can be blurry, but for me that's such structural change as to produce a new ballpark. In fairness, I should say I never saw the original and I've read the construction material was the *only* change because the rebuild exactly followed the original park's contours.

Named for fly-fighting bacteriologist Dr. Lewis McCormick, the original garnered immediate fame when Babe Ruth praised its beauty. The Babe boosted the fame when he became ill on the way to a 1925 exhibition game there (famously, the "bellyache heard 'round the world") and again when he and Lou Gehrig both homered in a 1931 game.

It hosted stock car racing in the 1950s and Crash Davis's fictional record-breaking homer in *Bull Durham* (1988). The Tourists saluted the film's thirtieth anniversary with Crash bobbleheads.

With mountainside logistics limiting construction envelopes, its thirty-six-foot-tall right-field wall is just 300 feet from home. Its souvenir shop is named Tourists Trap, and where in the world but on its scoreboard are Visitors and Tourists antonyms? Speaking of the scoreboard, it's manual – one of six in the Minors.

"Tourists" dates to 1915 – when nicknames were less formal and not trademarked – but is not original to Asheville; Augusta teams used it 1904-17.

Auburn Doubledays
Leo Pinckney Field at Falcon Park, Auburn, NY
Class A-Short Season New York-Pennsylvania League
Washington Nationals
Got: **July 13, 2013; Staten Island Yankees 6, Auburn Doubledays 1**

A $3 million renovation during the 2018-19 off-season made Cayuga Community College Spartans sports a Doubledays co-tenant, although winter weather interruptions virtually wiped out its 2019 college baseball season. The Spartans played their first home game there May 2, just two days before their last scheduled home game. Cayuga softball, soccer and lacrosse also use the field.

Renovations include artificial turf. "Carpet" failed miserably a generation ago, but a new form is taking hold in college and Minor League baseball that is said to feel more like natural grass-and-dirt. Those who hated earlier artificial turfs said it was like playing on concrete. I've walked on it, and it did feel more like outdoor carpet than sod – no doubt more so when running and diving. Plus: *hot*!

The Auburn/Abner phonetic play salutes an icon who spent much of his childhood in Auburn. Ballston Spa native Abner Doubleday did *not* invent baseball but *did* fire the first Union shot of the Civil War, serve heroically at Gettysburg, rise to the rank of general, and help create the San Francisco cable-car system.

Falcon Park salutes the social fraternity that built the 1927 original. Its 1959 professional team bought it, but folded in 1980. Auburn then assumed the team's debt, resurrecting the ball club in 1982 and replacing the park in 1995.

The field and an NYPL division are named for the circuit's third president, long-time Auburn *Citizen* Sports Editor Leo Pinckney. What is now Minor League Baseball – formed Sept. 5, 1901 – was originally headquartered in Auburn.

Augusta GreenJackets
SRP Park, North Augusta, SC
Class A South Atlantic League
San Francisco Giants
Got: **July 2, 2018; Columbia Fireflies 16, Augusta GreenJackets 8**

The only new Minor League ballpark to open in 2018 hit the drawing boards in 2012, when the city across the Savannah River from the Augusta we all know included a baseball stadium in a redevelopment project now called Riverside Park. The same year, a group bought the Georgia-based 'Jackets from Cal Ripken, Jr., to move them to this new park.

What took six years? Legal challenges, filed and cleared and appealed and cleared – mostly one at a time. Once the way was *finally* clear, high-end suites sold out nearly a week before the official groundbreaking May 25, 2017. Season ticket sales to the new park surpassed the old one's by mid-July. In August, SRP Credit Union (as in Savannah River Project, now Savannah River Site) bought naming rights.

Two area high schools christened it April 9, 2018, with the Clemson University Tigers and University of Georgia Bulldogs drawing 5,801 the next day. The Minor League team's home opener, on the 12th, topped both with 5,919.

The move at least nominally ended an Augusta, GA, professional baseball history that dated to 1885 and included the legendary Ty Cobb's 1904 pro debut. Crossing city and state lines notwithstanding, the shift was actually only about two linear miles, and east rather than north. The old Augusta facility was nice-looking but small and in a remote location – the second ballpark tried on that spot.

Batavia Muckdogs
Dwyer Stadium, Batavia, NY
Class A-Short Season New York-Pennsylvania League
Miami Marlins
Got: July 11, 2013; Batavia Muckdogs 1, Vermont Lake Monsters 0

Want to see a Minor League game here? Go soon.

The NYPL took over the franchise in December 2017. Already on the ropes, it was operated 2008-17 by the Rochester Red Wings under contract with its Genesee County non-profit ownership. However, when attendance jumped in 2019, the league (as owner) signed a three-year lease.

Still, the Muckdogs are one of two short-A teams in a saturated stretch of MiLB clubs within twenty miles of Interstate 90 between Erie, PA, and Syracuse, NY. The Jamestown Jammers moved away after the 2014 season, but from the west end of the cluster. Since then, the Auburn Doubledays and Batavia – each barely a half-hour from a Triple-A team – have been the league's two least attended.

Batavia's baseball-historic 1939 saw State Street Park, renamed MacArthur Stadium during World War II fervor, open and the city host the six-club meeting that created the Pennsylvania-Ontario-New York (PONY) League. Renamed after losing its Ontario team, the NYPL has six teams in "NY" and two in "P" but also one each in Vermont, Massachusetts, Ohio, Maryland, Connecticut and West Virginia. Make a pronounceable acronym out of that!

MacArthur, renamed for long-time club president Edward Dwyer in 1973, was replaced in 1996 under the Dwyer name. Despite Eisenhower-era gaps, Batavia claims to be the league's only in-place charter franchise. A *truly* historic claim? Organized Baseball's first black manager: Gene Baker, 1961. The long-time Clippers changed nicknames in 1998 to one fans chose that salutes farm-friendly Elba muckland.

Beloit Snappers
Pohlman Field, Beloit, WI
Class A Midwest League
Oakland Athletics
Got: July 30, 2014; Beloit Snappers 4, Peoria Chiefs 3, 11 inns.
Different in 2020: stadium; not yet, but something will happen soon

One of several teams that have stayed in an old park to the point of risking their existence, the Snappers finally seem headed toward a new park.

Major League Baseball wrote ballpark standards into the 1990 Professional Baseball Agreement that governs Major-Minor relations. This community-owned club's board of directors is less concerned about profit than most MiLB clubs, and has been getting waivers since 1990, but first the Milwaukee Brewers (2004) and then the Minnesota Twins (2012) cited the stadium in dropping the club.

Attendance is among the MwL's lowest, and in March 2017 Minor League Baseball told the board to fix the issue by 2020 or lose the team. On the last Friday of the 2018 campaign, directors signed plans to (1) sell the team to someone who promised to keep it in Beloit if a new ballpark is built and (2) to build that ballpark. In January 2019, MiLB said deadlines had been missed and things did not look good – but in September 2019 a new deal was struck with an existing MiLB owner.

Opened as Telfer Park in 1982, it landed a Brewers' farm team that used their nickname. Telfer was renamed in 1987 for longtime schoolboy and American Legion baseball coach Harry Pohlman.

In 1995, the team was renamed for snapping turtles. Turtle Creek, the town of Turtle and Beloit's original name – Turtle Village – all salute a turtle-shaped mound at Beloit College tribal people built over 1,000 years ago.

Pohlman appears in the film *Sugar* (2008).

Billings Mustangs
Dehler Park, Billings, MT
Rookie-Advanced Pioneer League
Cincinnati Reds
Got: **Aug. 6, 2014; Grand Junction Rockies 6, Billings Mustangs 5**

In 2006, after five decades of mostly affiliated baseball at Cobb Field, Billings voters passed a bond issue to replace it on the same piece of land. The $12.5 million ballpark went from a plan to reality, including the demolition of Cobb, entirely between the walk-off single that ended the 2007 season and 2008's first pitch.

The city owns the ballpark, but it is jointly managed by the city, the Mustangs, Montana State University Billings and American Legion Baseball. The MSUB Yellowjackets and Billings Royals Legion team also play there.

Fleetwood Gaming owner Jon Dehler bought naming rights to honor his father, Fleetwood founder Billy Joe Dehler. A grass berm and an outdoor suite – the 329 Club, located next to the left field corner's distance marker – augment the listed capacity, 2,571 individual stadium seats plus bleachers that can seat another 500. The playing field is eight feet below street level, with its 360-degree concourse above the seating bowl. This rare configuration provides great sightlines even on concession runs, but can offer challenges when it comes to drainage.

The Reds-Billings affiliation, which dates to 1974, is tied for the second-longest current partnership among parent-farm teams that are not commonly owned or operated.

Biloxi Shuckers
MGM Park, Biloxi, MS
Class Double-A Southern League
Milwaukee Brewers
Got: **July 2, 2015; Biloxi Shuckers 3, Mississippi Braves 1**

Good things can come from bad beginnings.

This beautiful Gulf Coast ballpark survived the second-worst Minor League baseball construction soap opera of this millennium. BP oil spill settlement money provided nearly half of the funding for an idea that had been kicking around the coast for about ten years, and the Beau Rivage casino named it – at least partly in exchange for the land, directly across the street from the casino.

Good start, but that's when the delays began. The incoming team was the Huntsville Stars, who ended up playing many of their 2015 first-half home games in the old facility back in North Alabama and the rest at the home of the opposing team. MGM Park finally opened almost halfway into the season, and even that was a close call: The certificate of occupancy was issued the very *day* the first game was finally played. Perhaps making up for having played so many home innings away, Biloxi took fourteen frames to beat Mobile 5-4. Despite such distractions, the Shuckers won their division's first-half title and had the league's best regular-season record.

The stucco-looking exterior lets the ballpark blend into its downtown surroundings. A statue of MGM's Leo the Lion guards the main gate.

Hurricane Irma nearly gave MGM a surprise 2017 playoff when the Southern League rescheduled games four and five of the South Division series from Jacksonville to MGM – but Pensacola won the series in three games.

"Shuckers" is for the local seafood industry.

Binghamton Rumble Ponies
NYSEG Stadium, Binghamton, NY
Class Double-A Eastern League
New York Mets
Got: **between June 22-28, 2002**

In 1991, the Mets bought the Williamsport Bills to move them to Binghamton. Media quoted the Bills' majority owner – also a New York Yankee minority owner – as saying the 1990 Professional Baseball Agreement forced that sale to that buyer.

The move came with the April 1992 opening of Binghamton Municipal Stadium, renamed in a 2001 deal with New York State Electric and Gas. The Mets soon sold to locals, who in 2010 called their Met affiliation "our most treasured asset."

In 2012, they denounced media reports that they'd sold the B-Mets to a group that would move them to Ottawa, ON. Nothing happened because Ottawa didn't renovate its stadium. In 2015, Wilmington Blue Rocks ownership sued the B-Mets for breaking a 2014 sale agreement that would have moved the B-Mets to Delaware. The suit proved the Ottawa story but was settled under seal just before mediation. That December brought a *third* buyer – who promised not to move them. His 2017 nickname change salutes the "carousel capital of the world."

Heisman Trophy and former National Football League quarterback Tim Tebow, a 2018 Rumble Pony, continued to boost attendance and became an All-Star – but a July 20 hand injury ended his season.

I got the B-Mets before I was even getting *Gets*, while umpiring in a nearby national tournament, but the Ponies' *Go-*

Back took two tries. On the first, after a seven-hour drive, the sky became a waterfall between gate-opening and first pitch.

The Eastern League was founded in Binghamton in 1923.

Birmingham Barons
Regions Field, Birmingham, AL
Class Double-A Southern League
Chicago White Sox
Got: **May 28, 2013; Tennessee Smokies 3, Birmingham Barons 2**

Most ballpark proposals go through a rough period of scrutiny while the usual suspects scream about tax dollars subsidizing private business. That's not what actually happens in these public-private partnerships; the city generally ends up owning, and collecting rent on, what it builds – and that idea usually wins out. This one was announced and done on an extremely quick timeline – and beautifully done. Outside, on 14th Street, a 286-foot long BIRMINGHAM sign in twenty-six-foot tall all-capital letters is visible from Interstate 65 and Willie Mays, who is from nearby Westfield, makes a leaping catch in bronze.

In 2013, Regions Field: lured the Barons back from twenty-five years in suburban Hoover; landed a four-year ChiSox affiliation extension, bringing their partnership to the seventh-longest among separately owned teams; won the league title; and drew nearly twice the fans. In 2015, the franchise's best attendance for a non-Michael Jordan season included the new ballpark's 1 millionth. By 2017, there was broad agreement that the ballpark was turning the Magic City's downtown around. It appeared in season three of TV's *Brockmire* (2019).

The Barons play one regular-season game a year at Rickwood Field (see **Birmingham, AL [LEGACY]**), their historic pre-Hoover home. The oldest standing stadium that ever housed professional ball is now as much museum as ballpark, but still hosts the Rickwood Classic and some other games.

Mays played his first games under professional contract at Rickwood in 1947, although he played infrequently – and unsigned – in 1945-46 for the Chattanooga Choo-Choos.

Bluefield Blue Jays
Bowen Field at Charles A. Peters Baseball Park, Bluefield, VA
Rookie-Advanced Appalachian League
Toronto Blue Jays
Got: **July 16, 1990; Bluefield Orioles 6, Huntington Cubs 0; Huntington Cubs 2, Bluefield Orioles 1**

Despite its West Virginia street address, Bowen Field sits on land that lies physically in Virginia but is owned by the city of Bluefield, WV, as part of Lotito City Park. The state line is only a few foul balls from home plate. The Ridge Runner train that runs around the city park once ran on the world's smallest interstate railroad.

There are actually two Bluefields, administratively two municipalities but effectively one community straddling the state line. Spotlighting the temperate climate in "Nature's Air-Conditioned City," free lemonade is passed out the day after any 90-degree reading – an idea originated in 1939 and first executed in 1941.

Bowen Field fits right into all this quaintness, featuring tree-covered mountains beyond its outfield, an old-style grandstand and a cinderblock office building. The winner of the season series with nearby Princeton, WV, gets the Mercer Cup.

Baseball came to Bluefield in 1882, professional ball in 1924. Opened in 1939, Bowen was rebuilt after a 1973 fire. The only city with a team in every Appy season since 1946 saw three affiliations in the mid-1950s, but 1958 started a record fifty-three-year run with the Orioles. Baby Birds, coined then, still fits. George Fanning became general manager in 1948, helped sign Boog Powell in 1959 and remained GM until he died at 86 in 1995. After attendance dropped eighteen percent 2009-13, the ball club resumed beer sales – but the gate fell another twenty-four percent through 2018 before a slight upward bounce in '19.

Boise Hawks
Memorial Stadium, Garden City, ID
Class A-Short Season Northwest League
Toronto Blue Jays
Got: **Aug. 10, 2014; Boise Hawks 17, Eugene Emeralds 3**
Different in 2020: stadium; not yet, but something will happen soon

Built with private funds on Ada County-owned land next to the Western Idaho Fairgrounds, Memorial Stadium opened two seasons *after* the former Tri-Cities Triplets moved from Richland, WA. Ironically, the Trips went from one high school field to another. They played at Richland High School's ballpark in 1986, then played 1987-88 as the Hawks at Borah High School's field – since named for Bill Wigle, who served as Borah's baseball coach for its first twenty-four seasons. Memorial opened in time for the Hawks' 1989 home debut.

Previous Boise professional baseball dates erratically to 1904. A long-running Pioneer League franchise folded in 1963, and Boise was in and out of the Northwest League in the mid-1970s. The Hawks reportedly talked to Hillsboro, OR, before the Yakima Bears moved there after the 2012 season. Two years later, the Chicago Cubs dropped their fourteen-year affiliation over the now substandard ballpark.

New ownership managed to hike Hawks attendance every year 2015-19 but still wants a new stadium. The city *might* see two: Boise State University is reviving baseball in 2020 and – after flirting with sharing a ballpark with the Hawks – decided to build its own on-campus facility. There were three big developments in 2019 – January: the Hawks acquired a United Soccer League franchise contingent on the Hawks getting a new ballpark; April – BSU said it would again consider sharing a stadium, but with hard conditions that would require serious negotiation; June – BSU again said it would build its own.

Bowie Baysox
Prince George's Stadium, Bowie, MD
Class Double-A Eastern League
Baltimore Orioles
Got: **June 19, 2010; Harrisburg Senators 5, Bowie Baysox 2**

Prince George's Stadium hosted the first game decided under Minor League Baseball's new extra-inning rule Opening Day 2018. The invented-runner rule, foisted by Major League Baseball to lessen the possibility of extremely long extra-inning games, places the last man to complete an at-bat the previous inning on second base at the beginning of any extra inning. The idea was first used in international play in 2008, although there it doesn't take effect until the eleventh inning.

The Birds-Baysox partnership, tied for the ninth-longest current affiliation among separately owned teams, is reflected in the Orioles-orange bleacher backs, handrails and other stadium trim. The Baysox even played at the Orioles' nest. After leaving Hagerstown, the franchise played 1993 as planned at Baltimore's Memorial Stadium – which had been vacated when Oriole Park at Camden Yards opened in 1992. When weather pushed Prince George's completion past the 1994 opener, the Baysox had to juggle their early homestands among the baseball playpens of the Frederick Keys, the Wilmington Blue Rocks, the US Naval Academy Midshipmen and the University of Maryland Terrapins.

With a stated capacity of 10,000, it's big for Double-A – and a few gates, including the 2000 Double-A All-Star Game, have topped that by more than 4,000. The Baysox, in the Washington Nationals' protected territory, pre-date them by eleven years.

Bowling Green Hot Rods
Bowling Green Ballpark, Bowling Green, KY
Class A Midwest League
Tampa Bay Rays
Got: **May 5, 2012; Bowling Green Hot Rods 2, Lake County Captains 0**

The Hot Rods date to 2001, when the Wilmington Waves and Lexington Legends joined the other Class A circuit, the South Atlantic League.

The Legends have been stable, but the Waves became a beach ball. After one season in the North Carolina city, it was on to Albany, GA, as the South Georgia Waves. The next year found them, without changing names, in Columbus, GA. Their first-ever second consecutive season in place, 2004, brought a name change to Columbus Catfish. Four seasons followed in that name and place, but the franchise opened the 2009 season in Kentucky as the Corvette City's first affiliated team in sixty-seven seasons.

The sell-out debut crowd of 6,886, at this writing unequaled, saw the starting Rods ride onto the field in locally owned vintage hot rods. The team store is, of course, The Body Shop.

In 2010, the Rods and Lake County Captains moved from the SAL to the Midwest. Their parks have the rare boast of hosting the same team in different still-operating leagues.

Goodbye, Columbus? The Caps also fled that Georgia city, six seasons earlier.

"Ballpark Blackout" for the 2017 solar eclipse had the Rods in moon-based uniforms and their visitors in sun-based garb. A banner 2018 saw fan number 2 million, the Rods revert to "Catfish" for an August game, the Bowling Green "Bootleggers" win the first Battle for the Barrel over the Peoria "Distillers" and – finally – a league championship, also over Peoria in its regular identity of Chiefs.

Bradenton Marauders
LECOM Park, Bradenton, FL
Class A-Advanced Florida State League
Pittsburgh Pirates
Got: **Aug. 21, 2013; Bradenton Marauders 4, Jupiter Hammerheads 3**

Like most Florida State League ballparks, LECOM has a more visible mission than hosting the Minor League team that plays the most games in it: hosting spring-training games of its parent team.

"Marauders" straddles the line between using an independent identity and their parent club's.

City Park, opened in 1923, was renamed in 1962 for Pirate great "Deacon" Bill McKechnie – who had retired to Bradenton – as he joined the Hall of Fame. While this might suggest the Pittsburgh-Bradenton affiliation dates to then, the Bucs actually didn't move their Florida operations there until 1969. The name of McKechnie, who died shortly after the 1965 World Series, remained on the ballpark until Lake Erie College of Osteopathic Medicine bought naming rights before the 2017 spring training schedule. Essentially rebuilt in 1993 and renovated in 2007, it is now more than triple its original capacity.

The Marauders resulted from the Pirates' buying and moving the Reds' Sarasota FSL club in 2010, a year after Cincinnati moved its spring operations to Arizona. That move by the Reds was significant in spring-training history, which has been drifting west for decades; the Reds became the fifteenth team training in Arizona, bringing the Cactus League to par with the Grapefruit League – or, depending on your perspective, dropping once-dominant Florida into a tie with nascent Arizona.

Bristol Pirates
Boyce Cox Field at DeVault Memorial Stadium, Bristol, VA
Rookie-Advanced Appalachian League
Pittsburgh Pirates
Got: **July 9, 1990; Huntington Cubs 4, Bristol Tigers 1; Huntington Cubs 7, Bristol Tigers 0**

Bristol's long Appalachian League history includes twenty-four of its 1911-55 seasons as a Class D league. The Appy shut down for 1956 and returned in the short season format in 1957. Bristol was not in the resurrected circuit until 1969, when this basic new stadium landed this franchise as a Tigers' team.

Following a White Sox' stint, the Pirates returned sixty years after ending a previous affiliation. A game of that era – not here – made baseball history: May 13, 1952, at old Shaw Stadium (see **Bristol, VA [VISITED]**), Ron Necciai struck out twenty-seven batters for the then-Bristol Twins. No other professional has ever done that in one game, but Necciai would last just six weeks in the big leagues.

"Twins" – far pre-dating Minnesota big-league baseball – referred to Bristol being one community but two cities straddling the Virginia-Tennessee line. Since rejoining the Pirates, Bristol has begun using BriBucs as an alternate nickname – a take-off on the Pirates' Bucs, short for Buccaneers. The stadium is named for long-time Appy President Charlton Ross "Chauncey" DeVault, the field for Boyce Cox. The Bristol, TN, native – whom I met as a visiting play-by-play guy – played two non-consecutive seasons (interrupted by World War II) for the Twins, helped bring Little League to town and in 1984 became president of the then-Tigers. Bristol's entire pro baseball history has been on the Virginia side of the line, but the BriBucs want a new stadium and all three sites identified by a 2016 feasibility study are in Tennessee.

Brooklyn Cyclones
MCU Park, Brooklyn, NY

Class A-Short Season New York-Pennsylvania League
New York Mets
Got: July 25, 2014; Vermont Lake Monsters 5, Brooklyn Cyclones 2

Long after the Dodgers fled to Los Angeles, both the Mets and Yankees came to want nearby affiliates, but both used their jointly held territorial rights to veto every effort the other made. In 1998, New York Mayor Rudy Giuliani offered a solution: If both big-league teams would withhold one such veto, the city would build each incoming Minor League team its own stadium.

Both ballparks opened in 2001. The Mets bought the St. Catharines Stompers, who played 2000 as the Queens Kings; the Yankee team is on Staten Island (see **Staten Island Yankees [CURRENT]**). The Kings' temporary home was also a product of deal-making. The Mets built a much smaller but quicker-to-construct ballpark on the campus of St. John's University, dubbed it The Ballpark at St. John's, played the one season in it, and after that donated it to the school for its baseball program.

Opened as KeySpan Park, the Mets' ballpark in the Giuliani deal lost that name when KeySpan Energy was sold. Municipal Credit Union bought naming rights in 2010.

Despite more Hurricane Sandy damage than any other Minor League park, MCU Park was ready for the 2013 opener – but, ironically, it was rained out.

In 2015, this franchise became the NYPL's first to draw 4 million fans in one venue. Only two other short-season clubs have done that, and neither did it faster.

Buffalo Bisons
Sahlen Field, Buffalo, NY
Class Triple-A International League
Toronto Blue Jays
Got: July 6, 2013; Syracuse Chiefs 4, Buffalo Bisons 3

First, don't tell 'em the plural of bison is bison – they *know*!

Opened as Pilot Field in 1988, Sahlen (SAY-luhn) is its sixth name – all but one under naming rights contracts.

Kansas City "downtown retro" architect HOK Sport (now Populous) later used the same design for Oriole Park at Camden Yards, making both itself and the design instantly iconic. Among those who think outside the big-league box, this Buffalo ballpark is usually cited as the first use of the design. This was HOK's third baseball stadium, following those opened as Riverside Stadium in Harrisburg, PA, and Stanley Coveleski Regional Stadium in South Bend, IN. Both had some elements of the design.

In 1985, by moving to Buffalo, the Wichita Aeros went from one venerable ballpark to another: Lawrence-Dumont Stadium had opened in 1934, War Memorial Stadium – "star" of the Robert Redford film *The Natural* – in 1937. The old yard was much of the reason Buffalo lost affiliated baseball in the 1970s, but the partial renovation for the movie made it serviceable as at least a temporary home.

Pilot was built with expansion in mind – its own, to land a big-league expansion team, but that never happened. The 1983 Louisville Redbirds were the first Minor League club to draw more than 1 million in a season, but the Bisons later did so six straight times (1988-93) – including the Minor League record: 1,240,951 in 1991.

It's also the home of the Buffalo Baseball Hall of Fame.

Burlington Bees
Community Field, Burlington, IA
Class A Midwest League
Los Angeles Angels of Anaheim
Got: **Aug. 21, 2014; Cedar Rapids Kernels 6, Burlington Bees 5**

Its baseball stadium is functional if unremarkable, but Burlington, IA, holds a unique status within Minor League baseball and sports a long history in it.

The Bees are the only MiLB club that shares both its location identifier and its nickname, while professional ball in the city dates to 1889. The other Bees, also an Angels' farm club but not corporately related, play in Salt Lake City. Burlington's team has been Bees longer this time around – since dropping their eleven-year practice of using their parents' nicknames in 1993, compared to Salt Lake's 2006 switch. The Lake's goes further back, 1915 (Pioneer League) over 1924 (Mississippi Valley League), but Burlington has used it in a far higher number of seasons. A third Burlington hosts a team, but that one goes by its state's name – the Vermont Lake Monsters. "Indians" is the only other nickname shared by separately owned Minor League teams.

An Illinois-Indiana-Iowa League member that survived the Three-I's collapse by joining the Midwest League in 1962, the Iowa Burlington has since developed ballplayers for twelve different parent clubs – two of them twice. The original stadium opened in 1947, but Community's grandstand burned down June 9, 1971. Not one playing date was lost the rest of that season or the next while volunteers rebuilt it.

The ballpark appears in the film *Sugar* (2008).

Burlington Royals
Burlington Athletic Stadium, Burlington, NC
Rookie-Advanced Appalachian League
Kansas City Royals
Got: **July 25, 1990; Burlington Indians 4, Huntington Cubs 3**

Minor League *teams* often move; this *stadium* did! Built in Danville, VA, after World War II, it was dismantled in 1958, moved forty-three miles south and reassembled near Burlington's Fairchild Park. Originally named, like the municipal park, for Fairchild Aircraft, it hosted Carolina League games. Although showing its age, its size and maintenance put it among its league's better facilities.

It took its current name in 1960, started hosting this franchise in 1986, and appears in the film *Bull Durham* (1988). June 24, 1988, the then-Indians' game with the Bluefield Orioles went twenty-seven innings; Richard Musterer's eight-hour-fifteen-minute WBBB play-by-play is the longest continuous one-game solo broadcast in Organized Baseball history.

The B-Royals are one of three MiLB clubs based in a city named Burlington, tops in the Minors; the others are the Burlington Bees and the Vermont Lake Monsters. The Bees, an Iowa Midwest League team, and their predecessors used that nickname for more than seventy of the seasons dating to 1924 but never overlapped with North Carolina's Burlington Bees (1942, 1945-51).

A memorable individual 1990 season saw Jim Thome – in *half* of a *short* season ended by promotion – bat .373 with twelve home runs and thirty-four runs batted in. That batting average would have won the league crown if he'd had enough plate appearances; extrapolating his home run and runs batted in suggest a Triple Crown if he'd played the full Appy season. In a year, Thome was in the Majors; in another twenty-eight, in the Hall of Fame.

Carolina Mudcats
Five County Stadium, Zebulon, NC
Class A-Advanced Carolina League
Milwaukee Brewers
Got: **(A-Advanced) May 13, 2012; Carolina Mudcats 3, Potomac Nationals 2 (A-Advanced)**

Carolina Mudcats
Class Double-A Southern League
First Get: **(Double-A) Aug. 14, 2011; Carolina Mudcats 6, Montgomery Biscuits 2**

The original Carolina Mudcats were unusual: a Double-A team in a city of Zebulon's size (1990 US Census: 3,421) that was not a suburb. Born of an effort to return affiliated ball to Raleigh, it landed here after the Durham Bulls' territorial veto forced ownership to find the closest possible place. "The 5Co" is in

Wake County, less than a mile from Franklin, Nash, and Johnston counties and just over seven from Wilson County.

Its 1991-2011 Southern League run ended when Organized Baseball told Minor League owners it would start enforcing the 500-mile rule, which requires air travel for all point-to-point team trips of more than that distance. With only Knoxville, TN, that close, Mudcats ownership faced with such an uptick in overhead sold and bought: its Southern League team, to a Pensacola buyer who moved the Mudcats there; a Carolina League team, from the owners of the Kinston Indians to move it to Zebulon and inherit the Carolina Mudcats identity. This created the oddity of a team named Carolina in a league named Carolina in a state named Carolina that then had eight other pro teams.

Some instability followed; after the Brewers became the third different Mudcat parent club in as many two-year affiliation cycles in the 2017 season, they bought the club – raising the number of parent-controlled Minor League teams in Triple-A through Rookie-Advanced leagues to, at the time, an even twenty percent.

Cedar Rapids Kernels
Perfect Game Field at Veterans Memorial Stadium, Cedar Rapids, IA
Class A Midwest League
Minnesota Twins
Got: **Aug. 4, 2014; Wisconsin Timber Rattlers 4, Cedar Rapids Kernels 3**

An earlier Veterans Memorial Stadium opened here in 1949, helping Cedar Rapids land an Illinois-Indiana-Iowa League franchise. The Cedar Rapids Braves were one of three teams that survived the collapse of the Three-I by joining the Midwest League in 1962. They played that season as the Red Raiders, began using their parent teams' nicknames in 1965, and in 1993 took Kernels.

The current park opened on the old one's parking lot in 2002. Veterans also hosted the 2004 and 2016 Midwest League All-Star games and the 2006 American Legion World Series. Before the 2009 season, the Cedar Rapids-based Perfect Game baseball development program bought naming rights to the playing field, prepending to rather than replacing the existing stadium name.

After twenty years with the Angels, the Kernels joined the Twins in 2013. The Twins had become the second straight big-league team to drop the Beloit Snappers from its farm system over Pohlman Field's condition, age, and lack of player and fan amenities. That cost the Snappers the positives of having a nearby parent team – their previous one had been the Milwaukee Brewers – but opened the door for Cedar Rapids to gain one.

Field of Dreams (1989) fans, the farm where the game scenes were shot is less than ninety minutes from Cedar Rapids and includes a museum to the film.

Charleston RiverDogs
Joseph P. Riley, Jr. Park, Charleston, SC
Class A South Atlantic League
New York Yankees
Got: **Sept. 3, 2011; Asheville Tourists 3, Charleston RiverDogs 1**

Here's how to get a ballpark named after you: Serve more than forty years as mayor, during which you get a ballpark built. Riley, Charleston's mayor 1975-2016, shepherded this ballpark to its 1997 opening. He says getting it done took a lot of work, among other things because he had to coordinate with and plan for *two* tenants; the 'Dogs share the playpen with The Citadel Bulldogs baseball. The school originally owned the land, and Riley's complicated deal included swapping this site with that of The Citadel's old College Park – where the 'Dogs played until "The Joe" opened.

Iconic stadium architect HOK Sport (now Populous) designed it. City Council unanimously voted to name it for Riley over his objection – he wanted to call it Ashley River Park, and his defense of that was strenuous, sincere ... and unanimously overruled when the council voted.

The Joe topped 300,000 in 2017, including three June sellouts for Heisman trophy and former National Football League quarterback Tim Tebow and a fourth for the Aug. 21 total solar eclipse. The house record remains the 8,255 for a game Yankees Alex Rodriguez and Eduardo Nunez played together during 2013 rehabilitations.

Owners include actor Bill Murray and Mike Veeck, son of legendary baseball promoter Bill Veeck. It also hosts the annual Legends of the South game between teams of ex-Yankees and ex-Braves, and the Charleston Baseball Hall of Fame.

Charlotte Knights
BB&T Ballpark, Charlotte, NC
Class Triple-A International League
Chicago White Sox
Got: **April 12, 2014; Charlotte Knights 4, Norfolk Tides 2**
Different in 2020: stadium name (name sponsor BB&T Bank merging with SunTrust to become Truist)

This gleaming downtown – or, as they say in Charlotte, Uptown – ballpark overcame years of legal challenges, mostly from a local lawyer who wanted baseball but only big-league baseball. It sits just a block from the stadium of the National Football League's Charlotte Panthers, with a parking deck between them.

Most Charlotte teams went by Hornets until the new owner of the 1976 Double-A club slapped the nickname of its parent Orioles on it. After the 1985 National Basketball Association expansion team took advantage by grabbing the longtime but dormant nickname, its owner bought the Double-A ball club and renamed it Knights. An arson fire sent its home stadium up in smoke in 1985, putting the team in a temporary ballpark that was thrown together on the old one's grounds.

Finally, land was found for a new park – in a Charlotte suburb across the state line in South Carolina. In 1990, another temporary park was quickly erected on what would become the parking lot of the team's future home. The 1993 Triple-A expansion team, playing there, drew a market-record 429,132 – but never matched that and spent 2002-13 in the bottom two of International League attendance.

BB&T opened to 10,231 in 2014. The 1993 season mark fell in forty-five dates as Knights attendance tripled to a Minors-leading 687,715. One August 2018 Saturday, they drew a combined 20,306 to a day-night double-header.

Charlotte Stone Crabs
Charlotte Sports Park, Port Charlotte, FL
Class A-Advanced Florida State League
Tampa Bay Rays
Got: **Aug. 24, 2013; Charlotte Stone Crabs 3, Jupiter Hammerheads 0, 5 inns., rain**

This same-site replacement of Rangers Stadium opened in 2009, six years after the Texas Rangers moved their spring training operations to Arizona and the Florida State League franchise – then the Port Charlotte Rangers, purchased the year before by Orioles great Cal Ripken Jr. – to Palm Beach.

Billed as a renovation, the project actually replaced everything above the concrete seating bowl. It was the first project completed by stadium-specializing architectural firm Populous after its January 2009 spinoff from HOK Sport. In August 2008 in Port Charlotte, the Rays and Ripken announced they would bring spring training and an FSL team from, respectively, St. Petersburg and Vero Beach.

The Rays' Minor League teams in the Florida State and Gulf Coast leagues had replaced the Dodgers at Vero when they moved their spring, Class A-Advanced and Rookie operations to Arizona – but they stayed only two seasons. Ripken had purchased the Vero Beach FSL franchise. The big Rays played its first professional baseball game, a spring-training contest Feb. 25, 2009.

In 2016, Ripken Baseball sold the now-Stone Crabs to a group that included one of the Tampa Bay Rays' owners. With that, he was down to one professional team from a high of three – backing off an announced plan to own ten teams in ten leagues in ten years.

Besides baseball, Charlotte Sports Park also hosted – one July 2015 Friday afternoon – a nine-foot alligator who camped in the visitors' dugout.

Chattanooga Lookouts
AT&T Field, Chattanooga, TN
Class Double-A Southern League
Cincinnati Reds
Got: Aug. 14, 2005; Chattanooga Lookouts 11, Mississippi Braves 0

In 1998, the Lookouts announced they would privately fund a new downtown stadium *if* they could pre-sell 1,800 season tickets and ten luxury boxes. Reaching those goals in January 1999, they broke ground the following March and opened it April 10, 2000. As befits its team's name, for a nearby historic mountain, it sits atop a hill that's accessed by a fifty-step climb from the street – which is appropriately named Power Alley. There are also, of course, elevators. Opened as BellSouth Park in 2000, its name changed when AT&T acquired BellSouth.

Lookouts ownership, since changed, is campaigning for a new ballpark. Coming up on twenty years is coming up on the short end of the expected life of a ballpark, but part of the new owners' case is that the privately built playpen wasn't designed very well.

Pro ball came to town in 1885 and has gone by Lookouts since 1897. Engel Stadium – which portrayed Brooklyn's Ebbets Field in the Jackie Robinson biopic *42* – hosted them for sixty summers. Pitching legend Satchel Paige's professional debut was with Chattanooga, as was the unofficial pro debut of Willie Mays. Paige's was with the Chattanooga Black Lookouts in 1926, Willie's with the Chattanooga Choo-Choos twenty years later. Mays played some games with them – without a contract, to protect his high school sports eligibility – while he was in the ninth and tenth grades.

Clearwater Threshers
Spectrum Field, Clearwater, FL
Class A-Advanced Florida State League
Philadelphia Phillies

Got: **Aug. 25, 2013; Clearwater Threshers 5, Lakeland Flying Tigers 4, 11 inns.**

Opened as Bright House Networks Field in 2004 and later shortened to Bright House Field, it took its coincidentally Philadelphia sports-echoing name in 2017 after Charter Communications bought Bright House Networks and put it under its Spectrum brand. (The National Basketball Association's Philadelphia 76ers and the National Hockey League's Philadelphia Flyers both played 1967-94 in an arena called The Spectrum.)

Like most Florida State League teams, the Threshers share their playpen with their parent club's spring training games – share in a theoretical sense, there being no overlap in those schedules – and also like most of those cases, they are owned by that parent club. They originally played at Jack Russell Stadium as the Clearwater Phillies, from their founding in 1985 until they changed nicknames via a fan contest when their new stadium opened.

It is in the protected territory of, but predates, the Tampa Bay Rays. The city of Clearwater, Pinellas County and the state of Florida built the ballpark as a joint project. It was designed by renowned "downtown-retro" ballpark architect HOK Sport (now Populous).

A May 2015 game saw both a no-hitter and a triple play – both, unfortunately for the hometown crowd, by the visiting Charlotte Stone Crabs. The 2017 Threshers became only the second Florida State League team ever to draw more than 200,000 in a season.

Clinton LumberKings
NelsonCorp Field, Clinton, IA
Class A Midwest League
Miami Marlins

Got: **Sept. 1, 2014; Cedar Rapids Kernels 3, Clinton LumberKings 1**

The Miami Marlins picked up Clinton for its low-A team after the much closer Greensboro Grasshoppers of the South

Atlantic League dropped their long-time parent for the Pittsburgh Pirates following the 2017 season.

The Works Progress Administration-funded project opened as Riverview Stadium in 1937. It first took a naming-rights sponsor in 2002, and the Clinton-based financial planning firm NelsonCorp Wealth Management became the third such sponsor nearly two months into the 2019 campaign.

The LumberKings nickname highlights local history; Clinton was the sawmill capital of the world when it first hosted professional baseball in 1895. In 1954, the Clinton Pirates joined the Mississippi-Ohio Valley League. Just two seasons later, the MOVL changed its name to the Midwest League, and the 'Kings are the only franchise that hasn't changed cities since. Along the way, they have played as the C-Sox, Pilots, Dodgers and Giants. The team is on the twelfth big-league parent of the MwL era, and the 1976 Pilots had players from two different big-league clubs.

The league actually dates to 1947, when it was founded as the Illinois State League. The 1949 addition of a Paducah, KY, team caused the first name change, with moves into Iowa causing the second. As reported in Chapter 8, **The Structure**, today's leagues are less mindful of their geography.

Columbia Fireflies
Segra Park, Columbia, SC
Class A South Atlantic League
New York Mets
Got: **April 16, 2016; Greenville Drive 5, Columbia Fireflies 3**

About ten years after Columbia's dilapidated Capital City Stadium drove the Capital City Bombers to South Carolina, talk about building a replacement facility turned serious. It got a shot in the arm when the owners of the Savannah Sand Gnats guaranteed the city a team. Although the owners, in announcing their guarantee, went out of their way to say they weren't necessarily talking about moving *that* team from antiquated Grayson Stadium, that is what ultimately happened. With the biggest question mark about spending millions of dollars to build a ballpark effectively erased, the city moved forward and iconic stadium architect Populous had it ready for the 2016 season.

Columbia professional baseball history dates to 1892, yet its all-time baseball attendance mark would fall in just forty dates. Due largely to huge crowds for Heisman and former National Football League quarterback Tim Tebow, the 2016 record fell in just fifty-three dates of 2017. A game planned around that year's solar eclipse drew a house record 9,629.

Then-Spirit Communications Park's debut drew 9,077 – versus Columbia's former team, now the Greenville Drive. Greenville, SC, had gone through the same lose-team/build-stadium/get-new-team scenario starting in 2004. That wasn't the only "homecoming" of the day, though; the Bombers were a Mets' affiliate when they left town.

Spirit Communications bought naming rights before the groundbreaking. Lumos Networks' parent firm bought Spirit in 2018, merged the two, rebranded them as Segra and in 2019 extended that to the existing stadium name contract.

Columbus Clippers
Huntington Park, Columbus, OH
Class Triple-A International League
Cleveland Indians
Got: **June 24, 2012; Columbus Clippers 4, Lehigh Valley IronPigs 0**

Opened in 2009, Huntington Park is the first stadium to host Triple-A baseball's top two showcases in the same season: in 2018, the Triple-A All-Star Game and the Triple-A National Championship. Its Clippers led Minor League baseball regular-season attendance in 2008, breaking the Sacramento River Cats' eight-season run, and again in 2013. The near big-league quality ballpark was fifth in attendance among the 160 affiliated clubs in 2018, fourth in 2014, second in 2012, and third the other five seasons.

These boys of summer play in their parent club's old hometown. The Columbus Senators joined the eleven-year-old Western League in 1896; two moves later, they were the WL's Cleveland Blues when the circuit rebranded as the American League in 1900. The AL declared itself a second major league, earned that status in a brief and intense war with the National League, and thus brought professional baseball into its modern era.

Founded in 1977, the Clippers returned pro ball to Columbus seven years after its Jets moved to West Virginia. The club having been a New York Yankees' affiliate for twenty-seven seasons, some assume "Clippers" salutes Joe "The Yankee Clipper" DiMaggio, but the Clippers debuted with the Pittsburgh Pirates. In fact, "Clippers" – like Columbus – honors a sailor named Christopher.

In 1932, nine-year-old Harold Cooper began his baseball career as a Columbus Red Birds clubhouse boy. He twice brought baseball back after Columbus lost it. He served as Columbus Jets general manager 1955-68 and International League president 1978-90.

Corpus Christi Hooks

Whataburger Field, Corpus Christi, TX

Class Double-A Texas League

Houston Astros

Got: **April 23, 2014; Midland RockHounds 3, Corpus Christi Hooks 1**

Architect HKS designed this coastal facility to feel like an old park and salute the cotton warehouses it replaced. The Hooks – named for the local fishing industry – have *twice* been reeled in: Hall of Famer Nolan Ryan's firm, Ryan-Sanders Baseball, bought the Double-A Jackson Generals in 2000 to move them to Austin; nearby Round Rock intercepted them with a better land-and-money offer. In 2005, R-S bought the Triple-A Edmonton Trappers to move them, bumping the Double-A club to this new park near Corpus Christi Bay, the Texas State Aquarium and the

USS *Lexington* ship/museum. June 2018 and May 2019 series as the Blue Ghosts saluted the ship.

Two 2018 giveaways of Astros' 2017 World Series replica rings drew 10,446, the house baseball record, and 9,612. The stadium's street number, 734, salutes Ryan: He threw a record seven no-hitters and wore uniform number thirty-four with the Rangers and Astros, both of whom retired that number. (Actually, he wore number thirty in his first four no-no's as a California Angel.)

Ryan-Sanders was founded by Ryan, his son Reid, and former Astro co-owner Don Sanders. Originally aligned with the Rangers, R-S went all-Astros after a falling out with Texas (see **Myrtle Beach Pelicans [CURRENT]**). In 2013, the Astros bought the Hooks and Reid became their president, the next year Nolan became an Astros' executive advisor, and in the 2018 affiliate shuffle the Round Rock Express flipped from the Rangers to the Astros.

In late 2019, however, Reid was reassigned and Nolan resigned.

Danville Braves
American Legion Post 325 Field, Danville, VA
Rookie-Advanced Appalachian League
Atlanta Braves
Got: **Aug. 31, 2011; Danville Braves 6, Johnson City Cardinals 3**

Nestled in Dan Daniel Memorial Park along the – you guessed it – Dan River in Danville, the stadium seats the second-most fans in the Appy League. The city built the rudimentary ballpark in 1992, landing the Pulaski Braves the next season. The D-Braves repeatedly led the league in attendance in the 1990s but didn't draw their first 3,000 single gate until 2017.

Danville professional baseball, which dates to 1905, was a memory 1958-93. In 1998, fans were treated to a season-and-a-half in one. The Durham Bulls of *Bull Durham* (1988) film fame, a Class A-Advanced Carolina League team displaced by Triple-A

International League expansion, chose Myrtle Beach, SC, as their new home. However, no existing Myrtle Beach ballpark could accommodate the team, nor could one be built quickly enough. The club played that season at Legion Field, nearly 250 miles from their future home city but right in the middle of the Caro footprint, as the Danville 97s. That moniker remembered the famed 1903 crash of the Old 97 mail train near Danville – an event immortalized in song (*The Wreck of the Old 97*, first released in 1924 and since done by country stars from Roy Acuff and Hank Snow to Johnny Cash and the Statler Brothers) as well as story.

Having poked fun at all those Dans, let me say the city is named for the river, which Virginia pioneer William Byrd named for a biblical city, and the municipal park is named for 1969-88 Congressman Dan Daniel.

Dayton Dragons
Fifth Third Field, Dayton, OH
Class A Midwest League
Cincinnati Reds
Got: **May 5, 2012; Bowling Green Hot Rods 2, Lake County Captains 0**

The stories of both the ballpark and the team begin and end around rather than on the field: attendance.

It opened, after construction delays, a few weeks into the 2000 season. With every single seat sold before even one pitch was thrown, it drew an A-record 581,853. Ever since, Dayton has led not only A but high-A in attendance – even, since 2006, Double-A. Incredibly, every Dragons game ever played has sold out, and it *averages* nearly 1,000 more than it *seats*. The string passed the longest in American professional sports history in 2011 and starts 2020 at 1,385. Dayton passed 10 million in its eighteenth opener – faster than any low-A team ever and fourth fastest overall. Its two Midwest League All-Star Games averaged an impressive 8,824 – but that's only about 800 more than its regular-season average.

Some question these numbers because they don't have trouble getting tickets, but the team is counting sold tickets – as its leadership has been quoted as saying in media. That said, I have attended two games there – a Saturday night and a weeknight – and there were plenty of people at both. The ballpark has a very high walk-around clientele, with folks socializing or exploring and sometimes seeming oblivious to the ballgame.

If the reported $40 million for the Dragons' 2014 sale is even close, this low-A club set a price record for *all* of Minor League baseball.

Daytona Tortugas

Radiology Associates Field at Jackie Robinson Ballpark, Daytona Beach, FL

Class A-Advanced Florida State League

Cincinnati Reds

Got: **May 26, 2012; Daytona Cubs 3, Clearwater Threshers 1**

One of professional baseball's most historic sites is of only two in the Minors that lie on an island. Pay attention going in or out, though; between the layout and the walkways, you just about have to know to notice! A Daytona Beach relative didn't believe it until she google-mapped it.

Baseball here dates to 1914. Then, it was just a piece of land – a diamond with a set of wooden bleachers. Soon known as Daytona City Island Ballpark, it's less something built than something that evolved. The original bleachers were replaced in the 1920s by a true grandstand and press box. Seats were added in the 1950s, today's grandstand and press box in 1962.

Arguably the full-season Minors' oldest active park – when did it become "this" park? – it's historic anyway. A year before breaking big-league baseball's color line, Jackie Robinson played the first integrated professional baseball game, aside from barnstorming exhibitions, since baseball segregated itself in 1887. Robinson played that season as a Montreal Royal, before moving up to the Dodgers. The ballpark was renamed for him before the 1990 season, and an open-air museum followed. Despite that, its 1998 National Register of Historic Places entry reads City Island Ball Park.

The Chicago Cubs ended a twenty-two-year affiliation over too many rainouts (thirty-three in three seasons) after the 2014 campaign; the team joined the Reds but adopted an independent nickname.

Hurricane Dorian knocked down much of the outfield wall, and the nearby Jacksonville Jumbo Shrimp helped with repairs.

Delmarva Shorebirds
Arthur W. Perdue Stadium, Salisbury, MD
Class A South Atlantic League
Baltimore Orioles
Got: **June 17, 2012; Kannapolis Intimidators 4, Delmarva Shorebirds 3, 10 inns.**

Named for the founder of Salisbury-headquartered Perdue Farms, this ballpark likely wouldn't exist without the Perdue family.

Arthur's son, Frank, threw out the ceremonial first pitch at its 1996 debut. He earned that honor and the right to name it for his father. After he succeeded Arthur as the head of the company, he was the driving force in getting his hometown a Minor League team – including donating the land on which the stadium sits and half of its construction cost. Frank played the game into college, and it became a true avocation to him.

The ballpark's 360-degree concourse debuted in 2019. The Maryland Eastern Shore Baseball Hall of Fame is next door. The team's location identifier is for the Delmarva Peninsula, so named because it contains parts of three different states: Delaware, Maryland, and Virginia.

Not as large as the Wicomico Youth & Civic Center, "The Perdue" long landed many events that otherwise would have gone there because a deed restriction was thought to prohibit alcohol sales in it. Research later showed the restriction ended when a 1971 property transfer omitted it, and that the original 1959 restriction was placed not by the couple who bequeathed the land to the county, but by the county in accepting it. The WYCC got an alcohol license in 2016.

Down East Wood Ducks
Grainger Stadium, Kinston, NC
Class A-Advanced Carolina League
Texas Rangers
Got: (A-Advanced) May 13, 2012; Carolina Mudcats 3, Potomac Nationals 2 (A-Advanced)

Kinston Indians
Class A-Advanced Carolina League
First Get: **Sept. 2, 2011; Frederick Keys 10, Kinston Indians 0**

This team is simultaneously a patience reward to Kinston officials and a favor from the Houston Astros to the Rangers.

In 2012, the Kinston Indians moved to Zebulon, NC, as Kinston's team moved to Pensacola, FL. While Grainger stadium (1949) was then one of the oldest still in use, it was in good shape. Its problem was geography, exacerbated by other events (see **Carolina Mudcats [CURRENT]**). Kinston leadership kept its sights set on a professional team, though, and in 2015 the Rangers asked for a renovation and a seventeen-year lease for a Rangers' O&O.

They had purchased the Wilmington Blue Rocks, whose owners had bought the Binghamton Mets – the latter two sales contingent on the first – but this didn't come to light until Wilmington ownership sued Binghamton ownership for not completing the deal. Soon after the suit was settled under seal, it became clear no one was moving. Kinston quickly quoted the Rangers as saying a team was coming anyway, eventually revealing an even more complicated Plan B: The Rangers and Astros would each buy a California League team and MiLB would transfer both to the Carolina League. Texas was that desperate to escape the windy, pitcher-killing home of its High Desert Mavericks, and the Astros agreed to bring another team along because a league swap required two.

The Mavs won the Cali title in their last season, leaving that circuit with no 2017 defending champion and, in a way, giving the Caro two.

The Ducks' mascot? DEWD, naturally.

Dunedin Blue Jays
TD Ballpark, Dunedin, FL
Class A-Advanced Florida State League
Toronto Blue Jays
Got: **July 4, 2014; Dunedin Blue Jays 5, Tampa Yankees 4**
Different in 2020: back home; team played 2019 elsewhere during complete renovation

One of the Florida State League's many O&Os, the D-Jays are also one of several in the protected territory of – but predating – the Tampa Bay Rays.

Dunedin Stadium at Grant Field opened in 1990. The Grant name derived from an existing ballpark that had been built in 1930, Grant Field, but only its playing field and clubhouses remained at the time. Naming-rights contracts made it Knology Park 2004-08 and Florida Auto Exchange Stadium 2010-17; the Grant Field reference was not retained after the latter deal expired. TD Bank picked up the rights in November 2019.

The Jays' other spring-training facilities are four miles away. That's a negative, but they haven't based their spring training anywhere else since joining the American League in 1977. Existing development makes unification of the facilities pretty much impossible. However, with help from the city, Pinellas County and the state, the big-league Jays renovated both stadium and complex in a project that was negotiated as part of a new twenty-five-year lease. The FSL Jays played most of their 2019 home schedule at Clearwater's Jack Russell Memorial Stadium (see **Clearwater, FL [LEGACY]**), which gave me a chance to add it to my collection. It became my 200th professional – including both Majors and Minors – ballpark.

The non-adjacent training facility is called the Bobby Mattick Training Center at Englebert Complex. Opened in 1978 with only the Englebert name, it was renamed in 2007 for a former Toronto manager who spent seventy-one years in baseball and is remembered as the "father of the Blue Jays."

Durham Bulls
Durham Bulls Athletic Park, Durham, NC
Class Triple-A International League
Tampa Bay Rays
Got: **Sept. 8, 2011; Columbus Clippers 8, Durham Bulls 3**

Triple-A's 1998 expansion bumped the film-famed Carolina League franchise (*Bull Durham*, 1988), now the Myrtle Beach Pelicans. Opened for those Bulls in 1995, the beautiful brick ballpark was designed by HOK Sport (now Populous), famous for Oriole Park at Camden Yards. Colloquially known as the DBAP, which locals pronounce dee-bap, its otherwise state-of-the-art scoreboard has a touch of quaint: manual score-by-innings and line-score functions on its main scoreboard.

The sign depicting a huge bull on the left-field fence is unusual for two reasons: 1) There was no such sign in the stadium that appeared in the movie – Durham Athletic Park – but because one was added in the film one was built into the new ballpark; 2) the sign in the flick was on the *right*-field wall. The old ballpark, where *Bull* was mostly set and largely filmed, is now a working museum.

The Bulls-Rays affiliation isn't yet among the longest in the Minors – in the 2019-20 cycle, it ranks twenty-seventh among Major-Minor partners without common ownership – but it is as long as possible: Each is the only partner the other has ever had. In that subset, only the Kansas City-Omaha tandem that dates to 1969 is older – and it's the longest of *any* current non-O&O partnership.

The 2018 International League champions earned that title entirely on the road because of Hurricane Florence.

El Paso Chihuahuas
Southwest University Park, El Paso, TX
Class Triple-A Pacific Coast League
San Diego Padres
Got: **April 29, 2014; Fresno Grizzlies 1, El Paso Chihuahuas 0**

At a glance, this affiliation dates to the 2014 debut of the Desert Dogs. Actually, it is the sixth-longest current affiliation among separately owned teams – dating to 1983 through a total of four Minor League cities.

The Tucson Padres' move here ended two baseball sagas and changed the face of the city: El Paso tore down its city hall so architect Populous could build SWUP.

The first saga was the absence of affiliated ball from El Paso, after the St. Louis Cardinals bought and moved its Diablos to Springfield, MO, in 2004. (The C's regularly use Diablos as an alternate nickname.)

The second saga was the wandering PCL franchise of 2010-13. The Portland Beavers unexpectedly lost their stadium after their owner landed an expansion Major League Soccer franchise. He intended to house both in then-PGE Park, but the MLS insisted PGE be made soccer-only. Planning started for a new baseball stadium, but when that effort failed the Padres bought their homeless affiliate. Their plan was to base the team in Tucson, AZ, which had recently lost its PCL team, until a new ballpark could be built in the San Diego suburb of Escondido. That stadium plan also failed, because a funding crisis caused the state to claw back development monies it had committed to municipalities. The Padres then sold the team to the El Paso group that moved it to West Texas. Even SWUP didn't open on time, and the Dogs played their first 2014 home series in Tucson.

Elizabethton Twins
Joe O'Brien Field, Elizabethton, TN
Rookie-Advanced Appalachian League
Minnesota Twins

Got: **July 2, 1990; Elizabethton Twins 8, Huntington Cubs 5; Elizabethton Twins 5, Huntington Cubs 3**

The Appalachian Mountains and Watauga River give this basic ballpark one of Minor League baseball's most picturesque settings. Then-Riverside Stadium, opened with the Twins in 1974, was renamed in 1980 for the man who landed the Twins as the parent club that first year.

One of affiliated baseball's smallest towns – population 14,000 – and its small*est* ballpark have seen twelve league crowns in their forty-six seasons, fifteen division titles during their seasons in which the Appy used the divisional format – including runs of six and five straight – and only nine losing campaigns.

The city operated the club until turning it over to a contractor in 2019, and either way among Minor League teams that are not owned and operated by their parent club the E-Twins/Twins partnership is now tied for the second longest. It is also the longest current partnership in a league in which half predate this century.

This almost iconic relationship nearly ended following the 2017 season, because a deal reached in the previous off-season went unsigned. Just before the 2018 opener, the two Twins extended their previous agreement for one year. After playing that season in limbo, the parties finally worked out and signed a five-year deal which included a renovation that got underway shortly after the 2018 campaign – which, amid all that negativity – was yet another championship season.

Erie SeaWolves
UPMC Park, Erie, PA
Class Double-A Eastern League
Detroit Tigers
Got: **June 21, 2012; Bowie Baysox 8, Erie SeaWolves 5**

After the Erie Sailors of the A-Short Season New York-Pennsylvania League fled Ainsworth Field to become today's Hudson Valley Renegades, the city knew it needed a new playpen to get back in the game – or, rather, to get the game back. Former minor-leaguer Gerard "Jerry" Uht Sr. set up a perpetual endowment with the Erie Community Foundation whose sole purpose was to fund the construction and maintenance of a professional baseball stadium in Erie.

The city broke ground in July 1994. When it opened in May 1995, it was named for Uht (rhymes with hut). The city first returned to professional ball in its old league, the NYPL, by luring the Welland Pirates to their new ballpark. The Bucs' affiliation came with the team, and the SeaWolves' nickname originally saluted the Pirates. It became so synonymous with Erie baseball it remained throughout later changes including the 1999 Angels' Double-A expansion franchise. Attendance runs in the low 200,000s and has never ranked higher than ninth in the twelve-team league.

The ballpark became known colloquially as "The Uht," but the official moniker changed when the University of Pennsylvania Medical Center bought naming rights after the 2016 season.

The 2017 club celebrated a 2016 Eastern League title it didn't win, among other things, in a creative promotion called Alternative Facts Night.

Eugene Emeralds
PK Park, Eugene, OR
Class A-Short Season Northwest League
Chicago Cubs
Got: **Aug. 13, 2014; Salem-Keizer Volcanoes 2, Eugene Emeralds 1**

PK Park is the home of the Ems, but they are actually its secondary team. The University of Oregon built and owns this ballpark. It is not only shared by the two teams, it shares its parking lot with Duck football's Autzen Stadium. PK literally "boasts" artificial turf that feels more like natural grass.

In an amazing story, the 2018 Ems had the Northwest League's worst record in overall regular-season games but slipped into the split-season league's playoffs when Hillsboro opened the door for an extra team by winning its division in both halves. The Ems then won out, sweeping Hillsboro and Spokane – clinching the crown on, just as amazingly, a walk-off bases-loaded *balk*.

In 2009, Ducks' Athletics Director Pat Kilkenny revived the school's dormant varsity baseball program and helped fund the stadium that bears his initials. In 2010, it welcomed the Ems from old Civic Stadium (see **Eugene, OR [VISITED]**). Earlier iterations of Ems baseball played at Bethel Park, but the 1969 Pacific Coast League team that was bumped by major-league expansion to Eugene from Seattle chose Civic. When the NwL returned in 1974, its club followed suit.

About five years after losing the Ems to PK, Civic burned down. Investigators found the June 2015 fire to be a case of arson by a group of boys. The very August night the Ems commemorated Civic, four Ems pitched a combined no-hitter.

Everett AquaSox
Funko Field, Everett, WA
Class A-Short Season Northwest League
Seattle Mariners

Got: **Aug. 19, 2012; Everett AquaSox 7, Eugene Emeralds 1**

Outside this 1984 ballpark, a plaque marks the landing spot of the first professional home run hit by future Hall-of-Famer Ken Griffey Jr. As easy as it would be to assume the famous future Mariner was playing at home, this was actually a road game for him: Everett's team was then a Giants' affiliate, even using their parent's nickname, and the future Seattle great was playing for the visiting *Bellingham* Mariners.

The Walla Walla Bears had moved into then-Everett Memorial Stadium when it opened, first as Giants but in 1995 taking the AquaSox nickname as they switched parent clubs. Logos include one based on frogs – the first thought for the team nickname, and still an informal alternate one. The main logo is the ingenious *E* morphed from the Mariner *M*.

The ballpark, which has artificial turf, revived the Northwest League All-Star Game in 2013. That showcase has an interesting history: The NwL first tried an ASG in 2004, next played the one here in 2013 and again in 2014, and then joined the advanced Rookie Pioneer League in playing the first inter-*level* pro baseball ASG in 2015. So far, that unique series continues and continues to be unique.

Felix Hernandez's 2016 rehabilitation start drew its largest crowd ever, 5,189. A rainout in that year's playoffs sent a game to Seattle's Safeco Field.

Before the 2019 season, the pop-culture retailer Funko closed a six-season deal to name the ballpark.

Fayetteville Woodpeckers
Segra Stadium, Fayetteville, NC
Class A-Advanced Carolina League
Houston Astros
Got: **July 24, 2019; Fayetteville Woodpeckers 4, Lynchburg Hillcats 3; Fayetteville Woodpeckers 3, Lynchburg Hillcats 0**

The erstwhile Bakersfield Blaze came home in 2019.

The Texas Rangers, to get their high-A players out of their High Desert Mavericks' windy, pitcher-killing ballpark, engineered moving two clubs from the California League to the Carolina – then bought their affiliate while the Astros bought the Blaze (actually Plan B; see Chapter 8, **The Structure**, and **Down East Wood Ducks [CURRENT]**).

The moves happened so quickly that the Mavs – having identified Fayetteville, NC – as their future home, had no suitable playpen. Their two-season stopgap was to play as the Buies Creek Astros (see **Buies Creek, NC [LEGACY]**) in nearby Campbellsville University's Jim Perry Stadium. The school got a field renovation out of the deal.

The Fayetteville park's most unusual feature may be outside it – the only one I recall with railroad tracks running past on *both* sides.

The BC-Astros having won the 2018 Carolina League championship in a series shortened to one game by Hurricane Florence, the 2019 Fayetteville Woodpeckers were simultaneously the league's newest brand and defending league champions. They made it back to the championship, but lost three games to two.

Fayetteville had affiliated ball continually 1909-2001, including a 1950-56 Caro run. The new team colors are not only the bird's but the Army Special Operations Command's – headquartered at nearby Fort Bragg. A July 3, 2016, regular-season game between the Atlanta Braves and the Miami Marlins, a salute to the military played in a temporary stadium at Fort Bragg, was the first Major League game in North Carolina history.

Florida Fire Frogs
Osceola County Stadium, Kissimmee, FL
Class A-Advanced Florida State League
Atlanta Braves
Got: **July 5, 2017; Jupiter Hammerheads 10, Florida Fire Frogs 2**
Different in 2020: team location, and probably branding

Opened in 1984, this ballpark has perhaps the most disparate history of its time. The Houston Astros' spring training, Florida State League and Gulf Coast League teams arrived in 1985. The Astros dropped their FSL team after the 2000 season, replaced in 2003 by United States Specialty Sports Association youth baseball.

In 2017, the Astros and Nationals triggered a game of musical ballparks by opening a joint West Palm Beach complex. The Nats and then-Brevard County Manatees had shared Space Coast Stadium in Viera, which promptly signed the USSSA – pushing the OSC and the 'Tees together. Heisman quarterback Tim Tebow drew its biggest crowd ever but disappointed them by having that day off.

Some facts: (1) Few big-league teams own their top five clubs, but the Braves own all except the Frogs; (2) they tried to buy their high-A affiliate in 2012, then changed high-A partners three times in four cycles; (3) they've opened a new spring-training ballpark in North Port, FL; (4) Osceola County paid the Frogs $500,000 to leave after 2019. Where better for the Frogs to go than North Port? The Charlotte Stone Crabs would have to agree, but that doesn't seem impossible. Yet in late October the new park's staff knew of no such plan. I wonder if the club might be forced to a road-only season in 2020.

Meanwhile, doesn't it take some coconuts to make your state name your geo-locator in a state with thirteen other affiliated teams?

Fort Myers Mighty Mussels

Hammond Stadium at the CenturyLink Sports Complex, Fort Myers, FL

Class A-Advanced Florida State League

Minnesota Twins

Got: **Aug. 23, 2013; Fort Myers Mighty Mussels 3, St. Lucie Mets 2, 7 inns, rain**

The southernmost US stadium hosting affiliated baseball, opened in 1991, anchored the then-Lee County Sports Complex.

CenturyLink bought naming rights in a 2015 deal that includes providing Wi-Fi.

The former Miracle announced the new team nickname in December 2019.

After Lee County built a new complex just ten minutes away for the Boston Red Sox – jetBlue Park at Fenway South – in 2012, the Twins demanded and got an extensive renovation of Hammond. Lee County also owns Terry Park and City of Palms Park, both former homes of professional baseball. May 23, 2018, the Miracle became the first pro team to play at home in all four by playing at Palms. The club had played eight home games at jetBlue during Hammond's 2014 renovation and one at Terry in 2006 to celebrate the 100th anniversary of the municipal park in which it lies.

The team's original 1962 brand – Miami Marlins – was not prescient of big-league expansion; it saluted the 1956-60 Triple-A Miami team that moved to Puerto Rico in 1961. "Miracle" could seem prescient, with a group including actor Bill Murray and legendary promoter Bill Veeck's son Mike buying a team in disarray in 1989 and turning it around, but it was about alliteration and the then-trendiness of a singular nickname.

The National League's 1993 expansion into Miami caused the Miracle's 1992 move to Fort Myers, but – like many a Minor League team in a city with a major team in another sport – it was already not drawing well.

Fort Wayne TinCaps
Parkview Field, Fort Wayne, IN
Class A Midwest League
San Diego Padres
Got: **June 25, 2012; Lansing Lugnuts 6, Fort Wayne TinCaps 2**

The Summit City – so nicknamed for being the highest point on the 1820s-era Wabash & Erie Canal – hosted *the* first baseball game ever played in a professional league in 1871 (May 4: National Association of Professional Base Ball Players, Fort

Wayne Kekionga 2, Forest City of Cleveland 0) but later went sixty years without pro ball.

In 1992, the Kenosha Twins were looking to move at the same time Fort Wayne was looking for a team. The city hastily threw together Memorial Field, and the club moved in as the Fort Wayne Wizards.

The old ballpark had all the problems inherent in haste making waste. That became a paradoxical positive by – just thirteen years later – making feasible the inclusion of a new stadium in a downtown revitalization plan. Parkview Health bought naming rights to the state-of-the-art Populous-designed ballpark before its 2009 opener, which sold out in thirty minutes, and later extended the deal through 2023. The rechristened TinCaps drew 4 million fans to "The View" in less than ten seasons, and the success of the revitalization is obvious.

"TinCaps" – as edgy a nickname at its debut as it is not today – salutes John "Johnny Appleseed" Chapman, who is buried in Fort Wayne. Legend says his cooking pot doubled as a cap. The team played as the Octane, the renaming contest runner-up, in a 2015 game.

Frederick Keys
Nymeo Field at Harry Grove Stadium, Frederick, MD
Class A-Advanced Carolina League
Baltimore Orioles
Got: **June 24, 2010; Frederick Keys 7, Winston-Salem Dash 4**

The team nickname salutes the Frederick County native whose battle-inspired poem *The Defence of Fort M'Henry* is somewhat better known as *The Star-Spangled Banner*. Francis Scott Key's birthplace *was* in Frederick County when he wrote the verse, but it is now in Carroll County – which was created in 1837.

Opened in 1990, Harry Grove Stadium lies in the Orioles' protected territory. Grove co-founded the Frederick Hustlers, the city's first professional baseball club, which initially took the diamond in 1915. (Nearby Baltimore would have a tussle over that nickname sixty years later, when the American Basketball Association forced the owners of the team they were moving from Memphis to change "Baltimore Hustlers" to something with "fewer negative connotations." I smile every time I juxtapose that with years of coaches yelling at players to hustle.) Grove's descendants covered a $250,000 shortfall in construction costs, and the stadium name was the quid pro quo even though stadium naming deals were at that time rare and in some municipalities illegal. The city approved the actual sale of naming rights in 2013, but required that the name "Harry Grove" remain in the resulting moniker. Nymeo Federal Credit Union made the deal in February 2015.

The Keys-O's partnership is the Carolina League's longest and tied for the ninth overall among separately owned teams.

Fresno Grizzlies
Chukchansi Park, Fresno, CA
Class Triple-A Pacific Coast League
Washington Nationals
Got: **May 19, 2013; Fresno Grizzlies 4, New Orleans Zephyrs 2**

How did teams in Washington, D.C., and California end up together? Geography isn't the only priority, but nobody wants players 2,000 miles and three time zone changes away.

The last teams left in the biannual affiliation shuffle are paired. The long-time Giants' affiliate lost that berth to Sacramento in 2014, landing the Astros for an obviously limited run; no Texas-based Triple-A team was then available but Round Rock would be in the 2018. Houston indeed left Fresno for the Express, bouncing the Texas Rangers – who surprised many by passing on San Antonio. The resulting domino effect forced the Nats to Fresno.

The 1998 Arizona Diamondback expansion put Fresno back in the Pacific Coast League by bumping the Phoenix Firebirds there – but not the longtime Phoenix club. Just a year earlier, the Phoenix and Tucson franchise owners had swapped.

The Grizzlies enjoy a million-dollar-a-year naming rights contract – which was nearly lost amid a 2014 Chukchansi tribe internal dispute over its Chukchansi Gold Resort & Casino, for which the tribe bought rights in 2007. Opened as Grizzlies Stadium in 2002, the HOK Sport (now Populous) ballpark is the only four-level stadium in the Minors.

An annual food-truck challenge that started in 2011 went phenomenal in 2015. The Grizz played The Taco Truck Throwdown as the Fresno Tacos to a house record crowd, and Taco Bell tweeted an offer to "buy tacos for all of Fresno" if that went permanent. It didn't, but "Tacos" is now a frequent alternate nickname.

Frisco RoughRiders
Dr Pepper Ballpark, Frisco, TX
Class Double-A Texas League
Texas Rangers
Different in 2020: possibly, stadium name
Got: **April 19, 2014; Frisco RoughRiders 6, Corpus Christi Hooks 0**

Technically, at this writing, this unique ballpark has no name. (Perhaps it should be called Clint Eastwood Ballpark?) Dr Pepper Snapple Group, which is based in nearby Plano, TX, did not renew its naming-rights contract after the 2017 season – but with no new name sponsor or announced replacement name, and twelve years as that, it has stuck. (The original 2003 name, Dr Pepper/Seven Up Ballpark, was shortened after the 2006 campaign.) There does not appear to be a default name. Of course, name signage is expensive so it may be a matter of waiting for something that will stay.

In late 2001, the Rangers bought the Shreveport Swamp Dragons to move them to Frisco. They completed that move in time for the 2003 season. In 2014, the Rangers' next owner – after having been forced out of the big club's ownership – bought the 'Riders. Through the 2019 season, they have led Double-A attendance for fifteen straight campaigns.

Frisco is in Rangers' protected territory, with the ballparks only about forty miles apart. Cowboys Stadium architect HKS created both; Pepper's unique design, which from some viewpoints looks more like a residential cul-de-sac than a ballpark, won baseballparks.com's 2003 Best New Ballpark. The nickname originally saluted the Texas Rangers, but a 2015 rebrand took on a Teddy Roosevelt look. The award-winning 174-foot Lazy River – which is *not* a swimming pool because its water flows – opened in 2016.

Grand Junction Rockies
Sam Suplizio Field, Grand Junction, CO
Rookie-Advanced Pioneer League
Milwaukee Brewers
Got: **Aug. 18, 2014; Grand Junction Rockies 5, Great Falls Voyagers 3**

This ballpark's main claim to fame is the Junior College World Series, which it has hosted since 1959. A side benefit for the Pioneer League's Rockies is having such a huge stadium for their class. It is also the regular-season home of Colorado Mesa University Mavericks baseball, and adjacent Stocker Stadium hosts CMU football. The towering building behind the first-base grandstands separates the two fields.

Sam Suplizio was the first University of New Mexico baseball player to be named an All American. Injury forced "the next Mickey Mantle" out of baseball in 1958, but he helped GJ land the JUCO the very next year. He would serve thirty-three years as tournament director. In 1991, he helped Denver land the National League expansion franchise that became the Colorado Rockies *and* was inducted into the Colorado Sports Hall of Fame.

In 2011, the big Rockies bought the Casper Ghosts to move them to the Junction in 2012. That made a ghost of Wyoming affiliated ball but ensured renovating the vintage 1949 GJ facility. A week after re-opening it, the co-tenant Mavs drew a Division II regular-season record 4,122. The Rockies' debut drew 5,312, but the post-renovation record – 12,014 – is for a 2014 JUCO game. Its 2010 all-time record crowd is 12,309, also for a JUCO game.

Great Falls Voyagers
Centene Stadium, Great Falls, MT
Rookie-Advanced Pioneer League
Chicago White Sox
Got: **Aug. 7, 2014; Orem Owlz 3, Great Falls Voyagers 1**

This venerable ballpark doesn't act its age, for two reasons: a great save story that has nothing to do with relief pitching, and a renovation some call a rebuild.

The Civilian Conservation Corps project opened as Legion Park in 1940, hosting as you may guess American Legion baseball, and remaining so until a 2007 naming-rights deal with managed-care giant Centene Corporation. Professional ball came to that stadium in 1948 as the Electrics – except two seasons as the Selectrics. Although some sources deny "Selectrics," I've found newspaper advertising and team promotional images with that name, which baseball-reference.com says they used 1949-50. Pro baseball in Great Falls dates to 1892, and all its other 1916-63 teams were called the Electrics. Its media market is the smallest in the US with affiliated ball.

The Dodgers' affiliation they landed in 1953 was lost to ballpark deterioration in 1963. Then came the *save* story: 100 baseball-loving business people pledged $1,000 each toward a renovation so extensive some say today's stadium was "built" on the site of – and replaced – Legion Park. The Giants came in 1969; the Dodgers returned in '84.

A $2.2 million renovation – just a quarter of that on taxpayers – began in 2003 as they switched to the White Sox, originally by that nickname. Five years later, they became Voyagers – for Legion Park's famed 1950 UFO filming; video is available on the Internet. As befits an older ballpark with such history, it also hosts an in-park museum: the Great Falls Historical Room.

Great Lakes Loons
Dow Diamond, Midland, MI
Class A Midwest League
Los Angeles Dodgers
Got: June 28, 2012; Fort Wayne TinCaps 10, Great Lakes Loons 0

The organization that is now the Loons spent a dozen seasons in Battle Creek, MI, but after three iterations there failed it was sold to the non-profit Michigan Baseball Foundation. Midland-based Dow Chemical had just created the MBF, and what it bought was then known as the Southwest Michigan Devil Rays. Next, Dow tore down its own headquarters and donated the land for the ballpark. Ground-up brick from the HQ is part of the warning track.

The playpen was designed by renowned stadium architect HOK Sport (now Populous). Its inaugural season, 2007, saw its field caretakers win Midwest Grounds Crew of the Year and its newly relocated team join the Dodgers' system and draw more than

320,000 fans. Less than two months later, it was named to host the 2008 Midwest League All-Star Game. Just before the 2008 season, the MBF bought WYLZ-FM, changed its format to all sports, put it in the ESPN radio network, and made it the Loons' flagship play-by-play station. Liberal use of a loon birdcall dominates the stadium's public address.

Its double-entendre name – "diamond" is slang for a ball field and Dow's logo is a red diamond – survived the Dow-DuPont merger and spin-off. Chemical giants Dow and DuPont merged in August 2017, creating the world's largest chemical company, but the plan all along was to split the resulting conglomerate into three firms – one of which would retain the Dow name, logo and Midland HQ. The Dow spinoff closed April 1, 2019.

Greeneville Reds
Pioneer Park, Greeneville, TN
Rookie-Advanced Appalachian League
Cincinnati Reds
Got: Aug. 21, 2011; Elizabethton Twins 14, Greeneville Astros 3

The only Appy stadium built in this millennium also hosts Tusculum University Pioneers baseball. Then-Tusculum College opened it in 2004. The Martinsville Astros moved from Virginia – and won the next eleven attendance crowns. The G-Astros lost the 2015 attendance title to the Pulaski Yankees while, ironically, winning the league championship.

Houston dropped Greeneville after 2017, but *Baseball America* soon reported the Reds would step in. Cincy confirmed that in a tweet, but TC promptly called it premature, saying "nothing has been signed" yet. The resulting intrigue lasted about three months, probably orchestrated to allow the signing and formal announcement to happen at a Greeneville stop that was added to the Reds' winter caravan.

The G-Reds played an August 2018 home game with the Johnson City Cardinals at the home of the Double-A Tennessee Smokies near Knoxville – the connection being that the three teams are commonly operated. Coincidentally, the G-Reds' manager in that game, Gookie Dawkins, was the first batter in Smokies Stadium history.

The Green*e*ville team – with one more E than in the color – is not to be confused with the South Atlantic League's Greenville Drive, 2½ hours south. It is the only thus-spelled Greeneville/Greenville of the thirty-odd across the United States, even though most if not all are named for Revolutionary War General Nathanael Green*e*.

Greensboro Grasshoppers
First National Bank Field, Greensboro, NC
Class A South Atlantic League
Pittsburgh Pirates

Got: **Aug. 26, 2011; Greensboro Grasshoppers 5, Delmarva Shorebirds 4**

Then-First Horizon Park, opened in 2005 and christened with their then-parent Florida Marlins before 8,540, was the trip that created the *Go-Back*. Until my visit there, I timed my arrivals to about an hour before the game – roughly when most parks open their gates. However, back when my GPS didn't factor in traffic, getting across Charlotte took more than an hour longer than it should have. I might still have made it, but no dedicated parking and no "Will Call" signage caused two more fatal delays; I walked into the seating bowl as the *bottom* of the first inning began. From then on, I aimed for *two* hours.

FHP became NewBridge Bank Park in 2007. In 2012, the 'Hoppers bought the ballpark. NewBridge merged with Yadkin Bank in 2016, but before any signage changes FNB bought Yadkin. NewBridge also remained the venue name in team-supplied box scores during that season. The new name finally went up in 2017.

The 'Hoppers broke the Lakewood BlueClaws' sixteen-year run as SAL attendance champions that year, repeating in 2018. "Grasshoppers" tied "Hornets" in 2019 as this franchise's most-used nickname at fifteen seasons, but it's not yet halfway to all-time Greensboro baseball leader "Patriots."

Their sixteen-year run with the Marlins was their longest affiliation, but they bolted to the Pirates for the 2019-20 cycle.

Greensboro team colors – unlike Greeneville, TN, and Greenville, SC – actually include green, although most if not all "Green"-based municipality names salute Revolutionary War General Nathanael Greene.

Greenville Drive
Fluor Field at the West End, Greenville, SC
Class A South Atlantic League
Boston Red Sox
Got: **Sept. 17, 2009; Lakewood BlueClaws 3, Greenville Drive 2**

Opened as West End Field in 2006 on land that was once a lumber yard, this beautiful brick downtown ballpark was re-christened two years later when the Fluor Corporation engineering firm acquired naming rights. One of a handful of ballparks in the Minors that was privately funded, it is owned by the team.

After the 2004 season, Greenville lost its Atlanta Braves Double-A O&O team to Mississippi because of the condition of Greenville Municipal Stadium; the new playpen was greeted with rave reviews then and later credited with the subsequent downtown turnaround. Its interior is modeled on Boston's Fenway Park, complete with a thirty-foot-tall "Green Monster" left-field wall, Pesky's pole in right field, and a manual scoreboard. The fans even sing *Sweet Caroline* on cue. With rehabilitating Red Sox second baseman Duston Pedroia in the lineup, the Drive boosted their one-game attendance record by about 100 on Opening Night 2019.

Greenville native "Shoeless" Joe Jackson earned his nickname as a 1908 Greenville Spinner. His boyhood home is now a museum across the street from Fluor, but a development project has it moving again — just a short distance this time.

This club is not to be confused with the Greeneville Reds, about 2½ hours north; neither Green(e)ville club uses green as a team color. Greenville is rare in that its official history says it *is* named for the color, although other sources say it – like most municipalities of that name – was named for Revolutionary War General Nathanael Greene.

Gwinnett Stripers
Coolray Field, Lawrenceville, GA
Class Triple-A International League
Atlanta Braves
Got: **2009 or 2010**

Gwinnett County, suburban Atlanta's most populous county – knowing the Braves were unhappy with their Triple-A club's Richmond, VA, digs – opened Gwinnett Stadium in Braves' protected territory in 2009. Coolray Heating and Air bought naming rights in the next season. Coolray's biggest crowd, 10,568, welcomed long-time Atlanta skipper Bobby Cox managing a team of Braves' farmhands in an exhibition game against the 2012 big club. Cox's club lost 5-4.

The Braves have *twice* bought and displaced their top farm team – first, when the Boston Braves bought the Milwaukee Brewers in 1952, moving them to Toledo, OH, and themselves to Milwaukee; second, when the Milwaukee Braves bought the Atlanta Crackers in 1965, moving them to Richmond, VA, and themselves to Atlanta.

The Triple-A team went by Braves during its entire tenure in Richmond and its first nine seasons in Gwinnett County, but it has drawn very poorly in its suburb. Its management convinced Braves ownership to try a new nickname – making it the first Braves-owned farm team *ever* to go by anything but Braves. The submitted name that won the resulting contest was Big Mouths, a reference to nearby Lake Lanier's largemouth bass, but management segued to Stripers because "we have to love the name." (I'll leave to your opinion and/or research whether largemouth bass and striped bass are from the same kettle.)

Coolray "played" a fictional New Orleans ballpark in season two of the TV comedy *Brockmire* (2018).

Hagerstown Suns
Hagerstown Municipal Stadium, Hagerstown, MD
Class A South Atlantic League
Washington Nationals
Got: **June 25, 2010; Hickory Crawdads 4, Hagerstown Suns 0**

Built in only six weeks of 1930, this ballpark's long history had perhaps its most historic moment before most of us were born: June 24, 1950, Willie Mays played his first game in affiliated baseball. The New York Giants had signed the "Say Hey Kid" from the Birmingham Black Barons, whom he had joined in 1947. The Hagerstown ballpark hosted Class-B teams until losing affiliated ball altogether in 1955.

It regained MiLB in 1981, stepping up to A-ball, when the Carolina League revoked the franchise of the Rocky Mount Pines – among professional baseball's worst teams ever – and put it in Hagerstown. The Orioles' Double-A franchise bumped that team to Frederick, MD, in 1989. In 1993, big-league expansion dominoed it to Bowie, MD – but H-town seamlessly replaced the team when the Myrtle Beach Hurricanes blew right in, returning Hagerstown to Class A with the franchise that is there now.

The Nats, as geographically attractive as the O's, are unhappy with the small, old, sparsely attended ballpark but haven't found a better option. The stadium is one of six in the Minors with a manual scoreboard, and I wouldn't be surprised if it's the original.

The Suns nearly moved to Fredericksburg, VA, but that three-year effort failed in 2016. Its largest crowd ever, 6,758, saw Stephen Strasburg pitch a rehabilitation start in 2011. No 2017 Tim Tebow crowd topped that, but his four-game Columbia Firefly series drew 1,754 more than the 2017 Suns' first twenty-three home games *combined*.

Harrisburg Senators
FNB Field, Harrisburg, PA

Class Double-A Eastern League
Washington Nationals
Got: **July 8, 2013; Harrisburg Senators 3, Bowie Baysox 2**

Harrisburg teams, mostly nicknamed Senators since 1904 and *ever* since '33, were *never* affiliated with either of the American League's Washington Senators franchises. Yet its partnership with today's DC ball club is just outside the top-ten longest current affiliations among separately owned teams.

Its ballpark is one of two in the Minors located on an island, City Island in the Susquehanna River. Playing on an isle has rarely been a problem, but 2011 flooding caused by remnants of Tropical Storm Lee forced the Sens to the road for the entire playoffs.

On the road in their 2018 opener, they won the first invented-runner game in US professional baseball history. Major League Baseball put the rule into effect in regular-season Minor League play in an effort to shorten extra-inning games. It places the last man to complete a time at bat in the previous inning on second base at the beginning of all extra innings. The Senators beat the Bowie Baysox 10-9 in a 13-inning game that ran more than four hours.

Opened in 1987 on land first used for baseball in 1907, the Eastern League's second oldest was HOK Sport's first professional baseball park; now Populous, and now iconic, it pioneered "downtown retro" parks made famous by Oriole Park at Camden Yards. Commerce Bank of Harrisburg bought naming rights in 2004, changing the name of both their bank and the park to Metro Bank in 2009. FNB acquired Metro in 2016 and changed the name again.

Hartford Yard Goats
Dunkin' Donuts Park, Hartford, CT
Class Double-A Eastern League
Colorado Rockies
Got: **July 2, 2017; Hartford Yard Goats 10, Portland Sea Dogs 2**

Different in 2020: possibly, stadium name (name sponsor Dunkin' Donuts changed its own name to just Dunkin' shortly before the 2019 season)

During the 2014 season, Hartford announced it would build a new downtown ballpark into which the New Britain Rock Cats would move in 2016. During that post-season's affiliation shuffle, the Minnesota Twins dropped the Cats. Maybe they saw this coming: the worst contracting soap opera in recent history.

The Colorado Rockies stepped in, but problems erased both the entire 2016 home season and the contractor – who was fired early that year. Yet, *before* construction resumed *after* the season, the Rockies renewed through the 2018 campaign. The Goats were scheduled to open 2017 away – but "The Dunk" opened on time.

The silver lining: 2017 would have been the first year since 1980 with no new Minor League stadium. Proving worth the wait, the beautiful ballpark sold out scores of games in its first three seasons. The Goats drew 400,000 in 2018, the first Connecticut minor-league team ever to do so – and repeated that in 2019. A huge Dunkin' Donuts coffee cup salutes home runs by ... steaming. The right field barrier is not a wall but in-play netting – the only way to squeeze seats into the construction envelope without a wall so close balls hit over it would be, by rule, only doubles.

Hartford baseball history includes an original-eight National League team – one of two such cities without MLB today – and the only big-league service of curveball inventor Candy Cummings; teen-aged Candy figured it out slinging clam shells.

In 2019, The Dunk became the first MiLB park to ban peanuts.

Hickory Crawdads
L.P. Frans Stadium, Hickory, NC
Class A South Atlantic League
Texas Rangers
Got: **Sept. 5, 2011; Greenville Drive 11, Hickory Crawdads 4**

After a record South Atlantic League attendance in their first year, 1993, the Crawdads became the first South Atlantic League club to draw more than 200,000 a year in their first three. The Rangers bought the Crawdads after the 2017 campaign.

Founded in nearby Gastonia in 1977, the franchise had seven affiliations with six teams – it was in its second go-round with the Rangers at the time of their purchase – and six different nicknames. It wore its parent club's nicknames except in 1985, when the unaffiliated team played as the Jets. The move to Hickory ended a set of shifts; by buying the Gastonia club in 1989, the owner of the Double-A Charlotte Knights – who had lost their home stadium to arson – eliminated a territorial challenge to putting them in Fort Mill, SC. In 1993, he replaced them with a Triple-A team and sold the Gastonia club to the owner who moved it to Hickory.

The ball club has been Crawdads ever since, and its baseball-pinching crawdad logo is among Minor League baseball's most popular.

The crawdad mascots, Conrad and Candy, became "engaged" on Mother's Day weekend in 2018 – when the Crawdads played as the Crawmoms – and "married" that June.

After a slow start, the Hickory ball club has a good post-season record: It made the playoffs ten times 1994-2015, including three straight 2002-04. That streak was bookended by league championships, with another in 2015.

Frans founded the local Pepsi-Cola plant, and his family keyed funding the ballpark.

Hillsboro Hops
Ron Tonkin Field, Hillsboro, OR
Class A-Short Season Northwest League
Arizona Diamondbacks
Got: **Aug. 14, 2014; Boise Hawks 7, Hillsboro Hops 2**

The Portland suburb built this small but beautifully modernistic ballpark for the Yakima Bears, who had tried for years to get a new or upgraded stadium in eastern Washington. Opened as Hillsboro Ballpark in 2013, its name was sold the next season to a local car dealership. "Hops" salutes Oregon's hop production while punning on what happens when a baseball is batted sharply into the ground.

The move from Yakima, WA, was a kind of homecoming; the franchise had been founded in nearby Salem, OR, as the Senators in 1977. It never succeeded there financially, changing hands three times in eleven years – the last time after the 1987 season to ownership that three years later moved it to Yakima.

Hillsboro is in its first foray into Minor League baseball, and the team appears to have found financial success – finishing third in the eight-team league in attendance every season at least through 2019.

There could be a cloud on the horizon, though. Portland had Triple-A baseball 1919-72 but has since lost five clubs: Two Triple-A teams were sold and moved, a third lost its ballpark, and incoming Triple-A teams twice bumped short-A clubs – like the Hops. Deja vu? Portland efforts to land major-league baseball, which seem near critical mass, could bump Hillsboro or the Salem-Keizer Volcanoes – or both.

Hudson Valley Renegades
Dutchess Stadium, Wappingers Falls, NY
Class A-Short Season New York-Pennsylvania League
Tampa Bay Rays
Got: July 27, 2014; Hudson Valley Renegades 9, Vermont Lake Monsters 5

Despite its address, Dutchess Stadium lies closer to Fishkill than to the Falls. Built in seventy-one days to attract the Erie Sailors east from Pennsylvania, its gates opened literally as the last seats were bolted into place for their *secon*d home game as the 'Gades. The fact that the ballpark was not ready for their scheduled home opener June 17, 1994, forced them to play that game at Wahconah Stadium in nearby Pittsfield, MA. (You may have missed that news, amid coverage of a white Ford Bronco.)

Wahconah, long but no longer home to affiliated teams, is arguably among the oldest standing parks in the US that have ever hosted professional baseball. Dutchess came in a 1990s wave of new stadiums; five of the NYPL's fourteen teams moved in 1994 alone. For emphasis, I'll risk redundancy and point out that's almost a third of the league's members! Overall, eleven teams moved that year – mostly into new-construction stadiums – in the second most active year in history, topped only by an even dozen in 1993.

The run of stadium construction started when Major League Baseball wrote ballpark standards into the 1990 Professional Baseball Agreement, which governs the Major-Minor relationship. The 'Gades switched from the Rangers to the Rays three years later. The owners include actor Bill Murray and Mike Veeck, son of legendary baseball owner/promoter Bill Veeck.

Idaho Falls Chukars
Melaleuca Field, Idaho Falls, ID
Rookie-Advanced Pioneer League
Kansas City Royals

Got: **Aug. 19, 2014; Grand Junction Rockies 2, Idaho Falls Chukars 0, spnd., 2nd inn.)**

The league's oldest continuous franchise has played on this piece of ground since 1940. The team used the nickname Russets its first nineteen years and the nickname of its parent clubs all but two years of 1962-2003, trying out and discarding Nuggets in 1985 and Gems in 1992.

When the club joined the Royals in the 2004-05 affiliation cycle, they decided again to rebrand. After a name contest yielded the "too common" Eagles and no other suggestions the staff liked, the broadcaster suggested this pun on chucker – baseball slang for a pitcher. What *is* a chukar? A grayish-brown partridge, indigenous to Europe but brought to the western US as a game bird. Although "Chukars" had an inauspicious debut, the moniker has worked. The team unveiled the name by releasing nearly two dozen chukars – who fly little better than *WKRP in Cincinnati* turkeys. They settled in center field, and staff had to chase them off before the opener could start.

My game here got rained out in progress. In fairness, I should say *no* stadium could have handled the rain that fell there that day. This is a go-back I tabled awaiting more need in the area – it's long way to go for one game.

It was in the Path of Totality of the 2017 solar eclipse, but was the only one of the six such Minor League parks whose team was away that day – so the stadium hosted a free watch event.

Indianapolis Indians
Victory Field, Indianapolis, IN
Class Triple-A International League
Pittsburgh Pirates
Got: **June 27, 2012; Indianapolis Indians 9, Toledo Mud Hens 6**

The only Minor League team that has played continuously in the same city with the same nickname since 1902 has been "Indians" thirteen years longer than Cleveland's Tribe.

The big Tribe bought its namesake in 1952, lost money on it in their first season together, and was about to move it when locals bought it back.

Opened in 1996, "The Vic" replaced Owen J. Bush Stadium. Originally Perry Field, it was renamed Victory Field amid 1942 World War II fervor – and folks kept calling it that after it was renamed for "Donie" Bush, a small-ball specialist in his playing days, in 1966. Bush had become president of the Indy club after the local buy-back.

The Tribe drew 13 million fans in its sixty-five years at the old yard but matched that in just over twenty seasons in their new ballpark by HOK Sport (now Populous).

Only Indy and Spokane, WA, use a big-league nickname that's not its parent's; just one other MiLB nickname – Bees – is shared by two separately owned teams.

How rare is it for a player to hit for the cycle – single, double, triple and home run in the same game? Such historical statistics aren't available for the Minors, but the MLB regular-season total from 1882 through Aug. 7, 2018 was only 319 – and never by teammates in the same game. Yet on that date two Indy Indians completed the cycle in the same *inning* at Victory Field.

Inland Empire 66ers of San Bernardino
San Manuel Stadium, San Bernardino, CA
Class A-Advance California League
Los Angeles Angels of Anaheim
***Got:* May 21, 2013; San Jose Giants 8, Inland Empire 66ers 0**

In the protected joint territory of the Angels and Dodgers, then-San Bernardino Stadium opened in 1996 for the then-San Bernardino Stampede. The nickname was chosen, as the club moved from Fiscalini Field, to replace "Spirit" because of the new ballpark's western motif.

HOK Sport (now Populous) designed the stadium, which in 2002 became the first in California League history with a naming rights deal. The San Manuel Band of Serrano Mission Indians picked up the expired contract in 2012 to promote their casino. Also in 2002, the club hosted its then-parent Mariners in the first visit by a Major League team to the Berdoo in thirty years. *Bull Durham* (1988), *Field of Dreams* (1989) and *For Love of the Game* (1999) star and well-known baseball lover Kevin Costner played shortstop and pitched for the Stampede. A year later, the club took its regional name and a nickname saluting the famed US highway that passes nearby.

The team agreed to append the city's name, a la its parent Angels, in the 2016 stadium lease renewal that required the city to put $2 million into the ballpark. The Angels' somewhat odd name was less direct and more workaround. Their lease requires "Anaheim" to appear in the team name but doesn't say what *can't* appear; the Angels, wanting the marketing value of the Los Angeles name, came up with "Los Angeles Angels of Anaheim." That probably inspired the 66ers' home city to suggest adding "of San Bernardino" to their location identifier.

Iowa Cubs

Principal Park, Des Moines, IA

Class Triple-A Pacific Coast League

Chicago Cubs

Got: **Aug. 31, 2014; Iowa Cubs 11, Oklahoma City RedHawks 8**

After a long history of Minor League Demons and Bruins, Des Moines (French for "the monks") had a dry spell through most of the 1960s. In '69, the city landed a Triple-A Oakland farm team that went by Iowa Oaks. That remained through a Chicago White Sox' hitch into their first Cubs' season, 1981, but the team adopted Cubs in '82 while retaining Iowa over Des Moines. The affiliation is now the fifth-longest current partnership between separately owned teams.

Opened in 1992 as a same-site, same-name replacement of Sec Taylor Stadium, this ballpark kept the name of the late *Des Moines Register* and *Tribune* sports editor until Principal Financial

Group bought naming rights in 2004. It opened as architect HOK Sport (now Populous) exploded onto the ballpark scene with Oriole Park at Camden Yards. The original, opened as Pioneer Park in 1947, was renamed for Taylor in 1959. Carrying the name over to the rebuild was posthumous, Taylor having died in 1965. Its otherwise modern scoreboard is manual for score by innings and line score. The Iowa State Capitol is visible beyond Principal's outfield.

Another diamond, Holcomb Park, hosted the first professional night baseball game played under permanent lights May 2, 1930 – almost nine years before Cincinnati premiered nighttime MLB action. That franchise folded with the Illinois-Indiana-Iowa League in 1961.

A 2008 game was played to empty seats; flooding had forced evacuations, but with no possible makeup dates the city agreed to let the game be played without admitting fans.

Jackson Generals
The Ballpark at Jackson, Jackson, TN
Class Double-A Southern League
Arizona Diamondbacks
Got: **2008 or 2009**

The Tennessee city of Jackson built Pringles Park to land the Memphis Chicks as their Southern League franchise was being displaced by Triple-A's 1998 Pacific Coast League expansion. The move and the ballpark opening took place on schedule that season.

After arriving as the West Tenn Diamond Jaxx, the club was sold in 2002 and again in 2008. In 2011, ownership made the team the second Jackson Generals in Double-A baseball history. Seven years later, the nearby Jackson State Community College Generals changed their nickname to Green Jays to end confusion – even though JSCC pre-dated the Jaxx in Jackson by more than thirty years and their use of the name Generals by forty-four.

The Pringles name died when Kellogg bought Jackson-manufactured Pringles from Procter & Gamble and didn't renew the naming contract. The club settled on The Ballpark at Jackson for its non-commercial name, but in December 2017 asked for bids on a new naming contract.

The Chicks and the original Nashville Sounds were born when the Eastern League's two Canadian franchises were moved to the Southern League after the 1977 season.

Who were the earlier Jackson Generals? They played in the South's other Double-A circuit, the Texas League, in another Jackson in the Southeast. Coincidentally also founded in Memphis, they moved to Mississippi's capital in 1975, initially going by Jackson Mets but becoming Generals in 1991. Having since moved twice, they are now the Corpus Christi Hooks.

Jacksonville Jumbo Shrimp
Bragan Field at the Baseball Grounds of Jacksonville, Jacksonville, FL
Class Double-A Southern League
Miami Marlins
Got: **Aug. 3, 2010; Jacksonville Suns 5, Birmingham Barons 0**

Baseball has been played here since 1954, when Samuel W. Wolfson Baseball Park opened. The game's long Jacksonville history includes mostly teams named Suns from just after World War II through 2016. In 2003, the city created the Sports Complex of Jacksonville by rebuilding Wolfson and building Jacksonville Veterans Memorial Arena west of the National Football League's Jaguars' field. "The Vet" has minor-league hockey.

The Baseball Grounds of Jacksonville, Wolfson's replacement, nearly doubled Suns attendance. The field was separately named for the club's long-time owner, Peter Bragan Sr., six months after his death. Bragan's older brother Bobby, a Dodger when Jackie Robinson broke MLB's color line, initially resisted the move but changed his mind after getting to know Jackie.

Renowned stadium architect HOK Sport (now Populous) gave the Grounds a unique outfield: a tiered seating terrace off left field called The Knuckle, a Southern League-longest 420 feet to center field, and a view of the Jaguars' stadium – then Alltell Stadium, now TIAA Bank Field – beyond right.

In 2017, the team's new owner changed the long-time Suns nickname. "Jumbo Shrimp" met with the usual resistance but has done well in terms of merchandising.

Ever wonder where spring training in Florida got started? Not at this ballpark, of course, but it was in Jacksonville: by the original Washington Nationals, in 1888.

Johnson City Cardinals
TVA Credit Union Ballpark, Johnson City, TN
Rookie-Advanced Appalachian League
St. Louis Cardinals
Got: **July 7, 1990; Huntington Cubs 13, Johnson City Cardinals 6**

Howard Johnson Field, named for the then-director of Johnson City Parks and Recreation, opened in 1956 – 100 years after Henry Johnson founded the city, which was originally called Johnson's Depot. "At Cardinal Park" was later appended; eventually, most folks came to use one name or the other but rarely both.

The JC-Cards shared the ballpark with East Tennessee State University Buccaneers baseball until ETSU opened Thomas Stadium in 2012. The ballpark has also hosted baseball games of Science Hill High School, which was founded in 1867 as the Science Hill Male and Female Institute.

In 2016, TVA Credit Union bought naming rights to "Howard Johnson Field at Cardinal Park" and replaced the whole name. Johnson City has had a big-league farm team every season save one since 1937. More than fifty of them wore Cardinal uniforms, including *all* of them since 1975 – making this the fourth-longest current partnership among separately operated Majors and Minors teams.

The Cards reported house record baseball crowds on consecutive 2018 nights in July and their first 4,000 crowd that August. They played an August 2018 road game with the Greeneville Reds at Smokies Stadium, home of the Tennessee Smokies – the connection being that all three teams are commonly operated.

Jupiter Hammerheads, Palm Beach Cardinals
Roger Dean Chevrolet Stadium, Jupiter, FL
Class A-Advanced Florida State League
Miami Marlins, St. Louis Cardinals

Got ('Heads home game): April 7, 2012; Palm Beach Cardinals 4, Jupiter Hammerheads 2

Got (Cards home game): April 7, 2012; Jupiter Hammerheads 2, Palm Beach Cardinals 0

This is the only American stadium that is the day-to-day home of six professional baseball clubs: the Miami Marlins' Class A-Advanced Florida State League farm team, the Jupiter Hammerheads; the St. Louis Cardinals' FSL team, the Palm Beach Cardinals; the Marlins and Cardinals themselves, during spring training; and their entry-level rookie teams, the GCL Marlins and the GCL Cardinals.* Jupiter Stadium LTD operates both FSL clubs for their parent teams.

"The Dean" opened as Roger Dean Stadium in 1998 for the Marlins and Hammerheads, with the Card clubs joining them in 2003. Designed by HOK Sport (now Populous), it became the first ballpark in Florida to house two organizations. Two more have since opened, and there are three in Arizona – but only Jupiter has six teams because none of the others has high-A.

Roger Dean, a successful car dealer and community leader, was credited with revitalizing Jupiter. The name has been said to be honorary rather than corporate, so media coverage of the 2018

---

* GCL teams included in this entry, only, because of the unique six-team situation. The reasons outlined earlier for not doing entry-level Rookie teams are just as true at Roger Dean as at all the others. While they rarely play on the big diamond, its stadium is where they use workout and dressing rooms.

addition of "Chevrolet" referring to the extension of an "existing" naming rights deal surprised me. I dug up a 2002 article that says it was named "in exchange for a donation of $1 million" by Dean's heirs.

The brick ballpark has two levels of fixed seats and *three* clubhouses: separate home clubhouses for the Marlins' and Cardinals' clubs and a third for the visiting team of the moment. Jupiter is in the Marlins' protected territory.

How was I going to handle this two-team stadium? Even if I got them playing each other, only one would be "home." Should I visit twice to get both teams at home? Incredible luck solved this. Its two FSL teams played a day-night double-header with each other on a Saturday, with one team home one game and the other home the other game, so I picked that day and scored a home game by both teams in one visit.

Kane County Cougars
Northwestern Medicine Field, Geneva, IL
Class A Midwest League
Arizona Diamondbacks
Got: **Aug. 22, 2014; Kane County Cougars 9, Clinton LumberKings 1**

Opened in 1991 as Kane County Events Park, it was in 1993 renamed Philip B. Elfstrom Stadium for the man who helped land its minor-league tenant. Its name was then sold, first to Fifth Third Bank but that went unrenewed.

The ballpark by HOK Sport (now Populous) drew a struggling franchise from Wausau, WI, into the shadow of *two* big-league teams. Could it survive, revive and thrive so close to the Cubs *and* White Sox? Either big-league Chicago club could have vetoed the move by the then-Orioles affiliate; neither did, although the Cubs became their parent team for one later affiliation cycle.

Given the risk, the Cougars' success has been startling. They drew more than 400,000 a season 1993-2016, posting increases in both Cubs' campaigns (2013-14). The Cubs then went to South

Bend, IN, where attendance promptly skyrocketed. During the first Cubs' season – their twenty-third in Geneva – the Cougars became the first club in their class to draw 10 million in one location. That feat has since been surpassed in less time, eighteen seasons, by the Dayton Dragons.

While most ballparks are owned by either the local municipality or the ball club, this one is the property of the Forest Preserve District of Kane County. Elfstrom was its president 1982-90.

I saw Kane County a day earlier than I originally scheduled it, because weather forecasts suggested I switch with Peoria. I got in both ballparks, but I would have anyway; both teams got in both games.

Kannapolis Intimidators

Intimidators Stadium supported by Atrium Health, Kannapolis, NC

Class A South Atlantic League

Chicago White Sox

Got: **Sept. 4, 2011; Greensboro Grasshoppers 5, Kannapolis Intimidators 3**

Different in 2020: stadium (assuming it is completed on schedule) and nickname

Opened partially finished in 1995 as Fieldcrest Cannon Stadium – for the textile giant that built the mill town that in 1984 incorporated as the city of Kannapolis – it landed the Spartanburg Phillies. Originally keeping the nickname but taking Piedmont as its location identifier, the club later changed nicknames to Boll Weevils.

After NASCAR legend and Kannapolis native Dale "The Intimidator" Earnhardt bought in following the 2000 season, the team adopted his nickname. He never saw a game as an owner. After his death in the 2001 Daytona 500, the Intimidators retired his car number – 3 – from their uniform roster. The team has since been sold twice, and current ownership decided to change nicknames with its scheduled move into a new downtown stadium in 2020. The I's will become the Kannapolis Cannon Ballers.

The city bought most of its downtown in 2016 for a revitalization plan that includes the new ballpark. Its mill-town history made that easier than it would have been for most cities. Because most of its downtown properties were still commonly owned, Kannapolis did not have to negotiate with scores or even hundreds of different property owners.

Carolinas Medical Center bought stadium naming rights in 2012, then changed its name to Atrium Health in 2018 and applied that to the ballpark.

Back when the Charlotte Knights played in a suburb across the South Carolina state line, a Kannapolis staffer pointed out to me that the Intimidators were actually closer to downtown Charlotte than the Knights were.

Kingsport Mets
Hunter Wright Stadium, Kingsport, TN
Rookie-Advanced Appalachian League
New York Mets
Got: **Aug. 20, 2011; Burlington Royals 17, Kingsport Mets 14**

Named for the five-term mayor whose administration built it, this rudimentary ballpark's first baseball game was the 1995 Hokie-Smokey Classic – a since discontinued annual contest between the University of Tennessee Volunteers and the Virginia Polytechnic Institute Hokies. Basically, it consists of two cinderblock sections arranged in an L with the elbow behind home plate.

Early Kingsport teams went by Indians or Cherokees but have used their parent club's moniker since 1957. Although no rule requires Appy teams to use their parent club's nicknames, every affiliated team has done so since the 1967 Pirate-affiliated Salem Rebels. During that time, the only ones *not* using a big-league nickname were three *unaffiliated* teams: the 1995 River City (Huntsville, WV) Rumblers, the 1990 Princeton Patriots, and the 1978 Paintsville Hilanders.

The K-Mets played opening day 2017 as the Kingsport Spirit, keying a day-long celebration of the centennial of the city's second and current charter. Kingsport's tourism bureau claims Long Island Iced Tea originated not on New York's Long Island but on the one in the Holston River; the K-Mets supported that by playing a 2018 game as the Long Island Iced Teas.

They played at Dobyns-Bennett High School's J. Fred Johnson Stadium 1969-94 except 1983, when a ballpark renovation led them to make a rare switch from one level to another by playing in the Gulf Coast League. In late 2018, Kingsport began serious consideration of a new downtown ballpark.

Lake County Captains
Classic Park, Eastlake, OH
Class A Midwest League
Cleveland Indians
Got: **June 29, 2012; West Michigan Whitecaps 4, Lake County Captains 2**

In 2010, the Captains and the Bowling Green Hot Rods changed circuits, leaving the South Atlantic League for the MwL. For the Caps franchise, that ended nineteen seasons of SAL play.

The city-built ballpark in a Cleveland suburb blends nostalgia into modern design, but its name is not descriptive; Classic Chevrolet owns naming rights. With its various specialty seating and standing room, crowds can top 10,000 for baseball and more for other events like concerts.

Goodbye, Columbus? Both transferring franchises had abandoned that Georgia city, the Caps for then-Eastlake Park in 2003 and the Rods for theirs in 2009. Their joint league jump allows their stadiums to boast hosting currently operating teams in two different leagues – unique today, and nearly so since the Negro Leagues folded. During their last seven Sally League seasons, the Caps were more than 250 miles from their nearest opponent; now, they are within 250 miles of five rivals.

Because Eastlake is in Cleveland's protected territory, the Indians could veto any other parent for the Caps – and they have partnered with this franchise its entire history, all the way back to its 1991 founding in Georgia. In fact, starting with the Canton-Akron Indians in 1989, the Tribe has consolidated nearly its entire non-Rookie farm system in the state of Ohio without owning a single one of their top-five tier teams. The exception is the A-Advanced Lynchburg Hillcats – a necessary exception given that there are no high-A teams in Ohio.

Lake Elsinore Storm

Pete Lehr Field at Lake Elsinore Diamond, Lake Elsinore, CA

Class A-Advanced California League

San Diego Padres

Got: **May 23, 2013; Lake Elsinore Storm 0, Modesto Nuts 0, spnd., 7th, light failure**

This ball club's most famous feature is its logo. Its best-selling cap, a youth-team favorite, features narrowed, glowing eyes under a furrowed brow. Why eyes for a Storm? The original logo, a storm cloud with lightning splitting the letters L and E, later added eyes overlooking the cloud. No one seems to remember why, or why they were pulled forth in 2000 to become this logo.

Founded in 1979 as the Santa Clara Padres, the franchise also played as the Redwood Pioneers and Palm Springs Angels before the Lake Elsinore Diamond opened in 1994. Then still an Angels' farm club, it rejoined the Padres in 2001. Part of a nationwide wave of new Minor League ballparks, the Diamond remains a fine stadium in a league that now has trouble building and renovating them due to California fiscal policy changes. It boasts the league's best backdrop; although its namesake lake is behind home plate, fans have an idyllic view of the Temescal Mountains.

The 2016 California-Carolina League All-Star Game, the Diamond's third, ended the interleague series. Both still play their mid-season classics on the same date, but each now has its own. Carolina team owners voted to opt out, and *The Press-Enterprise* of Riverside, CA, at the time reported "whispers dating back to the early 2000s of some dissatisfaction by Carolina League officials regarding the Cal League locales outside of Rancho Cucamonga and Lake Elsinore."

Lehr, a key developer of the city of Lake Elsinore, donated the land the stadium occupies.

Lakeland Flying Tigers
Publix Field at Joker Marchant Stadium, Lakeland, FL
Class A-Advanced Florida State League
Detroit Tigers
Got: **June 7, 2012; Charlotte Stone Crabs at Lakeland Flying Tigers, ppnd., rain**

Opened in 1966, the ballpark added a spring training-quality stadium to the existing spring complex that had been known as Tiger Town since its 1953 opening. The next year, the Bengals became the first big-league team to put spring MLB and a summer affiliated club in the same ballpark – now of course the norm in Florida. It is named for then-Parks and Recreation Director Marcus Thigpen "Joker" Marchant (1908-1983), who lived most of his life under a white cowboy hat, served as Lakeland's first P&R Director, and built the city's relationship with the Tigers – which will reach 100 springs during the current lease. That tenure predates '53; the Tigers started training in Lakeland in 1934 at Henley Field – which twice pinch hit in hosting the Lakeland FSL team while Marchant underwent renovations, in 2002 and 2016.

The FSL team added "Flying" in 2007 to honor both the US fighter squadron that flew for China early in World War II and the site's history as a World War II aviator school – which also accounts for "The Runway" (built over and mimicking one of the school's runways), logo, slogan ("Every game is a mission") and stencil-style uniform numerals.

The run-up to the 2017 reopening saw Publix Super Markets buy field naming rights, complete with statues of Marchant and Publix founder George Jenkins shaking hands. Also that year, the ballpark and the Tiger Town complex sheltered Hurricane Irma evacuees.

Lakewood BlueClaws
FirstEnergy Park, Lakewood Township, NJ
Class A South Atlantic League
Philadelphia Phillies
Got: **July 1, 2012; Hagerstown Suns 11, Lakewood BlueClaws 9**

Opened in 2001, this unique, very Jersey Shore, "simply clawsome" and largely wooden ballpark lured the Cape Fear Crocs – nee Fayetteville Generals – north. In fact, it is now the northernmost team in the *South Atlantic* League, by nearly 150 miles from the Delmarva Shorebirds to the south and by almost 200 from the Hagerstown Suns to the southwest.

The place blends entertainment destination and site of a baseball game – the key to filling Minor League seats – as well as anyone. The team and the township must be highly satisfied with each other: Their lease runs through 2055!

Relatively unscathed by Hurricane Sandy, it served as a staging area for recovery operations.

The BlueClaws led the SAL in attendance their first sixteen seasons in it – beating out fifteen other teams their first nine seasons and thirteen the last seven. They've packed it so full that they capped per-game sales at 8,000 in 2012 – although, after making some tweaks to plans and playpen, they later rescinded that.

The largest crowd ever was a legendary 13,003 Aug. 26, 2002 – a *Monday*, but also the home season finale. Even ticket-selling machine Tim Tebow didn't match that, but he did help draw more than 8,000 on consecutive 2017 nights. The 'Claws have hosted 8K well over 100 times, reaching all the million attendance increments faster than any Sally team. Oh – they've also won three SAL championships ...

Lancaster JetHawks
Lancaster Municipal Stadium, Lancaster, CA
Class A-Advanced California League

Colorado Rockies

Got: **May 21, 2013; Lancaster JetHawks 13, Rancho Cucamonga Quakes 12**

Opened in 1996 in Los Angeles Angels' and Dodgers' protected territory, the stadium has never hosted an affiliate of either – just Mariners, Diamondbacks, Red Sox, Astros and now Rockies.

"JetHawks" generated a ballpark nickname – "The Hangar" – which was included in new signage after a lost naming-rights deal. The facility's legal name, however, remains Lancaster Municipal Stadium – and that's what secondary tenant University of Antelope Valley Pioneers baseball calls it. Architect HOK Sport (now Populous) designed it.

The Santa Barbara Dodgers and Ventura Oilers merged in 1954, with the resulting Channel Cities Oilers dividing their home schedule between both cities. That lasted just one season, as the Oilers moved to Reno, NV, in 1955. They remained there as the only Cali team based outside California for nearly forty years, but their next stop was another brief one: Riverside, CA, 1993-95.

That ballpark's neighbors had blocked alcohol sales from its 1988 opening. The Riverside Red Wave gave up on making a profit in 1990 and moved to the Mojave Desert city of Adelanto. The Oilers-turned-Pilots met the same fate, not only leaving but playing twenty of their 1995 games at Palm Springs Stadium. They also played their first twelve days as JetHawks on the road while the Lancaster ballpark was being finished.

The franchise has been more financially successful in Lancaster, but the stadium's altitude and windiness have made parent clubs hard to come by – although the Rockies seem a good fit.

Lansing Lugnuts
Cooley Law School Stadium, Lansing, MI
Class A Midwest League
Toronto Blue Jays

Got: **June 22, 2012; Great Lakes Loons 4, Lansing Lugnuts 0**

Perhaps the most unusual thing about this downtown ballpark, especially for a team so far north, is that its top crowd came out not for a Midwest League regular-season, playoff, or even All-Star Game. Once a year, the Lugnuts and the Michigan State University Spartans play what is known as the Crosstown Showdown. The game draws well when weather allows, and set the house baseball record of 12,997 in 2012. Cooley also has the MwL All-Star Game event record, 10,334 in 2002. Because of Michigan's spring weather, the Showdown has since been moved to the MwL post-season and what college calls fall-ball.

It also opened with a college game: MSU and the University of Michigan Wolverines, April 3, 1996 – exactly one year after its groundbreaking. Its original name was Oldsmobile Park; GM dropped the Olds line in 2004 but left the paid-for name in place until losing naming rights in its 2010 reorganization. Western Michigan University's Cooley Law School picked up the naming contract the next season.

The ballpark's construction envelope limited its foul lines to only 305 feet, although each wall angles to an elbow and soon reaches more conventional distance. The Nuts & Bolts store is open year-round. The apartment complex beyond the outfield is called ... The Outfield Apartments.

Las Vegas Aviators

Las Vegas Ballpark, Las Vegas, NV

Class Triple-A Pacific Coast League

Oakland Athletics

Got: **June 23, 2019; Sacramento River Cats 4, Las Vegas Aviators 3**

One of three new 2019 stadiums with affiliated teams, Las Vegas Ballpark is the state-of-the-art envy of all. In one of baseball's hottest places, it boasts mesh-backed seats – some of which swivel 360 degrees. Architect HOK, with the end of its non-compete with its 2009 spinoff Populous, returned with this ballpark; both names are iconic in baseball.

The former Las Vegas 51s also changed nicknames and parents, with the Aviators even using "A's" as a short-hand nickname to play on "Oakland A's." After the New York Mets escaped parenting far-off Vegas by buying the Syracuse Chiefs, the 51s signed the first new affiliation of the 2019-20 cycle. However, the twenty-six-year-old spring-training Big League Weekend was a one-season casualty of their leaving Cashman Stadium. It is expected to return "maybe bigger and better" in 2020.

The Howard Hughes Corporation, which bought the 51s in 2017, built the ballpark in Summerlin – a planned community HHC also built that's technically in Vegas. In a town where money flows, HHC projected LVB to cost $150 million and the Las Vegas Convention and Visitors Authority paid $80 million to name it – *both* unprecedented figures in the Minors.

It actually snowed in Vegas the February 2018 day ground was broken. The 2019 debut game sold out in ten minutes.

The National Hockey League's Golden Knights' practice facility is close enough to be hit by LVB home runs – but the good-neighbor A's put up towering netting. Vegas welcomes the National Football League's Oakland Raiders in 2020.

Lehigh Valley IronPigs
Coca-Cola Park, Allentown, PA
Class Triple-A International League
Philadelphia Phillies
Got: July 12, 2013; Buffalo Bisons at Lehigh Valley IronPigs, ppnd., rain

This 2008 playpen landed the Ottawa Lynx. The local Coca-Cola bottler bought naming rights more than a year before it opened.

Taking a nickname saluting the local steel industry, the Pigs lost their first eleven games that season playing to Triple-A's worst record – yet won Minor League Operation of the Year and drew nearly six times as many fans as the 2007 last-in-IL-attendance Lynx.

A flash in the pan in Ottawa, the 1993 expansion team actually broke the IL's nearly fifty-year-old one-season attendance record but crowds dwindled quickly and steadily – with an odd upward blip in 2000 – into the low 100,000s. Even though "BaconUSA" has fewer than 8,100 fixed seats, the Pigs have *averaged* more than that every year and topped 9,000 in five straight seasons while leading the IL 2010-12. They cap per-game ticket sales at 10,100 – and they hit it often.

This club's promotions are usually among post-season award nominees, including their productions of the 2010 Triple-A All-Star Game and the 2013 Triple-A Championship, a long list of food-based promotions that pre-date the current run of them, and cross-promotions like their fan-decided "Bacon versus Tacos" grudge match with the Fresno Grizzlies. If you follow Minor League ball at all, you may see some trendsetters in there.

The Pigs' arrival ended a long baseball drought. Even though Allentown baseball history dated to the 1800s, the city hadn't had a team since 1960.

My first game here was rained out after I went in but before the first pitch.

Lexington Legends
Whitaker Bank Ballpark, Lexington, KY
Class A South Atlantic League
Kansas City Royals
Got: **Aug. 13, 2009; West Virginia Power 12, Lexington Legends 6**

Kentucky's Bluegrass country got an early start in professional baseball, in the 1880s, but it went blank in 1954. Lack of a suitable stadium stalled return efforts until a group pooled enough private money to build one *and* buy a franchise. Season tickets went on sale less than fourteen months before the first pitch. Despite morning temperatures in the thirties, more than 200 people were in line thirty minutes before sales started at 9 a.m.; 1,950 full season tickets were sold by 4 p.m.

Then-Applebee's Park opened in 2001, with Whitaker Bank becoming name sponsor in 2011. The parent team has also changed once, with the Kansas City Royals taking over from the Houston Astros with the 2013 season. The ballpark is at once beautiful and typical of those designed in the late 1990s. Parking is close but limited, and the ballpark has what is today a drawback – a non-downtown location. Talk of building a new stadium near legendary Rupp Arena, which *is* downtown, seemed to take hold in 2017 but later stalled.

Perhaps Whitaker's most unusual feature is the stadium restaurant, the Kentucky Ale Taproom, which is located directly behind home plate but at ground level rather than somewhere atop the stands. Despite the name, it is a full-service restaurant with a variety of food.

Louisville Bats
Louisville Slugger Field, Louisville, KY
Class Triple-A International League
Cincinnati Reds

Got: **July 23, 2011; Pawtucket Red Sox 4, Louisville Bats 3**

In 1982, the American Association franchise and St. Louis Cardinals' affiliate then known as the Springfield Redbirds moved for the third time in six seasons. Leaving tracks in New Orleans, LA, and Tulsa, OK, as well as the Illinois capital, the ball club moved into the cavernous University of Louisville football stadium.

That first season, it shattered the Minors' attendance record with 868,418. The next season, the Redbirds found a new way to make news by becoming the first MiLB team ever to draw 1 million – to be exact, 1,052,438.

They lost the Cards' affiliation to Triple-A expansion into Memphis in 1998, that same year joining the International League as the American Association was disbanded (again). They joined the Brewers for one two-year cycle, then in 2000 joined the Reds and opened this intimate ballpark – designed around an old train shed – where a million would require a full house every day with no rainouts. They became River Bats in 1998, just Bats in 2002.

Louisville is one of two original-eight National League cities without big-league baseball today. The ballpark, which bumped Memphis as my favorite the moment I walked inside, helped a United Soccer League team take hold by hosting matches while a soccer-specific stadium was planned and built. The Bats' lease largely funds the Louisville Downtown Development Corporation.

The Bluegrass World Series, a tournament featuring one team of retired big-leaguers and seven collegiate wood-bat teams, got off to a good start in 2018.

Lowell Spinners
Edward A. LeLacheur Park, Lowell, MA
Class A-Short Season New York-Pennsylvania League
Boston Red Sox
Got: **July 23, 2014; Vermont Lake Monsters 8, Lowell Spinners 6**
Different in 2020: just possibly, locale name and/or nickname

Several short-season ball clubs share ballparks with a college; the Spinners say theirs was the first *built* to do so – although it was the Spinners who first played in it June 22, 1998. The beautiful brick ballpark was designed by HOK Sport (now Populous), which specializes in "downtown retro" parks that blend modern function and nostalgia. The city of Lowell and the University of Massachusetts Lowell then built the ballpark jointly for Spinners and UMass Lowell River Hawks baseball. The ballpark is next to a campus residential area.

The Elmira Pioneers were a Boston affiliate 1973-92, before spending the last of their days with the then-Florida Marlins. In 1996, they moved to Lowell and rejoined the BoSox, who because of Lowell's location could veto any other parent. The Spinners played their first two campaigns at Stoklosa Alumni Field, a high school park that was renovated to be their temporary home. Once the Spinners got into their permanent new playpen, the professional club sold out a then-Minor League record 413 straight games 1998-2010.

LeLacheur, a twenty-four-year legislator who helped create the ballpark, died of Lou Gehrig's disease in 2010. "Spinners" derives from the area's textile manufacturing history; the team says it sells "spinnertainment." Parking for the stadium, no matter which team is playing, is on campus and controlled by the university.

With a Triple-A team swooping into nearby Worcester, MA, in 2021, Spinners ownership has talked about rebranding to regionalize its club.

Lynchburg Hillcats

Calvin Falwell Field at Lynchburg City Stadium, Lynchburg, VA

Class A-Advanced Carolina League

Cleveland Indians

Got: **Sept. 1, 2011; Potomac Nationals 5, Lynchburg HillCats 1**

This is the only one of the Tribe's top-five tier affiliates not located in the state of Ohio, but for a very good reason: Ohio has no Advanced-A teams. In this nearest high-A league, only the Salem

Red Sox and Potomac Nationals are closer to Cleveland – but the former are owned outright by the Boston Red Sox and the latter have much closer big-league fits in the Washington Nationals and the Baltimore Orioles. (The P-Nats are moving to Fredericksburg, VA – but that won't appreciably change this.)

In 2012, the then-parent Atlanta Braves bought their only non-owned farm club to move it to Wilmington, NC – *if* that city built a new stadium. Voters kicked that, the Braves didn't renew, and Lynchburg changed tribes in the next affiliation cycle.

In 1966, Calvin Falwell founded the non-profit Lynchburg Baseball Corporation to save baseball for his city, which was having a bad run: The Lynchburg Senators moved to Wytheville, VA, after the 1959 season; the Savannah White Sox moved in for the 1964 season, but the next year fled racial tensions for Evansville, IN. The LBC seamlessly replaced that franchise, but the 2012 experience with the Braves led the LBC to sell in 2016 to a buyer who promised to keep the team in Lynchburg. The club promptly announced a nickname change contest, but a landslide fan vote said they wanted to keep "Hillcats." However, a new color scheme and logo followed.

Appomattox Court House is just thirty minutes away.

Mahoning Valley Scrappers
Eastwood Field, Niles, OH
Class A-Short Season New York-Pennsylvania League
Cleveland Indians
Got: **June 21, 2012; Jamestown Jammers 6, Mahoning Valley Scrappers 2**

The Steel Valley's dominant city is Youngstown, with nearby Niles perhaps best known as the birthplace of President William McKinley. The nickname salutes the scrap component of the steel business and also, the team says, the "scrappy" local populace. Opened as Cafaro Field in 1999, the ballpark landed the former Erie SeaWolves – who had been bumped by the Double-A Eastern League expansion franchise that now wears that name.

Eastwood Field is located on the grounds of the Eastwood Mall, which opened thirty years earlier. The ballpark's name was changed from that of the mall developer to the mall itself in 2003. The stadium looks tremendous from the outside, especially at night with its superb lighting, but the inside looks dated.

Most baseball diamonds are sodded with Bermuda grass, but Eastwood uses Kentucky Bluegrass. The warning track is composed of crushed red brick. It can seat more than 6,000 for baseball and can get close to 10,000 for other events – and there a lot of them, many involving Youngstown State University and big-name concerts.

With lots of free parking at the largest retail facility between Cleveland and Pittsburgh, the Scrappers charge a "walk-in" fee on anyone entering the stadium on foot. If you like pinching your dollar bills, you should know that before you get there – because there's no kind of notice or warning until you get to the gate.

Memphis Redbirds
AutoZone Park, Memphis, TN
Class Triple-A Pacific Coast League
St. Louis Cardinals
Got: **June 16, 2003; International League All-Stars 13, Pacific Coast League All-Stars 9**

This ballpark became my instant favorite – of about three dozen at the time. It was the first HOK Sport-designed stadium I'd ever seen, and the brick exterior and ornate entry had me at "Wow." Opened in 2000 to replace Tim McCarver Stadium, AutoZone is among many ballparks credited with revitalizing their downtowns. Among *none* other, however: It drew 10 million faster than any PCL club ever.

The Redbirds were a 1998 expansion team as *both* surviving Triple-A leagues got bigger because Organized Baseball shut down the American Association. (This is why the *Pacific Coast* League has teams in Tennessee, Louisiana, Iowa, Nebraska, and Oklahoma.) The Cards promptly moved their Triple-A affiliation here. The community owned both team and ballpark, and although the team operated in the black the stadium debt service kept both strapped. In 2014, the Cards bought the team in a deal that also transferred the stadium to the city. When attendance plummeted, they sold a majority interest. Attendance rose the next two seasons, with former President Jimmy Carter and fan 10 million at the same August 2016 game.

"The AZ" also hosted the first two Major League Baseball Civil Rights Games in 2007 and 2008.

Goin' to Jackson? Incoming Triple-A clubs twice bumped Double-A teams from Memphis, and both ended up in a Jackson: the 1997 Memphis Chicks in Jackson, TN, as the West Tenn Diamond Jaxx; the 1973 Blues – after one financially disastrous season in Victoria, TX – in Jackson, MS, as the Jackson Mets.

Midland RockHounds
Security Bank Ballpark, Midland, TX
Class Double-A Texas League
Oakland Athletics
Got: **April 20, 2014; Midland RockHounds 7, San Antonio Missions 4, 12 inns.**

Like several western ballparks, this one seems to arise from nowhere as one drives to it. The beautiful facility, by renowned ballpark architect HOK Sport (now Populous), has some serious history for one built in this century.

In 2017, the RockHounds became the most recent affiliated team to accomplish the rare feat of four straight league championships. The last of those sneaked into the Texas League playoffs as a sub-.500 wild card, and the streak ended when the 'Hounds (finally) failed to make the 2018 post-season.

Financial institutions have named this playpen since its 2002 opening. That came thirty years after the 1972 San Antonio Missions fled to a twenty-year-old ballpark – now home to Midland College Chaparrals baseball – that was variously named for the farm club's parent teams or, as it is today, oilman Max H. Christensen.

In 2006, a 'Hound made history in the American League Championship Series: his was the first modern post-season big-league debut. Something even more unusual followed. Oakland called up Mark Kiger, mostly with Midland 2004-06, after losing four players to free agency or injury going into the playoffs. Injuries can't be helped, of course, and the A's would have had to sign the free agent to a 2007 contract. Kiger played in Game 3 of the series but, incredibly, never carried a bat to the plate nor crouched on defense in a regular-season big-league game. Ever. Released the following November, he retired after three more seasons in the Minors.

Mississippi Braves
Trustmark Park, Pearl, MS
Class Double-A Southern League
Atlanta Braves
Got: **April 29, 2011; Mississippi Braves 6, Mobile BayBears 4**

In 2005, four years after stadium dissatisfaction cost Jackson, MS, its Generals, the Atlanta Braves were as dissatisfied with their Double-A team's playpen in Greenville, SC. After fruitless efforts to get that ballpark renovated or replaced, the Braves helped fund what became Trustmark Park in the Jackson suburb of Pearl. It already had a naming rights contract with Trustmark Bank when it opened.

In 2007, the annual non-conference Mayor's Trophy game between the University of Mississippi and Mississippi State University moved into Trustmark as the renamed neutral-site Governor's Cup. In 2015, the University of Southern Mississippi Golden Eagles joined the Rebels and Bulldogs to create the Mississippi College Series. The MCS lasted just three seasons, but the annual MSU-Ole Miss Governor's Cup game continues.

The ballpark – designed by "downtown retro" architect HOK Sport (now Populous) – has 5,500 seats and the team states its capacity with berms, suites, and other standing room as 8,480. Collegiate games have drawn its largest baseball crowds – topped by 8,542 at the 2016 Governor's Cup. The largest ever to see an

M-Braves game, through 2019, was 8,217 – however, that was not a Southern League regular-season or playoff game but a March 2013 exhibition game with the big-league Braves. M-Braves staff say the top crowd for a regular SL game was 7,652 for "the second Chipper Jones rehab start Aug. 12, 2006."

Missoula PaddleHeads
Ogren Park at Allegiance Field, Missoula, MT
Rookie-Advanced Pioneer League
Arizona Diamondbacks
Got: **Aug. 16, 2014; Missoula Osprey 3, Idaho Falls Chukars 2; Idaho Falls Chukars 6, Missoula Osprey 2**
Different in 2020: nickname

Missoula's new nickname salutes kayaking, canoeing, and moose antlers.

The Salt Lake City Trappers, bumped by a Triple-A Pacific Coast League club, moved to Pocatello, Idaho, in 1993. Pocatello had several clubs 1926-91, but this was the last; the Pocatello Posse crossed into Canada to become the Lethbridge Mounties in '93. Finally finding a parent club, the D-backs, they became the Lethbridge Black Diamonds in '96.

Their 1999 move to Missoula didn't change the affiliation but did bring a parent-independent nickname – Osprey. Ospreys mate for life; a pair usually summer in the OPAF. Yet in January 2019 the team announced a 2020 nickname change, revealed in November 2019.

Opened in 2004 as Play Ball Park, it landed a possibly unique *joint* naming-rights deal in 2006. Many ballparks have separately named field and stadium, but here a company benefit management firm and a car dealer share putting both names on the whole facility.

That *M* on the side of Mount Sentinel stands not for Missoula or Mount but for *Montana* – as in *University of*. The next mountain to the left's *L* (for Loyola Sacred Heart Catholic High

School) creates a pun opportunity: "Did you know Missoula alphabetized its mountains?"

Not counting the ospreys, the millionth Osprey spectator visited the OPAF in 2013.

Rain washed out my game just before I left my hotel; because of travel time to and around the upper Rockies, I stayed for the next day's. The domino effect is part of why I ended 2014 one ballpark short.

Mobile BayBears
Hank Aaron Stadium, Mobile, AL
Class Double-A Southern League
Los Angeles Angels of Anaheim
Got: **July 9, 2011; Mobile BayBears 10, Mississippi Braves 4**
Different in 2020: new stadium (Toyota Field, Madison, AL) and nickname

Opened in 1997, "The Hank" gave a Southern League nomad a home.

The Double-A Charlotte Knights were bumped by Triple-A expansion and blocked from their intended next home of New Orleans by the Triple-A Denver Zephyrs. They played 1993-94 as the Nashville Xpress in Greer Stadium and 1995-96 as the Port City Roosters at the University of North Carolina at Wilmington.

Aaron's boyhood home, moved to The Hank in 2010, is an in-park museum. Outside, Satchel Paige Drive salutes another Mobile great. (They met once, in a 1968 exhibition between the Atlanta and Richmond Braves; after Paige got ahead with a strike, Aaron soft-lined to the third baseman.)

Remarkably for a city its size, Mobile has *five* baseball Hall of Famers but is losing Minor League baseball. Madison, AL – a Huntsville suburb – is finishing a ballpark into which the BayBears are to move in 2020 as the Rocket City Trash Pandas. The fan-chosen name is so popular the club's *temporary* store – first opened in November 2018 – was expanded, moved to a larger location and expanded again – for a club that starts play in April 2020!

The team announced the stadium name Oct. 11, 2019: Toyota Field, with naming rights revenues divided between team and city.

The BayBears drew more than 300,000 to their first season, but never again – eventually falling under 70,000, an arc that's well beyond the natural novelty-wears-off drop. As it continued, the ballpark deteriorated noticeably as less was spent on upkeep.

Modesto Nuts
John Thurman Field, Modesto, CA
Class A-Advanced California League
Seattle Mariners
Got: **May 17, 2013; Modesto Nuts 12, Lake Elsinore Storm 7**

Opened as Del Webb Field in 1955, the playpen was renamed in 1983 for a local state assemblyman who died less than a year after retiring.

After the 2016 season, the Mariners bought fifty-one percent of the team.

Founded as an independent in 1946, it joined the St. Louis Browns (now Baltimore Orioles) farm system two seasons later. It has since partnered with seven other big-league teams, one of them twice: the Athletics in Kansas City and again in Oakland – less than eighty miles from Modesto. Despite sixteen seasons using the nickname Reds, it was never a Cincinnati farm team. Like many Minor League teams, though, it was using its parent teams' nickname in the 1970s. The club joined the trend toward a unique brand in 2005, after parting ways with the Athletics. "Nuts" salutes Modesto's status as a leading producer of almonds and walnuts. The ballpark shows its age but has all the fun and intimacy of the Minors.

Where (and who) were *they* in '62? The 1973 film *American Graffiti* about that "Geez, what a night!" didn't mention a local professional baseball team, but the city did have one. The then-Houston – no, not Astros; Colt .45s – farm club played as the Modesto Colts. As Curt was heading off to school, and Steve wasn't, and who knows what was going on in that T-Bird, the Colts were finishing up a 75-65 season – second only to the San Jose Bees.

Montgomery Biscuits
Montgomery Riverwalk Stadium, Montgomery, AL
Class Double-A Southern League
Tampa Bay Rays
Got: **April or May 2007**

A terrific example of the "downtown retro" concept developed by HOK Sport architects (now Populous) anchors the Montgomery nightlife district. One end of the three-mile Montgomery Riverwalk along the Gun Island Chute of the Alabama River is a block away.

Opened in 2004 for the former Orlando Rays, it's built into an old railroad station that later housed the Riverfront Inn. The terminal became six suites along the first-base line, with fourteen more suites and the wonderfully named Biscuit Basket souvenir shop along third. An American flag flies in a notched-in curve in right field, and out front of the ballpark a twenty-five-foot-wide baseball graphic is embedded in the pavement of the Coosa-Tallapoosa-Jefferson traffic circle.

Professional baseball had been in and out of Montgomery for decades, usually as Rebels. In a phenomenon that's found more often the farther south one travels, its pro team does not own its baseball single-game attendance record. The MAX Capital City Classic, the annual University of Alabama-Auburn University baseball rivalry game, scored a new house record and then broke it not once but twice: 2009, 2017, and 2018.

Interested in non-baseball icons? The Hank Williams Museum is a four-minute walk from the ballpark – whose exhibits include the baby-blue Cadillac in which the country music legend died – and the Rosa Parks Museum is just another five minutes beyond.

Myrtle Beach Pelicans
TicketReturn.com Field at Pelicans Ballpark, Myrtle Beach, SC
Class A-Advanced Carolina League
Chicago Cubs
Got: **Sept. 7, 2011; Myrtle Beach Pelicans 4, Kinston Indians 1**

A stadium that is beautiful on its own merits but also because of its surroundings, this blend of urban ballpark and palm-enhanced site a mile from the beach opened as Coastal Federal Field in 1999. Its name changed when BB&T Bank bought Coastal Federal Bank in 2007 and again when BB&T didn't renew the rights deal after the 2011 campaign. I don't have the paperwork but assume from the replacement name that "Pelicans Ballpark" is now the generic name if it ever goes unsold. The TR deal was announced as a one-year contract, but the name remained through at least the 2019 season.

In the first season of a four-year affiliation, Pelicans principal owner Chuck Greenberg and Hall-of-Fame pitcher Nolan Ryan led the group that won a bankruptcy auction for the Pelicans' parent Rangers in August 2010 – but Greenberg was forced out in March 2011. The Pelicans honored the affiliation contract but switched to the Cubs when it ended. Ryan left the Rangers in October 2013, cutting other Rangers ties as they expired (see **Corpus Christi Hooks [CURRENT]**).

The Pelicans were the film-famed Durham Bulls until the Triple-A International League bumped them. In 1998, while Myrtle Beach built a ballpark, they played in Danville, VA, as the Danville 97s – named for the 1903 train wreck near Danville remembered in the song "The Wreck of the Old 97."

Nashville Sounds
First Horizon Park, Nashville, TN

Class Triple-A Pacific Coast League
Texas Rangers
Got: **April 20, 2015; Nashville Sounds 11, Colorado Springs Sky Sox 4**

Opened as First Tennessee Park in 2015, its name changed as First Tennessee Bank's parent company unified its subsidiaries' brands. A rare Populous-designed ballpark that does not have a mostly brick exterior replaced antiquated Greer Stadium. It features an open 360-degree concourse. The high-definition guitar-shaped video scoreboard dominates the right field wall. The Band Box full-service bar's board and bar games including ping pong, cornhole, foosball, shuffleboard and nine-hole miniature golf course are near the right-field corner.

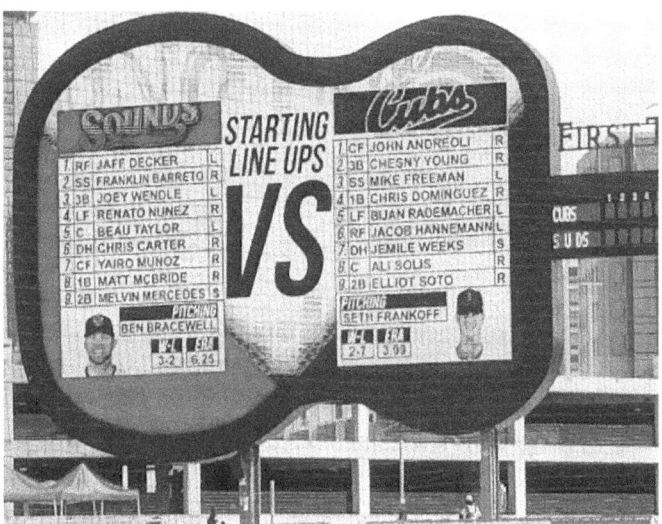

Attendance jumped seventy-five percent from Greer in its debut year, surprisingly dropped eleven percent in 2016, then spiked to consecutive Sounds regular-season records: 593,679 in 2017 (with the last home date rained out) and 601,135 in 2018. The 2017 Eclipse Party drew about 10,000 in a separate gate from the subsequent home game (not counted in the 601k).

FTP returned professional baseball to its 1870-1963 Sulphur Dell site, and a home plate replica off right field shows where batters stood at the Dell. (I can't believe anyone tore down a century-old ballpark!) In another nod to history, the Sounds got the city to change the ballpark's address to 19 Junior Gilliam Way to honor the name and number of the Dodgers' Nashville-born regular second baseman 1953-63. Gilliam, who died at just forty-nine, is the only Dodger with a retired uniform number who is not in the Hall of Fame.

Nashville is the easternmost city in the Pacific Coast League – only three of whose sixteen teams are actually in a state with Pacific coast.

New Hampshire Fisher Cats
Northeast Delta Dental Stadium, Manchester, NH
Class Double-A Eastern League
Toronto Blue Jays
Got: **July 22, 2014; New Hampshire Fisher Cats 3, Trenton Thunder 0**

In 2004, the New Haven Ravens were set to move to Manchester and become the New Hampshire Primaries – with an elephant-and-donkey-in-stars-and-stripes logo – but the local populace famously shouted that down. "Fisher Cats" won the resulting name-the-team contest. A fisher, a type of weasel that is prized for its pelt, is often called a fisher cat – especially in New England, and oddly so given that fishers don't eat fish.

The club played that first season at Gill Stadium, winning the Eastern League crown in a historic 3,000-capacity ballpark that had hosted four previous Minor League seasons since its 1913 opening – not to mention a handful of American Legion World Series. Fisher Cats Ballpark opened in 2005 and is now on its second sold name. The new playpen, a brick beauty with an impressive drive-up, proved worth the wait. Long-time Atlanta Brave superstar John Smoltz bulged the place – 8,903 – in a 2009 injury rehabilitation start for the Portland Sea Dogs during his partial season with the Boston Red Sox. A significant improvement came with the 2008 addition of one of the largest sports bars in the Minors. Hosting the 2017 Eastern League All-Star Game spurred the largest renovation to the city-owned facility since it opened.

"Primaries" has been used as a team nickname as special promotions, first in August 2007. The team also sometimes plays as the Granite State Mountain Men, a naming contest also-ran.

New Orleans Baby Cakes
The Shrine on Airline, Metairie, LA
Class Triple-A Pacific Coast League
Miami Marlins
Got: **July 10, 2011; New Orleans Zephyrs 2, Iowa Cubs 1**
Different in 2020: both stadium, in Wichita, KS (assuming it is completed as expected), and brand, Wichita Wind Surge

The Cakes expect to move into a new stadium in Wichita, KS, that replaces iconic but antiquated Lawrence-Dumont Stadium, in 2020. Cakes ownership had agreed to bring a Double-A team to NOLA, but another group emerged to work on that after the 2019 season.

Opened for the then-Zephyrs as Zephyr Field in 1997, it staged Hurricane Katrina relief efforts. A rare Populous ballpark that has not worn so well – also rare in that it is not downtown – its tenant has been the subject of moving rumors for years. Ironically, the state-owned stadium loses Triple-A shortly after just missing a potential makeover. In 2016, the state committed to renovate the Zephyrs' home to specifications that would have been set by the collegiate Southeastern Conference *if* NOLA landed the SEC's annual baseball tournament. It didn't; Hoover, AL, retained the event by building an entire sports complex around Hoover Metropolitan Stadium. Later that year, the Zephyrs were sold and the new owner's initial message was the team would stay – which the 2017 Baby Cakes rebrand *seemed* to support.

NOLA baseball history is full of Pelicans; why Zephyrs? In 1993, the expansion-bumped Triple-A Denver Zephyrs and Double-A Charlotte Knights both aimed for New Orleans. The dust settled with the Triple-A team there but the rights to "Pelicans" owned by the National Football League's Saints – who held them until buying and rebranding NOLA's National Basketball Association team.

The ballpark appears in the films *Mr. 3000* (2004) and *Failure to Launch* (2006).

Norfolk Tides
Harbor Park, Norfolk, VA
Class Triple-A International League
Baltimore Orioles
Got: **June 18, 2012; Norfolk Tides 7, Buffalo Bisons 5**

The city-owned downtown ballpark on the Elizabeth River opened in 1993 – when the Tides dropped "Tidewater" in favor of "Norfolk" as a location identifier. Another HOK Sport (now Populous) "downtown retro" stadium, it salutes seafaring with flags and light towers that echo masts and cranes – as do the colors and seahorse logo. The nickname Tides dates to 1962, preceded by the equally seafaring Tars.

The stadium went from idea to groundbreaking between the summer of 1990 and February 21, 1992. Like most ballparks built then, especially by that architect, the playpen took its team downtown. The team lists its ballpark's total capacity for baseball at 11,856, but its baseball record is 14,263 Aug. 31, 1996. The year before, *Baseball America* named it the best Minor League stadium in the US.

Hits at the Park, one of the Minors' finest full-service restaurants, offers up to 225 diners a panoramic view of the diamond from off deep right field. It has a full bar and while it isn't regularly open during the off-season it can be booked for special events. Predecessor Metropolitan Memorial Park, built in 1970, had the Minors' *first* full-service restaurant.

Triple-A ball arrived in 1969, when Norfolk lured the Jacksonville Suns north from Florida. Then three seasons into their affiliation with the Mets, they stayed thirty-eight more before switching to the Orioles.

Northwest Arkansas Naturals
Arvest Ballpark, Springdale, AR
Class Double-A Texas League
Kansas City Royals
Got: April 21, 2014; Springfield Cardinals 5, Northwest Arkansas Naturals 2

Designed by HOK Sport, which pioneered "downtown retro" ballparks, this brick stadium landed a naming-rights deal with Arkansas-based Arvest Bank before opening in 2008. In fact, this was the last HOK Minor League ballpark to open before its stadiums division split off into a new firm called Populous.

The former Wichita Wranglers moved into Arvest and adopted a six-foot-nine Sasquatch, Strike, as their mascot. Their pocket schedules until recently referred to the Arkansas Travelers as NLR instead of ARK – which a staffer confirmed to me was a dig at the Travs for "claiming" the whole state from North Little Rock.

"Naturals" simultaneously salutes the state of Arkansas, whose nickname is "The Natural State," and the 1984 film *The Natural*, much of which was shot at the first home of the Naturals' corporate sibling Buffalo Bisons – who were the Wichita Aeros before moving to Buffalo. There, they played in old War Memorial Stadium until moving into the last ballpark HOK designed before striking fame with Oriole Park at Camden Yards. The two commonly owned teams both played their Wichita eras at Lawrence-Dumont Stadium, built in 1934 and thought to be both why Wichita twice lost affiliated ball and too historic to replace – until now. Wichita signed the New Orleans Baby Cakes in 2018 to move to town, then tore down L-D and broke ground for a new stadium on the same site. The Cakes will become the Wichita Wind Surge.

Norwich Sea Unicorns
Senator Thomas J. Dodd Memorial Stadium, Norwich, CT
Class A-Short Season New York-Pennsylvania League
Detroit Tigers

Got: **July 23, 2014; Tri-City ValleyCats 1, Connecticut Tigers 0**
Different in 2020: team locale name, nickname; possibly stadium name

In 2009, the Atlanta Braves pulled their Triple-A club from the fading Diamond in Richmond, VA, to suburban Atlanta. A season later, two dominoes followed: The Connecticut Defenders of the Double-A Eastern League moved to Richmond as the Richmond Flying Squirrels and the Oneonta Tigers of the short-A New York-Penn League replaced them in Norwich, CT, as the Connecticut Tigers.

Founded in Wellsville, NY, in 1942, the club moved to Oneonta, NY, in 1966. In '67, the NYPL went short-season. That same year, the franchise that would become the Defenders was founded in Binghamton, NY. Three cities later, in 1995, it moved into this brand-new stadium – as the Norwich Navigators until 2006.

In 1991, the Oneonta ball club started playing one regular-season game annually at Doubleday Field in nearby Cooperstown, NY, on Hall of Fame Induction Weekend – but ended the series after its first Norwich season.

As part of a lease extension negotiated in 2019, the city agreed to allow the sale of ballpark naming rights provided "Dodd" remains in the new moniker and the team agreed to revive Norwich as its locale name. That December, the club announced "Sea Unicorns" as its new nickname.

HOK Sport (now Populous) designed Dodd Stadium, built in 1995 and named for the Connecticut native US representative and senator and father of former US Senator Christopher Dodd. It remains a Double-A quality facility, but short-season ball is perhaps a better fit given New England's springtime weather.

Ogden Raptors
Lindquist Field, Ogden, UT
Rookie-Advanced Pioneer League
Los Angeles Dodgers

Got: **Sept. 5, 2014; Orem Owlz 8, Ogden Raptors 3**

The Raptors have led the league in attendance every single season since opening the downtown ballpark in 1997. Digitalballparks.com's 2007 Ballpark of the Year was expanded for the 2008 season – most notably, and in a highly unusual move for the second lowest level of professional baseball, extending seating from just past the home dugout all the way to the left-field wall.

My visit there was several years later, and I came in wondering whether these attendance numbers could be true at this level. Its interior openness and perfect sightlines, the buzz of a Friday night crowd, and its external backdrop – a view of the Wasatch Range that more than one trophy distributor has named the best view in baseball – convinced me before I had my scorebook out. The Raptors moved in after playing three seasons as the Angels at Serge Simmons Field in Ogden, which was then new but was never intended for professional baseball.

One of the formerly Canadian clubs, the franchise was founded in 1977 as the Calgary Cardinals. Its move to Ogden came in 1994, the year after the film *Jurassic Park* came out. Amid that craze, the team was renamed for the velociraptor. This ballpark was a 2014 bonus toward my ballparks quest; I ended that regular season with three *Gets* to go, but when the Raptors and nearby Orem Owlz met in the first round of the Pioneer League playoffs over a Friday-Saturday-maybe Sunday, I flew to Utah and got both.

Oklahoma City Dodgers
Chickasaw Bricktown Ballpark, Oklahoma City, OK
Class Triple-A Pacific Coast League
Los Angeles Dodgers
Got: **April 27, 2014; Nashville Sounds 8, Oklahoma City RedHawks 5**

This amazing HOK Sport (now Populous) stadium triggered an OKC growth spurt – according not to fans like me but its mayor: "No city in America has come as far as fast as Oklahoma City, and the ballpark was the beginning of that." In Bricktown, OKC's downtown district, it also revived the Triple-A championship, as the Bricktown Showdown, in 2006. It and Tulsa's ONEOK Field host some Oklahoma State University-University of Oklahoma "Bedlam Series" games, which often outdraw pro games.

"The Brick" replaced All Sports Stadium – which once hosted more than 15,000 for a Bedlam game – in 1998. It's bounded by Mickey Mantle Drive, Johnny Bench Drive and Joe Carter Avenue. (But sir, but sir, that's only three sides! True. What should be a street but does look like an alley runs past the outfield wall and is signed Flaming Lips Alley – not a reference to a hard-throwing spit-baller but to an alternative rock band.) A statue of a great greets fans at each of the three main entrances: Mantle, Bench and Warren Spahn.

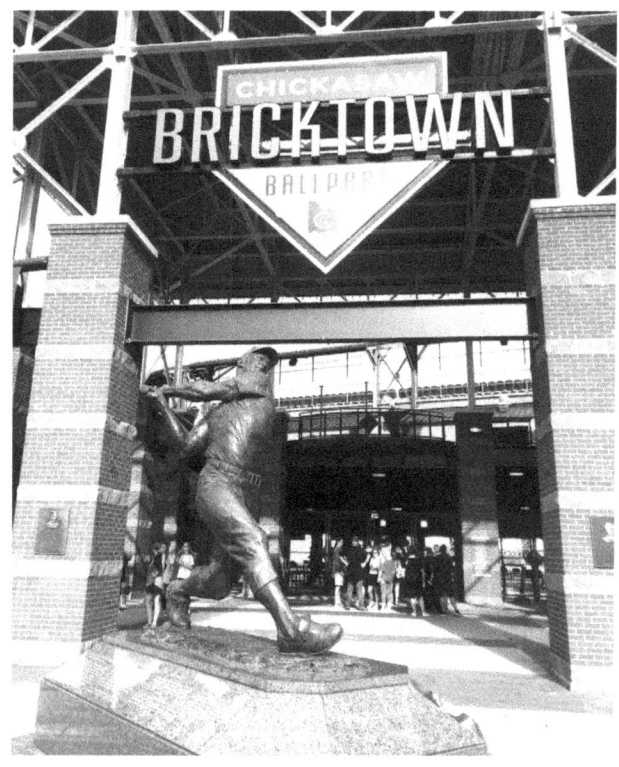

In 1998, the then-'89ers – founded in 1962 – rebranded as RedHawks. It was always an Astro or Ranger farm team until 2015, when a Dodger-led group bought and rebranded it with an ingenious OkLAhoma logo.

Newcastle Casino's tribal owners bought naming rights in 2012 but switched to the tribal name amid controversy – I remember news coverage of objections to tying baseball and gambling, but some say the real fight was over having a suburb's name on an OKC-owned facility.

Omaha Storm Chasers
Werner Park, Papillion, NE
Class Triple-A Pacific Coast League
Kansas City Royals
Got: **Aug. 5, 2014; Iowa Cubs 7, Omaha Storm Chasers 4**

Two professional baseball teams founded in 1969 and calling themselves Royals have built a partnership that has outlasted winning seasons and losing ones, expansion, new ballparks, and a couple of nickname changes to become the longest between teams not commonly owned. The affiliation cycle that starts in 2021 will tie the longest ever. The mid-cycle renewal was announced after a 2019 parent/affiliate exhibition game; I suspect the coming of a team to Wichita hastened it.

The Chasers report sellouts as 9,023, and they report them so often it's obvious they could draw more to this beautiful Populous-designed "retro downtown" style ballpark ... that isn't downtown. A statue of Omaha native and St. Louis Cardinal pitching legend Bob Gibson greets fans. The franchise has drawn more than 15 million between Werner, the PCL's smallest park, and the Minors' biggest for four decades. Johnny Rosenblatt Stadium also hosted the College World Series until separate playpens opened in 2010.

Omaha-based Werner Enterprises bought naming rights to the Chasers' new playpen, and the O-Royals decided to rebrand – again. A 1998 nickname change to Golden Spikes, for the transcontinental railroad, having flopped, the team reverted to Royals. This time, they involved fans in the process. Ironically, rain and snow postponed their Werner Park debut.

Sarpy County Tourism's office is in the ballpark.

Orem Owlz
UCCU Ballpark, Orem, UT
Rookie-Advanced
Pioneer League Los Angeles Angels of Anaheim
Got: **Sept. 6, 2014; Orem Owlz 7, Ogden Raptors 4**

By comparison with the big leagues, Minor League teams move a lot. Sometimes, though, they start to move – and then not. June 20, 2018, the Owlz announced a 2020 move to Pueblo, CO – still as Owlz. In less than a month, the move fell apart.

At the other end of their timeline, we find Brewers becoming teetotaling Angels. The Helena Brewers became the Provo Angels in 2001, expecting a new stadium but meanwhile using Brigham Young University's Larry H. Miller Field on condition of no alcohol sales or home Sunday games.

With then-Utah Valley State College in the process of moving to NCAA Division I, the idea of a shared ballpark emerged. Ideas change, though, and the resulting ballpark ended up on the campus of, and owned by, the renamed Utah Valley University. It opened in 2005, and the newly sold and rebranded Owlz moved in that June – secondary to UVU Wolverines baseball. After two naming-rights sales fell through, the Owlz dubbed it "Home of the OWLZ." They ignore UVU's two later name deals in box scores and team literature.

Baseball isn't the park's only beautiful sight; Mount Timpanogos and the Wasatch Range tower beyond the outfield.

This ballpark was a 2014 bonus for my project; I ended that regular season with three *Get*s to go, but when the Owlz and Ogden Raptors met in the first round of the Pioneer League playoffs over a Friday-Saturday-maybe Sunday, I flew to Utah and got both. So then there was one!

Palm Beach Cardinals
Roger Dean Chevrolet Stadium, Jupiter, FL

Class A-Advanced Florida State League
St. Louis Cardinals

The Palm Beach Cardinals share Roger Dean Chevrolet Stadium with the Jupiter Hammerheads – and, actually, four other teams. Let's save a tree here. If you skipped the Jupiter Hammerheads' entry, please pop up there and read all about it.

Pawtucket Red Sox
McCoy Stadium, Pawtucket, RI
Class Triple-A International League
Boston Red Sox
Got: **July 20, 2014; Pawtucket Red Sox 3, Buffalo Bisons 2**
Different in 2020: nothing, but should open Polar Park in Worcester, MA, in 2021

A lot of age and a pinnacle of history are what this ballpark is all about.

Opened in 1942 – easily the oldest stadium in Triple-A – it has hosted BoSox teams since 1970. First came a Double-A club from York, PA – changing parents on the way, from the Pittsburgh Pirates to the BoSox. After only three seasons, it moved to New Britain, CT, as the Triple-A Louisville Colonels invaded Pawtucket.

Despite dating to World War II, its two top crowds came in 2009 and 2017. Efforts to replace it having failed, the PawSox will move to Worcester, MA, in 2021.

It hosted professional baseball's longest game – and it *started* late! A problem with the lights delayed the April 18, 1981, game with the Rochester Red Wings. The Wings scored once in the seventh; the PawSox answered in the ninth. A league rule should have stopped it during the midnight hour, but the umpires did not have that rule in writing. The teams swapped goose eggs until the twenty-first. Rochester scored in the top of the inning – I once saw my team lose a twenty-four-inning game, and I can tell you it was almost a relief – but Wade Boggs drove in a run in the bottom of the frame. IL President Harold Cooper, unavailable earlier because of his daughter's wedding, was finally reached by telephone in the middle of the night. He ordered the game suspended at the end of "this" inning. At 4:09 a.m., the thirty-second ended with the score still 2-2. The June twenty-third finish took but eighteen minutes: After Rochester mustered only a Cal Ripken single, the PawSox loaded the bases with no outs, and Dave Koza ended it with a clean single. Time: 8:26; innings: thirty-three.

Irony – in 2018, McCoy hosted the first International League game to go extras under the man-on-second rule instituted by MLB to prevent just such a game from ever happening again.

Pensacola Blue Wahoos

Blue Wahoos Stadium, Pensacola, FL

Class Double-A Southern League

Minnesota Twins

Got: **April 8, 2012; Pensacola Blue Wahoos 7, Montgomery Biscuits 5**

The reason I don't like ranking ballparks, and also don't like – although I have here – naming a favorite is that it's too subjective. You can read more about this in Chapter 9, **What's Your Favorite?** Yet I must say this Populous-designed place is beautiful, especially its inside spaces and its view of Pensacola Bay. It reminds me of Oracle Park in San Francisco.

If I have a complaint, it's a logistical one: The ballpark's openness enhances its beauty, but during baseball season the Florida sun scorches. My right ear blistered during my first visit. They didn't sell sunscreen then, or at my second; maybe they do now. By the way, it sports affiliated baseball's only pink foul poles – not sunburn pink, breast cancer awareness pink.

Originally designed to hold 3,500 for an independent team, it was retooled when that team's owner bought the Double-A Carolina Mudcats. Opened in 2012, it reports sell-outs as 5,038. The ball club and the municipal agency that owns the ballpark were supposed to name it jointly. When they couldn't agree, the agency called it Maritime Park Stadium – which appeared on one small plaque near the entrance – while the team website labeled it Blue Wahoos Park. Yet its 2012 Stadium of the Year trophy reads Pensacola Bayfront Stadium. In 2015, the team bought the city's share of the naming rights and dubbed it Blue Wahoos Stadium.

Peoria Chiefs
Dozer Park, Peoria, IL
Class A Midwest League
St. Louis Cardinals

Got: **Aug. 23, 2014; Wisconsin Timber Rattlers 11, Peoria Chiefs 7, 11 inns.**

The most unusual thing about this park may be its ability to transcend a rivalry. The brick "downtown retro" ballpark by HOK Sport (now Populous), fits into its urban surroundings – as that design always tries to do.

Affiliates change, and I could name one in which fans went from watching future Cubs to future White Sox, but this is the only baseball palace I know of where fans went, in the short stretch of eight seasons, from watching future Cardinals to future Cubs *and back*. In the debut of then-O'Brien Field May 24, 2002, legendary Card-then-Cub broadcaster Harry Carey's widow Dutchie led the seventh-inning stretch at 8:36 p.m. as the Chiefs blanked the Kane County Cougars, 3-0.

The Chiefs once played in front of 32,103 – but that was at Chicago's Wrigley Field. Their top crowd at their own home so far is 9,692. Caterpillar, Inc., bought naming rights in 2013. This was my last *Get* of the 2014 regular season; I thought at the time it was my last of the year and that I would open 2015 with three to go (see **Orem Owlz** and/or **Ogden Raptors**, both **[CURRENT]**). This was also one of two cases of rolling the dice against Mother Nature, switching consecutive dates with the Kane County Cougars based on weather forecasts. I needn't have bothered – both teams got in both games – but that's 20/20 hindsight.

Portland Sea Dogs
Hadlock Field, Portland, ME
Class Double-A Eastern League
Boston Red Sox
Got: **July 28, 2014; Portland Sea Dogs 2, Reading Fightin' Phils 0**

You'd think this team would *always* have been a Red Sox affiliate, based on its stadium's location and what you see edging left field there, but when it was founded in 1994 that privilege for this class belonged to New Britain, CT.

The easternmost stadium that hosts a team in a US-based affiliated league opened to Sea Dogs who were at that time in the then-Florida Marlins' farm system. The Dogs replaced a Triple-A club that played in a Portland suburb before moving to Moosic, PA, in 1988, to become the Scranton/Wilkes-Barre Red Barons (see **Scranton/Wilkes-Barre RailRiders [CURRENT]**). A likeness of Fenway Park's Green Monster was added when the Dogs joined the BoSox farm system in 2003. Edson J. Hadlock, Jr., coached Portland High School baseball for twenty-eight seasons ending in 1978.

Hadlock has a rarity and an item that is unique to baseball fields: elevated bullpens, and a lighthouse that rises from the center-field fence upon a Sea Dog homer or victory. I have seen this, but during a day game. I'm sure it's a lot more impressive after dark.

In 2007, the Dogs played before nearly 35,000 at Fenway Park.

Not surprisingly, this team is accustomed to dealing with severe weather. Hit with a foot of snow twenty-three days before its 2017 opener, the club laid "black sand" that Saturday and the snow was nearly gone that Monday. The Dogs did open as scheduled.

Potomac Nationals
Northwest Federal Field at Pfitzner Stadium, Woodbridge, VA
Class A-Advanced Carolina League
Washington Nationals
Different in 2020: both stadium, in Fredericksburg, VA (assuming it is completed as expected), and brand, Fredericksburg Nationals
Got: **June 20, 2010; Potomac Nationals 15, Carolina Mudcats 2**

Remember reading about standards being written into the 1990 Professional Baseball Agreement? Only waivers kept this substandard playpen open after 2012. My chief memory is metal bleachers and reminiscing about broadcasting high school games. As I approached it, I thought I'd gotten misdirected to a football field.

A new ballpark in Fredericksburg, VA, is expected to open in 2020 – even though the city-team contract says by April 1, 2021. A December 2018 "Founders Day" event there drew nearly 200 fans braving a rainy, chilly forecast to buy season ticket pledges. Those fans reserved, and made deposits on, more than 600 full-season tickets. A team store opened July 5, 2019, and the nickname and colors were announced Oct. 5, 2019.

Woodbridge, which according to the US Census Bureau was the smallest US community with an affiliated team, used Prince William County as its location identifier until going to a regional name in 1999. This can be a negative; I've read articles placing the team in the actual city of Potomac, MD.

Except Cannons 1989-2005, the team has used its parents' nicknames. Opened in 1984 as Davis Ford Park, the playpen landed the Alexandria Dukes. Soon renamed Prince William County Stadium, it in 1994 took the name of G. Richard Pfitzner, the county supervisor who scored the Dukes. In May 2018, Northwest Federal Credit Union bought prepended field naming rights even though the ballpark was by then an obvious lame duck as far as affiliated baseball is concerned.

Princeton Rays

H.P. Hunnicutt Field, Princeton, WV

Rookie-Advanced Appalachian League

Tampa Bay Rays

Got: **July 22, 2012; Princeton Rays 13, Johnson City Cardinals 3**

In 1988, Princeton's schoolboy baseball Tigers and a new Appalachian League franchise, affiliated with and called the Pirates, started play at a brand-new ballpark. Calling it a wooden ballpark, although it was, conjures up old-style places that it was not. It was more solid and much more modern. However, in only twelve seasons its not-for-profit ownership replaced it on the same site in concrete-and-steel.

The Bucs dropped the affiliation after 1989. The franchise – now playing as Patriots – clung to life in 1990 as a "co-op," using players unassigned within their own farm system. The vast majority of Princeton's surplus players were Phillies, leading this broadcaster to dub the club "Philliots" when we played each other.

The franchise seemed at death's door when Jim Holland became general manager. He led the club back from that precipice and for the next twenty-five seasons. League and Mercer County rival Bluefield's Bowen Field, which despite its street address lies in Virginia, is just twelve miles away – inspiring Holland to create the Mercer Cup traveling trophy for the Princeton-Bluefield season series winner.

The 1999 Rays literally played "under construction" – but was Hunnicutt renovated or replaced? Of the original wooden ballpark, Holland says, only the four outfield light poles remain. If that's so, I don't see how they can be considered the same ballpark.

The Devil Rays changed their nickname when their parent Tampa Bay Devil Rays became the Tampa Bay Rays in 2008.

Pulaski Yankees
Motor Mile Field at Calfee Park, Pulaski, VA
Rookie-Advanced Appalachian League
New York Yankees
Got: **July 17, 1990; Huntington Cubs 6, Pulaski Braves 2**

The Appalachian League's oldest stadium hosts its youngest continuous franchise. The 1935 Works Progress Administration project joined the National Register of Historic Places in 2000. It's had affiliated baseball since 1942, this franchise since 1982 – but it was "inactive" 1993-96 and 2007.

An odd number of teams in leagues that play nearly every day, in series, is a scheduling nightmare that was nearly repeated in 2014. The owners of the Appy operating agreement (which amounts to the team owners; this unique Appy arrangement is laid out late in Chapter 8, **The Structure**) sold out to retire and the Mariners didn't renew. New owners acquired the stadium by renovating it, landed the Yankees as a parent team, and started spending – keyed by a thirty-five-by-twenty-two-foot video scoreboard.

The P-Yanks sold out opening day and went on to break the Greeneville Astros' eleven-year run atop Appy season attendance. (Ironically, that same year the Astros won their first league championship in Greeneville.) The 2018 club broke its house record crowd three times in August alone *and* Danville's 1993 season record with 91,226 – the first Appy team ever to draw 90,000. The third record crowd of August was also the first 4,000 in the ballpark's history: 4,068 for the home finale. I was among the then-record 3,217 July 4, 2017.

It is unusual, but not unique, in having single-family homes beyond the outfield. I broadcast a game from one of those front porches – just for the novelty … and $25 to the resident.

Quad Cities River Bandits
Modern Woodmen Park, Davenport, IA
Class A Midwest League
Houston Astros
Got: **April 12, 2015; Quad Cities River Bandits 7, Clinton LumberKings 2**

Davenport first hosted professional baseball in *1879* and opened this ballpark as Municipal Stadium in *1931*. Municipal hosted pro teams 1931-37 and 1946-58, with today's franchise arriving when the Davenport Braves joined the Midwest League in 1960. The club took the group location identifier in 1961.

Renamed for longtime Davenport *Times-Democrat* sports editor John O'Donnell in 1971, the park took only the third name of its long history in a 2007 deal with a financial service. It sits nearly under Centennial Bridge, which dominates the drive-up. Home runs often splash down in the Mississippi River, but fouls never hit fans – amid the recent push for more safety netting, this is the first Organized Baseball park where *every* fan seat is protected. Proceeds from its amusement park-style rides – a mini-midway of Ferris wheel, bumper cars, and Iowa's first double-decker carousel – go to charity.

This ballpark, the home field in the film *Sugar* (2008), is what "downtown retro" ballparks retro *to*. The concept – perfected by HOK Sport (now Populous) – didn't exist in 1931, of course, but HOK renovated it in 2004. That remodeling also successfully protected it from flooding, but 2019 was a different problem: access. Historic flooding, followed by the Canadian Pacific Railway raising its tracks and thus blocking high-water access, followed by a levee breach, wiped out all but three of its April 4-May 11 home games.

Which are the "quad" cities? Don't count these: Davenport, IA; Moline, IL; Rock Island, IL; Bettendorf, IA and East Moline, IL.

Rancho Cucamonga Quakes
LoanMart Field, Rancho Cucamonga, CA
Class A-Advanced California League
Los Angeles Dodgers
Got: **May 15, 2013; San Jose Giants 4, Rancho Cucamonga Quakes 3**

When construction workers building a ballpark learned the team that would play there would be called the Quakes, they started calling their project "The Epicenter." When it opened in 1993, that stuck – with a whole lot of other words around it. The City of Rancho Cucamonga Epicenter Entertainment and Sports Complex was the official name of what everybody called just the Epicenter for the next ten years. That mouthful changed with a 2013 naming-rights deal. In fact, that's the season I visited, and I didn't know the name had changed until that May game.

Founded in 1966 as the Lodi Crushers, the team lost its first affiliation when the Cubs decided to consolidate their farm teams east of the Mississippi River. "Inactive" in 1985, it was sold and moved to Ventura County. Unable to get a suitable stadium there, it was sold and moved again – becoming the San Bernardino Spirit in 1987. With the Spirit's move to Rancho, the Salinas Spurs moved in and bought the name. The club, in the protected territory of the Los Angeles big-league clubs, joined the Dodgers in 2011.

This ballpark taught me a lesson in climatology. It's forty miles from LA – so who needs a jacket, right? It's also a thousand feet higher. That cost me a stadium blanket. It's a nice stadium blanket, though.

Reading Fightin Phils
FirstEnergy Stadium, Reading, PA
Class Double-A Eastern League
Philadelphia Phillies
Got: **Aug. 9, 2013; Reading Fightin Phils 6, New Britain Rock Cats 5**

The league's oldest park – by thirty-six years! – opened as Reading Municipal Memorial Stadium in 1951. Yet, in its sixty-fifth season, it *twice* topped its one-game attendance record. Speaking of attendance, it's the first American baseball stadium to draw 15 million to only Double-A or lower games.

How successful is this beautiful old place? Successful enough to get away with promoting itself as "Baseballtown" and "America's Classic Ballpark." The former Reading Phillies changed their nickname after the 2012 season; Fightin Phils was another aka of the big Phillies in their "Whiz Kids" days. Affiliation and franchise changes buffeted Reading – in Phils' protected territory – until the Phils affiliated with them in 1967 and bought them in 2008.

You've probably noticed that when I rank long affiliations, I limit them with some form of "not commonly owned." It just doesn't make sense to me to include O&Os we know aren't going to change parents. Sort of like, right down the road in Philadelphia, saying Connie Mack was baseball's longest-tenured manager; he *owned* the team, so who was going to fire him? If you've noticed the Reading/Philly partnership is two years older than Omaha/Kansas City, which I list as longest, that's why. If you don't share my foible, the oldest pairing – if you include O&Os and track through city-to-city moves – is Pawtucket/Boston. The BoSox have partnered with the same Triple-A franchise in Toronto, ON, 1965-67; Louisville, KY, 1968-72; Pawtucket, RI, 1973-now – and it's moving to Worcester, MA, in 2021.

Reno Aces
Greater Nevada Field, Reno, NV

Class Triple-A Pacific Coast League
Arizona Diamondbacks
Got: **May 12, 2013; Reno Aces 9, Iowa Cubs 8**

Opened as Aces Ballpark in 2009, this stadium and the former Tucson Sidewinders key a retail/dining/nightlife complex. Greater Nevada Credit Union bought naming rights in 2016.

When the 'Winders were shedding their skin for the last time, a naming contest drew more than 3,500 submissions with about 1,100 different names; more than fifty of those pitched Aces. It's no surprise that won, having the kind of double entendre marketing folks love. It recognizes both a primary local industry of the team's home city and the team's game – the ace playing card ties to gambling, and a baseball team's best pitcher is known as its ace.

The city had lost affiliated baseball in 1992, after nearly forty years as the only non-California club in the California League, and was in danger of doing so again when the stadium was refinanced in 2012. That said, the area around the stadium is fulfilling redevelopment projections. Why did a successful ballpark need refinancing? Nothing operates in a vacuum, especially economics; what else was going on 2009-12? The Great Recession.

One of my chief memories of this park is the scenic drive to it. I was coming from California and that drive is awesome. If you're into history, make time for the Donner Pass and a museum to the Donner Party along the way.

Richmond Flying Squirrels
The Diamond, Richmond, VA
Class Double-A Eastern League
San Francisco Giants
Got: **June 16, 2012; Richmond Flying Squirrels 3, Portland Sea Dogs 1**

The same-site replacement of Parker Field opened in 1985 for the Richmond Braves, the Braves-owned Triple-A club now in suburban Atlanta. At that time, the R-Braves had already been in Virginia's capital city for two decades.

The new stadium wasn't much older than that when the Braves dumped it because of its condition, but it had some unusually hard moments along the way. In 2003 Hurricane Isabel damaged its roof, in 2004 part of a concrete beam fell onto the stands, and in 2008 the R-Braves went back to Greater Atlanta after forty-two years.

Both my visits to this ballpark were after those problems, and it seems structurally sound and is full of high energy – but I'm ahead of myself: The former Connecticut Defenders moved in for 2009. They say they were promised a new stadium by 2014; the city doesn't contest that but says the Great Recession killed the idea. Attendance slipped under 400,000 in 2016, and the Giants have expressed concern about the facility's condition.

I'm not sure of the value of a non-binding resolution in this situation, but one exists among the Squirrels, the city and Virginia Commonwealth University – which also plays home games at The Diamond – that says a new stadium should be built. Maybe they'll name it the Duh-amond.

Rochester Red Wings
Frontier Field, Rochester, NY
Class Triple-A International League
Minnesota Twins
Got: **July 7, 2013; Rochester Red Wings 12, Pawtucket Red Sox 7**

Rochester professional baseball dates to 1877, this franchise to 1899 – the Minors' oldest continuously operating one. The downtown park replaced Silver Stadium in 1996.

Morrie Silver led the 1956 charge to save baseball for the city; the St. Louis Cardinals, who owned both stadium and team, were about to sell the former and move the latter. The nonprofit Silver established during that effort, headed by his daughter, still owns the club.

Frontier's first event was actually not a baseball game, but it *was* something else you'd associate with summer: a Beach Boys concert, July 12, 1996. Frontier's largest crowd for a regular-season IL game didn't see the Wings; in 2012, Frontier was one of several stadiums hosting "Empire State Yankees" games. The Scranton/Wilkes-Barre Yankees used that moniker while playing a whole season on the road as Lackawanna County Stadium was rebuilt – and New York Yankee Andy Pettitte's rehabilitation start at Frontier drew its house record 13,584.

Even such a long-running operation can have a close call: A ten-year lease announced in August 2017 went unsigned until February 2018 – close enough to the season that the league put together an alternate stadium(s) plan.

Rochester-based Frontier Communications owns naming rights and provides free Wi-Fi. Speaking of names, "Red Wings" is not only old, it's older than the Red Wings that come to the minds of most sports fans: Rochester's baseball team has used this since 1929, pre-dating the Detroit Original Six National Hockey League team by three years.

Rocky Mountain Vibes
UCHealth Field, Colorado Springs, CO
Rookie-Advanced Pioneer League
Milwaukee Brewers
Got: **June 29, 2019; Rocky Mountain Vibes 7, Orem Owlz 5**

Colorado Springs Sky Sox
Security Service Field
Pacific Coast League
Got: **Aug. 20, 2014; Albuquerque Isotopes 7, Colorado Springs SkySox 4**

Opened as Sky Sox Stadium in 1988, the new ballpark brought the Hawai'i Islanders back to the mainland as the Colorado Springs Sky Sox. Its 2005 renovation followed Security Service

Credit Union's naming-rights purchase, but that expired in 2018 and UCHealth picked up the rights.

It and San Antonio's Wolff Stadium came into 2019 as *Go-Back*s, because the Sox franchise began a new tenure as the new, now Triple-A San Antonio Missions, and the short-season Pioneer League's Helena Brewers became the Rocky Mountain Vibes. "Vibes" derives from "Happy Campers," a nominee from the naming contest, and is aimed to play on the area's laid-back lifestyle.

"Sky Sox" reprised a 1950s team named in a contest whose winner said he was thinking of the altitude of the Springs and that team's parent club, the Chicago White Sox. The Cleveland Indians parented the Triple-A team at its 1988 move from Hawai'i, but the 1993 expansion Colorado Rockies brokered a switch. They later soured on the ballpark's location and age. Things seen as pluses in 1988 had become minuses – primarily, the fact that it is not downtown. I enjoyed my visits to this ballpark, but I understand its challenges in today's MiLB world. Those challenges will be less, er, challenging for a short-season club.

Like the Sky Sox who moved to Texas, the H-Brewers who moved to the Springs have been and continue to be a Brewers' farm team.

Rome Braves
State Mutual Stadium, Rome, GA
Class A South Atlantic League
Atlanta Braves
Got: **2010**

This ballpark is a small-town salute to big-league Braves baseball. Its street number is the career home run total of legendary Brave Hank Aaron, and its field dimensions mirror those of Turner Field – the home of the Atlanta Braves when they moved their low-A team from Macon, GA, to Rome in 2003.

The brand-new ballpark was named in a deal with Rome-based State Mutual Insurance. It appears in season three of TV's

Brockmire (2019), becoming the third Georgia stadium used in that series – following Luther Williams Field in Macon and Coolray Field in Gwinnett County. Score yet another success for the Georgia Film Commission, whose "credits" range from the film *Deliverance* (1972) to TV's *The Walking Dead* (2010-).

State Mutual's restaurant and bar, The Three Rivers Club, has indoor-outdoor ground-level seating directly behind home plate.

The big Braves own this and all but one of their farm teams. Their 2014 game here against a team of their farmhands, managed by long-time skipper Bobby Cox, drew the stadium's single-game record attendance: 6,314.

Every Braves' O&O club at or above Rookie-Advanced ball has moved since 1993, and Rome's Braves are especially well-traveled; between 1967 and its 1991 Macon debut, this franchise played in Lexington, NC, and three South Carolina cities – Greenwood, Anderson and Sumter.

The invented-runner-on-second-in-extra-innings rule led to an otherwise impossible two-pitch inning Aug. 10, 2018; two batters lined out on their first pitch, the first into a double play. Great pitching, huh?

Round Rock Express
Dell Diamond, Round Rock, TX
Class Triple-A Pacific Coast League
Houston Astros
Got: **April 24, 2014; Round Rock Express 6, Memphis Redbirds 2**

In 2000, Round Rock's offer of a $7 million site and a thirty-eight-year lease led Hall-of-Famer Nolan "The Ryan Express" Ryan's company to divert its just-purchased Jackson Generals from Austin to undeveloped farmland. Fifteen years later, I went to the wrong hotel – because there were two of the same brand within five miles of the park!

In 2005, Ryan-Sanders Baseball brought the Triple-A Edmonton Trappers to Round Rock, moving the Double-A club to Corpus Christi, TX. Round Rock's 2019-20 affiliation with Houston completed moving all Ryan-Sanders ties from the Rangers to the Astros (see **Myrtle Beach Pelicans [CURRENT]**) – possibly not for long; see **Corpus Christi Hooks (CURRENT)**.

Dell Computer owns naming rights. Ryan's eight-foot statue outside the main entrance sat at the Nolan Ryan Foundation's offices in his hometown of Alvin, TX, until the foundation moved to Round Rock. *The* round rock is only ten minutes away – just south of the Old StageCoach Inn on Chisholm Trail Road. The Dell appears in TV's *Fear the Walking Dead* (2018); the Express drew a near-record crowd as the show's fictional Armadillos.

Affiliation changes nearly created an interesting twist in the Round Rock "Dance Halls"-Nashville "Honky Tonks" trophy series for Austin-Nashville music supremacy. The Express won the first two – as the Rangers' Triple-A affiliate. In the 2019-20 cycle, Nashville is the Rangers' affiliate. Would the Sounds be trying to break the Express streak – or were their *players* trying to *extend* theirs? The question went from fascinating to moot when the teams dropped the series.

Sacramento River Cats
Sutter Health Park, West Sacramento, CA

Class Triple-A Pacific Coast League
San Francisco Giants
Got: **May 18, 2013; Sacramento River Cats 6, Oklahoma City RedHawks 3**

Opened in 2000, the ballpark was privately financed – mostly by Raley's Supermarkets' purchase of naming rights – and filled by the purchase and move of the Vancouver Canadians. Raley's held the rights for twenty seasons, but Sutter Health signed a fifteen-year deal effective after the 2019 campaign.

A Sacramento-based group bought the Canadians in 1998 to move them to the California capital. That marked the last time Vancouver had full-season professional baseball, mostly named Mounties in previous iterations, but the subsequent Northwest League short-season club is always a threat to win both the championship and the attendance race.

This is one of only a handful of Minor League ballparks I would describe as Majors-quality except for capacity. I stayed at a hotel directly across the Sacramento River and walked to the game. That was an experience in itself, strolling over the river on the golden vertical-lift Tower Bridge. During their first eight seasons, the then-Oakland Athletics' farm club won an unprecedented six straight division titles, back-to-back PCL titles two different times, the first back-to-back Triple-A championships ever *and* Minor League baseball's top attendance all eight years.

As recently as 2014, *Forbes Magazine* ranked this the most valuable ball club in the Minors. Yet when the 2013-14 affiliation cycle ended, the Cats dumped Oakland and the Giants dropped the Fresno Grizzlies for each other.

The stadium, across the river from the state capitol and Sacramento proper, replaced warehouses and railyards.

Salem Red Sox
Haley Toyota Field at Salem Memorial Ballpark, Salem, VA
Class A-Advanced Carolina League
Boston Red Sox

Got: **April 14, 2012; Salem Red Sox 8, Myrtle Beach Pelicans 6**

Part of the James E. Taliaferro Sports and Entertainment Complex southeast of downtown Salem, this ballpark boasts an impressive view of the Blue Ridge Mountains. "Memorial" in the stadium name remembers Salem's veterans – suggested by Taliaferro, Salem's mayor at the time. The Salem Civic Center and the Salem Football Stadium comprise the rest of the complex. Construction delays pushed its 1995 debut four times. It finally opened Aug. 7 – less than a month from the end of that season.

The ball club and its playpen had a banner 2017: its 50th straight season in the Carolina League; new division, moving from the Southern to the Northern because of two new teams in North Carolina; new stadium naming-rights contract; its third record crowd in three seasons – 8,847, May 19 (broken again in 2018); and the Caro's All-Star Game – the second time it hosted an ASG.

The BoSox bought the team in 2009, to get their high-A players out of Lancaster, CA – a high altitude, windy ballpark that could derail pitchers climbing the Minor League ladder. In their affiliated rather than O&O days, Salem nicknames were: Friends, Rebels, Pirates (w/Pirates), Redbirds, Buccaneers (w/Pirates) and Avalanche (w/Rockies). Now, think of the possibilities for a Salem-Boston partnership.

Salem-Keizer Volcanoes

Volcanoes Stadium, Keizer, OR

Class A-Short Season Northwest League

San Francisco Giants

Got: **Aug. 12, 2014; Salem-Keizer Volcanoes 14, Hillsboro Hops 11**

The first professional ballpark built in Salem or Keizer since pro ball's 1940 arrival opened in 1997. The former Bellingham Giants moved in, promptly winning the 1998 Northwest League title. In 1999, the stadium won a design award from the American Institute of Architects. It soon expanded the souvenir store and added the Home Run porch beyond left field, the Children's Play

Area, and the Lava Lodge Sports Bar. The Volcanoes Stadium Pro Shop later expanded, and the Volcano-tron video board erupted in 2006.

Mondays are typically slow gate days in Minor League baseball, but this club *asked* its league to schedule it at home Aug. 21, 2017. Why? Of the six Minor League teams lying in the path of the 2017 total eclipse, five of whom ended up being at home, the Volcanoes were the first to see that day's promotional potential.

"Total Eclipse of the Park" scheduled a morning game whose start was timed to include the first "eclipse delay" in professional baseball history – and filled the place. The delay lasted fifty-eight minutes in front of a sell-out crowd of 5,297. A time capsule will be opened June 25, 2069, re-sealed, re-buried and permanently reopened 100 years later – the day of the area's next eclipse. Perhaps needless to say, the Volcanoes won the 2017 Minor League Baseball Promotion of the Year Award.

Salt Lake Bees
Smith's Ballpark, Salt Lake City, UT
Class Triple-A Pacific Coast League
Los Angeles Angels of Anaheim
Got: **Aug. 11, 2014; Salt Lake Bees 8, El Paso Chihuahuas 7**

Opened in 1994, the home of the Bees is named per a contract with Smith's Food and Drug, Kroger's Utah division. That is the ballpark's fourth name, all of which have been corporate. The HOK Sport (now Populous) ballpark has the exceptional view one would expect of a stadium in Utah's Wasatch Range of mountains. It also has, for Minor League baseball, an extremely large upper deck.

The same-site replacement of Derks Park lured the Portland Beavers south, where they became the Salt Lake Buzz and drew a Pacific Coast League-record 713,224. Leading the league the next five seasons as well, they hit the 10 million attendance mark faster than any other PCL team to that time – a record later broken by the Memphis Redbirds.

Owner Joe Buzas dropped "Buzz" for "Stingers" in 2001 to settle the Georgia Institute of Technology's lawsuit over its sports mascot's name. After his death, the club resurrected Salt Lake City's 1915-65 and 1969-70 baseball nickname.

Angels farm-mate Burlington, IA, also goes by Bees – but despite the coincidence of their parent team there is no corporate relationship between them. Only one other nickname is shared by unrelated Minor League clubs not using that of their big-league parent – Indians, by Indianapolis of the International League and Spokane of the Northwest League.

San Antonio Missions
Nelson W. Wolff Municipal Stadium, San Antonio, TX
Class Triple-A Pacific Coast League
San Diego Padres
Got: **April 14, 2019; San Antonio Missions 5, Nashville Sounds 4**

San Antonio Missions
Nelson W. Wolff Municipal Stadium, San Antonio, TX
Class Double-A Texas League
Got: **April 25, 2014; Midland RockHounds 2, San Antonio Missions 1**

The Alamo City was in the Texas League or related circuits for 118 seasons between its 1888 charter member club and the 2018 San Diego Padres' affiliate's playoff exit, but Missions ownership – the Elmore Sports Group – moved three of its seven MiLB teams during the 2018-19 off-season. The long-time Double-A Missions became the Amarillo Sod Poodles in a new stadium, the Triple-A Colorado Springs Sky Sox became the San Antonio Missions, and the Rookie-Advanced Helena Brewers became the Rocky Mountain Vibes in the Springs.

The Triple-A Brewers' affiliation and a 7,000-mile trail of franchise moves thus came to San Antone: Portland, OR (1903), to Sacramento, CA (1918), to Honolulu, HI (1960), to the Springs (1988), to San Antonio. The ballpark's history includes a unique event: In 1998, Arkansas Traveler Tyrone Hearne homered with one, three, none and two on – professional baseball's only home run cycle ever.

ESG says "The Wolff" is *not* a Triple-A stadium, but the mayor opposes public money to replace it. It is a rare HOK Sport ballpark: designed after 1988 but not located downtown. Although this move is voluntary and part of a bigger picture, S.A. – seemingly, given its history, a perfect baseball town – lost affiliated teams in 1965 to Amarillo and 1971 to Midland, TX. It appears clear this one arrives with a cloud over its head; any city west of longitude eighty-five or so can probably have it by building a Triple-A quality park. Or upgrading one such as, say, New Orleans.

San Jose Giants
Excite Ballpark, San Jose, CA
Class A-Advanced California League
San Francisco Giants
Got: **May 11, 2013; San Jose Giants 5, High Desert Mavericks 2**

Opened as Municipal Stadium, this 1942 Works Projects Administration project cost just $90,000 and originally seated only 2,900. Today's SJ Giants date to 1988, and in its current configuration the ballpark has held well over 5,000. The Triple-A Pacific Coast League tried it 1977-78 but drew poorly – fewer than 100,000 fans in either year. Even when the Cali League returned, the playpen didn't break 100,000 until the Giants became the parent club in 1988.

How the market has changed: The Oakland Athletics spent 2011-16 trying to move to San Jose, now a major city in its own right and averaging 191,376 over the past ten years – but still in Giants' protected territory. They used their veto to block it, winning a resulting court battle, but the possibility was serious enough that the SJ club picked a future home – Fremont, an earlier Oakland option. All two-team MLB markets have jointly protected territories – except this one.

My visit there was in 2014, and even though it couldn't hold much more than 5,000 even then, the place did feel like a higher-than-high-A ballpark. That was perhaps influenced by a parking fee of $10. It doesn't seem like a lot now, especially not if you're all about the Majors, but it was the most I'd ever seen in a Minor League park at that time.

Excite Credit Union bought three years' worth of naming rights just before the 2019 season and just after changing its own name from Alliance Credit Union.

Scranton/Wilkes-Barre RailRiders
PNC Field, Moosic, PA
Class Triple-A International League
New York Yankees
Got: **July 5, 2013; Scranton/Wilkes-Barre RailRiders 3, Buffalo Bisons 2**

Lackawanna County Stadium, opened in 1989, was rebuilt in 2012 while the then-SWB Yankees played their entire season on the road as the Empire State Yankees. The SWB Red Barons had joined the Yankees, taking their new parents' nickname, after the Philadelphia Phillies dropped them during the 2006 affiliate shuffle. The Phils partnered with the Ottawa Lynx, who would become the Lehigh Valley IronPigs a year later. Coincidentally, that same season, PNC Bank bought naming rights to the stadium in Moosic.

In 2010, the Yankees and a partner bought the ball club – but the deal took more than a year to close. The day after it did, the renovation was set. During that all-road season, they played their "home" games in six stadiums around the Northeast. What was billed in advance as a "renovation" produced a "brand new" ballpark – so called at the open house that introduced it – that is spacious, round, immaculately landscaped, and with an approach that will make you think you're driving to a mansion.

Instead of resuming SWB Yankees, the ball club then became the SWB RailRiders – saluting Scranton as the birthplace of the electric streetcar.

Founded in Reading, PA, in 1919, the SWB franchise previously played in Albany, NY; Jersey City, NJ; Ottawa, ON; Columbus, OH; Charleston, WV; and suburban Portland, ME.

The 2017 Riders came within one playoff series of being the first team to play at home in the Triple-A Championship Game.

South Bend Cubs
Four Winds Field at Stanley Coveleski Stadium, South Bend, IN
Class A Midwest League
Chicago Cubs
Got: **June 27, 2012; Great Lakes Loons 11, South Bend Silver Hawks 6**

Opened in 1987, Stanley Coveleski Regional Stadium was named for a spit-balling pitcher (legal when he came to the Majors, and he was among those grandfathered after the spitball was outlawed) who played fourteen seasons 1912-28, retired to South Bend, and in 1989 was inducted into the Hall of Fame by its Veterans Committee.

This first US baseball stadium designed by HOK Sport pre-echoes the "downtown retro" design, such as brick exterior, which was later made famous by Oriole Park at Camden Yards. HOK Sport, originally a division within the Kansas City firm HOK that rose to prominence building schools, became such a force in ballparks that it spun off as Populous in 2009.

The South Bend ball club premiered in 1988 as a Chicago White Sox' team, originally using their name. They localized the nickname in 1994 with Silver Hawks, a nod to the locally built Studebaker automobile. The 'Hawks lost the ChiSox affiliation two seasons later, when their parent club consolidated its farm teams in the Southeast.

In 2013, Four Winds Casino Resort bought naming rights to Coveleski Stadium, altering the name and adding a life-size statue of Coveleski. The 'Hawks landed the other Chicago team for 2015, rebranded and quickly joined the elite club of clubs that average more than their park seats.

The Ivy at Berlin Place apartments beyond left field mimics those beyond the Cubs' Wrigley Field.

Spokane Indians
Avista Stadium, Spokane, WA
Class A-Short Season Northwest League
Texas Rangers
Got: **Aug. 17, 2012; Yakima Bears 6, Spokane Indians 1**

One set of their jerseys reads Sp'q'n'i – the Spokane Tribe's name in its language, Salish. This is the tribe that inspired the nickname, first used in 1903. As such names began to become controversial, the federally recognized Spokane Tribe of Indians and the team began working together. A 2006 logo redesign was followed by the introduction of the Sp'q'n'i uniform in 2013.

Built in 1958 for the Triple-A club the Brooklyn Dodgers acquired and bumped as they moved to Los Angeles, it lost that team to Albuquerque, NM, in 1971 and its 1973 replacement to Las Vegas, NV, in 1982. The legacy, of course, is a large Triple-A stadium for a short-season team. When it opened, contemporary newspapers called it Spokane Indians Baseball Stadium, but the team history refers to Fairgrounds Recreational Park. Seafirst Bank settled that with a 1994 naming-rights purchase; the utility followed in 2000.

It hosted the first inter-*level* All-Star Game, the 2015 ASG between stars from its short-A league and the high-Rookie Pioneer League.

Spokane and Indianapolis are the only Minor-league teams that use a big-league nickname which is not its parent's. The only other one shared by separately owned teams is Bees.

A 1946 Spokane Indians team bus crash that killed nine and hurt six remains the worst team transit accident in US professional sports history.

Springfield Cardinals
Hammons Field, Springfield, MO
Class Double-A Texas League
St. Louis Cardinals
Got: **May 18, 2014; Arkansas Travelers 9, Springfield Cardinals 3**

Hotel mogul John Q. Hammons funded this ballpark to anchor a downtown development project. It opened as the home of Missouri State University Bears baseball, a year before the Cardinals bought the El Paso Diablos and moved them to Springfield in time for the 2005 campaign. The two continue to share the facility, with the Cards the primary tenant.

The Hammons name is on so many Springfield buildings that comedian Bob Hope once said the city should be called Hammonsville.

The first full high-definition scoreboard in Class Double-A went up in 2016. Head Groundskeeper Brock Phipps won an unprecedented seventh Sports Turf Manager of the Year Award in 2019; he is the *only* person to win the award four straight years, 2013-16. Originated in 2002, the award honors four grounds-crew managers each year – one in Triple-A, one in Double-A, one in the two full-season levels of Class A, and one for the short-season levels.

The stadium has no dedicated parking and the team recommends paid lots across Trafficway Street or the Jordan Valley Park Parking Garage. Or it has; both jumped their rates before the 2019 season and the team was plainly not happy with them.

The Texas League's most-traveled franchise has also called home: Galveston, TX; Waco, TX; Galveston again; Shreveport, LA; Victoria, TX; Ardmore, OK; Albuquerque, NM; and El Paso.

St. Lucie Mets
First Data Field, Port St. Lucie, FL

Class A-Advanced Florida State League
New York Mets
Got: **May 27, 2012; St. Lucie Mets 2, Charlotte Stone Crabs 1**
Different in 2020: possibly, stadium name (name sponsor First Data is being acquired by Fiserv)

First Data hosts the New York Mets' spring training in February and March, then the St. Lucie Mets' April-September Florida State League season. Opened as Thomas J. White Stadium, named for the real estate developer who led building it, the county-owned stadium and the FSL club debuted together in 1988. It has gone through three previous naming-rights contracts: Tradition Field, 2004-09; Digital Domain Park, 2010-12; Tradition again, 2013-16. The Mets signed the commerce technology firm to the fourth – a ten-year deal – in February 2017. The playpen's name may change again, though, with Fiserv having acquired First Data in 2019.

After Heisman and former National Football League quarterback Tim Tebow's June 2017 promotion from the low-A Columbia Fireflies, attendance at First Data spiked from its normal annual path to a season record in less than six weeks. For the third time in four levels, Tebow homered on his first day. The first time was in the same complex in 2016 – in the Florida Instructional League, during his first at-bat since his junior year of high school. He also homered in his first at-bat for Columbia, and would later make it four out of five when, at Double-A Binghamton, he went yard on the first *pitch* he saw.

The Mets made the FSL playoffs five times in their first eighteen years – in a league of fourteen teams most of those seasons – and went on to win the title every time.

State College Spikes
Medlar Field at Lubrano Park, State College, PA
Class A-Short Season New York-Pennsylvania League
St. Louis Cardinals
Got: **July 4, 2013; State College Spikes 13, Batavia Muckdogs 1**

Although Pennsylvania State University built and owns the ballpark, and PSU Nittany Lions baseball is therefore its primary team, the Spikes hosted its first regular-season baseball game June 20, 2006. The then-Cardinals' farm club joined the Pittsburgh Pirates' system a year after moving from Augusta, NJ. When that partnership ended after three two-year affiliation cycles, the Cards and Spikes remarried.

The franchise dates to the New York-Penn League's two-team 1983 expansion, as the Newark Orioles. In fact, it was quite the nomad in its early years: five seasons in Newark, NJ; five in Hamilton, ON; just one in Glens Falls, NY; then twelve years going by New Jersey in Augusta. The move from Ontario back to New Jersey between the 1993 and 1994 seasons was one of *five* in the fourteen-team NYPL during that off-season.

Except for the 18.55-foot right-field fence that commemorates the year of Penn State's founding, Medlar mimics the Pittsburgh Pirates' PNC Park – despite the fact that it was built while its team was in the middle of a player development contract with the Cardinals.

It was Penn State's baseball team, not its national power football team, that first used "Nittany" – which is Algonquin for "single mountain" – in its sports nickname.

Staten Island Yankees

Richmond County Bank Ballpark at St. George, Staten Island, NY

Class A-Short Season New York-Pennsylvania League

New York Yankees

Got: **July 19, 2014; Staten Island Yankees 7, Jamestown Jammers 1**

Different in 2020: nickname, possibly; team considering changing it to Pizza Rats

This neighborhood first hosted professional baseball in 1886! The New York Metropolitans of the American Association, during the period it was considered a major league, played the

1886-87 seasons at the St. George Cricket Grounds. They sold out to the National League's Brooklyn Dodgers after the '87 campaign.

More than a century later, the modern Mets and the Yankees each wanted a nearby farm team, but both repeatedly vetoed each other's every effort to acquire one. In the Majors' two-team protection territories, either team can veto activities by anyone – including each other, even though they're in the same territory.

Finally, in 1998, New York Mayor Rudy Giuliani offered to build a separate stadium to house a farm team of each big-league club in exchange for one withheld veto. The Mets' team is in Brooklyn (see **Brooklyn Cyclones [CURRENT]**; the Yanks bought, moved, and renamed the Watertown Indians. The College of Staten Island hosted them until their playpen, designed by HOK Sport (now Populous), opened in 2001.

They played six 2018 home dates as the Pizza Rats, one of the nominees in their aborted 2016 nickname-change. While not specifying that nickname, the club has hinted that it might go through with a change at a later date.

The big-league Yanks sold their interest in the Baby Bombers in 2012 but still have the territorial veto.

Stockton Ports
Stockton Ballpark, Stockton, CA
Class A-Advanced California League
Oakland Athletics
Got: **May 24, 2012; Visalia Rawhide 9, Stockton Ports 2**

The Ports call this Banner Island Ballpark, but its signage and its owner – which is the city of Stockton, not the team – say Stockton Ballpark. Its 2005 opener sold out; in four years, it hosted its 1 millionth fan.

The ballpark is a great walk-around venue, with many food and other options to explore on its 360-degree concourse. Stockton Arena was built at the same time, as part of a waterfront revitalization project.

Mudville of "Casey at the Bat" fame *may* be Stockton; the team used "Mudville Nine" instead of Stockton Ports 2000-01. Author Ernest Thayer, who published the 1888 poem under a pseudonym, never disclosed where "Mudville" was – but both Stockton and Holliston, MA, claim it. Thayer was born near Holliston but was working in San Francisco when "Casey" was published.

Banner Island – which lies in Athletics' protected territory – may have been surrounded by the San Joaquin River when it was named, but today it's a peninsula. Its history includes Charles Weber inspiring its name by flying the US flag after Union victories, Coxey's Army camping before marching on Washington about the Panic of 1893, the building of World War II ships – and professional baseball as early as 1886.

Syracuse Mets
NBT Bank Stadium, Syracuse, NY
Class Triple-A International League
New York Mets
Got: **July 10, 2013; Syracuse Chiefs 3, Buffalo Bisons 2**

The Mets lost the luxury of having their Triple-A team in their home state when the Buffalo Bisons decided to join the geographically closer Toronto Blue Jays for the 2013-14 affiliation cycle. Injury added itself to insult when that affiliate shuffle forced the Mets to far-off Las Vegas, NV. Otherwise unable to extract themselves in the next two shuffles, they bought the Syracuse Chiefs in late 2017 to make it their Triple-A farm team starting in 2019. Strangely, as the Mets honored the Chiefs' player development contract with the Washington Nationals, one big-league team ran the business operations of another's farm team. They announced the branding change from Chiefs to Mets Oct. 16, 2018.

Heisman and former National Football League quarterback-turned Minor League player Tim Tebow started 2019 with the 'Cuse, coming off his 2018 All-Star but injury-ended season with the Double-A Binghamton Rumble Ponies. Injury also ended his 2019 campaign.

The ballpark, designed by HOK Sport (now Populous), opened in 1997 with different names for both it and the team: P&C Stadium hosted the SkyChiefs. P&C Foods later fell into bankruptcy; Alliance Bank landed naming rights in 2005 but merged into NBT Bank in 2013.

The team had been Chiefs 1934-96 but added Sky in 1997 because of, in its then-general manager's words, "political correctness." The "Sky" fell in 2007 as they returned to Chiefs but took on a train motif.

Tacoma Rainiers

Cheney Stadium, Tacoma, WA

Class Triple-A Pacific Coast League

Seattle Mariners

Got: **Aug. 20, 2012; Reno Aces 6, Tacoma Rainiers 5**

Opened in 1960, the "100-Day Wonder" was built in three months and fourteen days to land the Phoenix Giants. Lumber king Ben Cheney, who standardized the eight-foot two-by-four, drove both the stadium building and team acquisition efforts. A statue of Cheney has the best seat in "The House that Ben Built."

The Giants moved back to Phoenix in 1966, but Tacoma seamlessly replaced them with a PCL franchise that moved from Salt Lake City. Early in its history, that one went through parents like a hummingbird – Cubs 1966-71; Twins, 1972-77 (the Mariners joined the American League in 1977); Yankees, 1978; Indians, 1979-80; Athletics, 1981-94; Mariners, 1995-present. Tacoma had taken its historic nickname, Tigers, in 1980, but when they joined nearby Seattle they took the nickname most of its teams had used in its PCL days: Rainiers. You'd think it would have happened sooner; they are geographically closer than any other Major/Triple-A tandem in baseball.

The playpen underwent a 210-day renovation during the 2010-11 off-season, reducing its seat count to 6,500. It can hold about 1,000 more than that. In exchange for that makeover, the Rainiers signed a thirty-year lease. Making the 2010 playoffs, the Rainiers made it possible for the stadium facelift to start on time by putting playoff ball in Seattle's Safeco Field for the first time since 2001.

The first city to lose a PCL team (1905) is now the dean of the league, with a continuous entry since 1960.

Tampa Tarpons
George M. Steinbrenner Field, Tampa, FL
Class A-Advanced Florida State League
New York Yankees
Got: **June 10, 2012; Daytona Cubs 4, Tampa Yankees 3**

The home of Yankees spring training and the FSL's Tarpons features a World Trade Center tribute and the greatest-Yankees Monument Park that both make it well worth coming early.

Opened as Legends Field in 1996, the stadium was renamed for the retired-to-Tampa Yankees owner two years before his death. A 2011 Steinbrenner statue that was placed a few steps west of Monument Park six months after he died greets fans heading for the souvenir store from outside the stadium.

The Yanks have drawn as many as 170,000 to their one-month spring training. Founded as the Tampa Yankees in 1994, the T-Yanks returned Tampa to Florida State League ball six seasons after the Tampa White Sox moved to Sarasota and four years before the big-league Tampa Bay Devil Rays arrived in what is now the Rays' protected territory. The original plan was to tear down and replace Al Lang Field, but the National Football League's Tampa Bay Buccaneers objected and Legends ended up across Dale Mabry Drive from their stadium.

During the 2017-18 off-season, the T-Yanks announced they would return to the long-time moniker of Tampa's previous FSL franchise. The 2018 man-on-second-in-extra-innings rule caused the Tarps to lose a game despite not allowing their opponent to put anyone on base except by fielder's choice – which should of course be impossible. Essentially, they lost a perfect game – which should also be impossible.

Tennessee Smokies
Smokies Stadium, Kodak, TN
Class Double-A Southern League
Chicago Cubs
Got: Aug. 13, 2005; Carolina Mudcats 4, Tennessee Smokies 2

Opened in 2000 as Smokies Park, it made a slight name change in 2016 to end confusion with the Great Smoky Mountains National Park – although the last time I checked (2017), no changes had been made to the stadium's name signage.

Among the last teams to flee city for suburb, the Smokies are within twenty-five miles of the GSMNP, Dollywood, Gatlinburg, and World's Fair Park in downtown Knoxville. That has been cited as a reason the club succeeded despite bucking the downtown trend, but new ownership that took over in 2013 has bought land downtown – less than a mile from the site of the stadium the team left. Knoxville's mayor confirmed media reports of talks to bring the team back into the city, but said ownership bought, with the team, a lease through 2025.

The 2015 club broke its one-game attendance record three times, and – via a day-night double-header – hosted 10,000 fans in one day. A Jimmy Buffett Tribute Night in 2017, featuring Jimmy Buffett stuff but no Jimmy Buffett, drew a house baseball record 8,164. Smokies Stadium hosted a 2018 Appalachian League game between the Greeneville Reds and the Johnson City Cardinals. Why? Why not? All three are commonly operated.

You know the old joke about "free beer tomorrow" – well, tomorrow actually came to Smokies fans Aug. 22, 2018. The promotion was free beer until the visitors scored; the Jackson Generals prevented any potential problems by scoring two runs in the first inning.

Toledo Mud Hens
Fifth Third Field, Toledo, OH

Class Triple-A International League
Detroit Tigers

Got: June 20, 2012; Lehigh Valley IronPigs 2, Toledo Mud Hens 1

Unless you grew up in the Ohio-Michigan-Indiana tri-state, chances are you never heard of a mud hen until TV's *M*A*S*H* made Cpl. Max Klinger a big fan of this Minor League team. The nickname is now iconic – and it dates all the way to 1902, although somewhat intermittently before nicknames became formalized.

"Mud hen" is colloquial for the American coot, a duckish bird that's common around Lake Erie. Klinger's Hens moved away in June 1952 – *during* the show's setting, but the writers never noticed. The Triple-A Milwaukee Brewers moved to Toledo in 1953, but took the new nickname Sox; Klinger would have been a Sox fan the last four months of the Korean Conflict – say, 50 episodes of the show. The Sox stayed only through 1955.

Today's franchise moved to suburban Maumee, OH, from Richmond, VA, in 1965. The franchise was once Jack Dunn's storied Baltimore Orioles, the only professional baseball club ever to win seven consecutive pennants. Not even the New York Yankees have won more than five straight.

"The 5/3," opened in April 2002, drew the Hens downtown and into Tigers' protected territory. This fourth Toledo-Detroit stint, since 1987, is the eighth-longest current affiliation among separately owned teams.

Mike Hessman broke the *real* home run record for the affiliated Minors here in 2015 (as opposed to the fictional mark portrayed in the film *Bull Durham* [1988]). His first big-league hit was a homer, his record 433rd both his last and a grand slam. He retired after that season and became a batting instructor in the Tigers' farm system.

Trenton Thunder

Samuel J. Plumeri, Sr. Field at Arm & Hammer Park, Trenton, NJ

Class Double-A Eastern League
New York Yankees
Got: **June 19, 2012; Trenton Thunder 3, Richmond Flying Squirrels 2**

Construction delays caused mostly by an extra-wintry winter pushed then-Mercer County Waterfront Park's debut a month into the 1994 season, with the homes of the Wilmington Blue Rocks, Reading Phillies and Philadelphia Phillies pinch hitting. Even then, rainouts – often after day-long sunshine – plagued the brick-exterior ballpark because of sod so bad it was entirely redone after that first season. I'm not missing the double irony of this problem at a ballpark with the word "waterfront" in its name and hosting a team nicknamed "Thunder" – if you're curious, the water that's fronted is the Delaware River.

My visit was many years after that, and my chief memory of the place is high energy and a midway-like atmosphere. (Lest that read like a negative, I'm a big kid; I *like* midways!) Had I been plopped into the concourse without knowing where I was, I'd have guessed Coney Island.

Founded in 1980 in Glens Falls, NY, the franchise moved to London, ON, in 1989 but on to Trenton just five seasons later. Derek Jeter's 2011 Independence Day Eve rehabilitation drew its record crowd – 9,212.

Arm & Hammer added stadium naming rights to its existing sponsorship in 2013. Plumeri's son, Joe, is a Thunder co-owner. Plumeri the father is honored not only with the field name but also a statue in front of the ballpark.

Tri-City Dust Devils
Gesa Stadium, Pasco, WA
Class A-Short Season Northwest League
San Diego Padres
Got: **Aug. 9, 2014; Vancouver Canadians 11, Tri-City Dust Devils 1**

Opened in 1995, this ballpark originally hosted an independent professional club, the Tri-City Posse. In 2001, the Triple-A Albuquerque Dukes moved to Portland – bumping the Northwest League's Portland Rockies, who then invaded Pasco. Although they changed nicknames during that move, they remained with the Rockies through 2014.

The Devils first called the ballpark Tri-City Stadium, then Dust Devils Stadium, before selling Gesa (pronounced GEE-zah) Credit Union naming rights starting in 2008. "Tri" aside, *one* city owns it. Pasco's lease still lets the team sell naming rights, but there have been two modifications: (1) When there's no naming-rights contract, the default name is Pasco Stadium. (2) The team cannot name the ballpark for itself.

In the early 1970s, the Padres parented a now-defunct NwL club in nearby Kennewick that also went by Tri-City. The other "tri" city is Richland, which despite never having built a pro-quality stadium did host the 1983-86 Tri-Cities Atoms at Richland High School's baseball field. Not surprisingly, that franchise was sold and moved to Boise, ID – where it played two seasons at Borah High School until Memorial Stadium opened.

Perhaps confusingly only to someone trying to get them all, another Minor League team goes by Tri-City. It's also a short-A team, but on the other side of the continent: the Tri-City ValleyCats of the New York-Pennsylvania League.

Tri-City ValleyCats
Joseph L. Bruno Stadium, Troy, NY
Class A-Short Season New York-Pennsylvania League
Houston Astros
Got: **July 26, 2014; Tri-City ValleyCats 16, Staten Island Yankees 3**

Opened by Hudson Valley Community College on its campus in 2002, its primary team is HVCC Vikings baseball. The two-tone brick and stone front, with twin towers on either side of the main entrance, does present a collegiate feel. The location identifier refers to Troy, Albany and Schenectady – also known collectively as the New York Capital District.

The stadium's name and campus location warrant anti-confusion notices, and you're gonna need a scorecard for them. Another affiliated club uses Tri-City as its location identifier (thankfully, on the other side of the continent) – the Tri-City Dust Devils of the Northwest League – and *still* another uses Hudson Valley (not so thankfully, less than 100 miles away in not only the same league but the same river valley) – the Hudson Valley Renegades, and they've played each other for this league's title!

"The Joe" has squeezed in more than 7,100 – within shouting distance of twice its stated capacity. The team was founded in Little Falls, NJ, in 1977 with one of the two franchises the NYPL issued as part of the American League's Seattle/Toronto expansion. Then with the New York Mets, the team moved to Pittsfield, MA, in 1989, moved over to the Astros farm system in 2001 and into the Joe in 2002.

Tulsa Drillers
ONEOK Field, Tulsa, OK
Class Double-A Texas League
Los Angeles Dodgers
Got: **April 26, 2014; Northwest Arkansas Naturals 2, Tulsa Drillers 1**

The 1998 opening of Bricktown Ballpark in Oklahoma City made quite an impression on the Drillers' ownership. Fortunately for them and their idea, Tulsa's mayor wanted to develop the downtown. Populous designed the sleek facility, whose main entrance salutes the oil industry with a stylistic oil derrick.

Idea to public announcement took ten years and construction another two, but its ultimate success is undeniable. Before it opened, the Tulsa natural gas utility (pronounced ONE-OAK) bought naming rights – and that was just the beginning of the money flow. Within five years of the June 2008 announcement that the stadium would be built, more than $700 million worth of development projects was announced and/or finished around the site.

University of Oklahoma-Oklahoma State University "Bedlam Series" games own its top four baseball crowds.

An earlier Tulsa team is now the Arkansas Travelers; in 1966, the owners of the Triple-A Travelers and the Double-A Tulsa Drillers swapped franchises. Arkansas ownership wanted to reduce its travel costs by downsizing from the Pacific Coast League to the Texas League, an idea that has worked – the Travs have been stable ever since. The new Oilers, however, moved three times between 1976 and 1982 – finally stabilizing in Louisville, KY.

After the 1976 move-away, country music star Roy Clark and a partner bought the Lafayette Drillers to move them to Tulsa. Founded as the San Antonio Bronchos, the franchise had also played in Amarillo, TX. It joined the Dodgers the year they bought the Triple-A Oklahoma City RedHawks.

Vancouver Canadians
Nat Bailey Stadium, Vancouver, BC
Class A-Short Season Northwest League
Toronto Blue Jays
Got: **Aug. 18, 2012; Everett AquaSox 2, Vancouver Canadians 0**

Capilano Stadium, opened in 1951, was renamed in 1978 for a tireless baseball-promoting Vancouver restaurateur. Scotiabank owns naming rights to the field, in a rare stadium that is at the same time stately and high-energy. "Raincouver" has twice lost Triple-A teams, but short-season works – its attendance averages in the high 90s as a percentage of its capacity.

"The Nat" is both the northernmost and westernmost ballpark hosting a team in a US-based affiliated league – and the only remaining non-US club in such a league. Since 1999, in order, these moves reduced that figure from seven to one: the Lethbridge Black Diamonds to Missoula, MT; the Triple-A Vancouver Canadians to Sacramento, CA; the St. Catharines Stompers to Brooklyn, NY; the Calgary Cannons to Albuquerque, NM; the

Medicine Hat Blue Jays to Helena, MT; the Edmonton Trappers to Round Rock, TX; the Ottawa Lynx to Allentown, PA. I asked a staffer from a team in another league that has had teams move across the border why this has happened. The two reasons he gave had nothing to do with weather: (1) the currency exchange rate hurts US citizens playing in Canada (something that could vary with time); and (2) the disparity of health care insurance – a US citizen injured in Canada (say, during a sporting event) has a large and immediate coverage problem.

Remember to allow for border crossing time – from hitting the back of the line to getting waved through took me an hour!

Vermont Lake Monsters
Centennial Field, Burlington, VT
Class A-Short Season New York-Pennsylvania League
Oakland Athletics
Got: **July 21, 2014; Hudson Valley Renegades 3, Vermont Lake Monsters 2**

Located on the University of Vermont campus, Centennial Field is so named because it is part of a complex that was dedicated during UVM's centennial in 1904, but the existing ballpark isn't that old. It was added to the complex in 1906, and that wooden structure burned down in 1913. It was rebuilt in concrete and steel in 1922, though, and so is the oldest active baseball park in Minor League Baseball.

I can't say the old yard is aesthetically beautiful from the outside, but it is surprisingly so inside. It is also the first ballpark that hosted both a collegiate team and a short-season Minor League team – an arrangement that works flawlessly because there's no overlap between their seasons – starting in 1994. Unfortunately, UVM dropped baseball in 2009.

Also in 1994, *five* of the NYPL's fourteen teams moved – including the Jamestown Expos to Burlington. The Expos were immediately replaced by the Jamestown Jammers, who have since moved to West Virginia. Ten years before, then-Mayor Bernie Sanders brought professional baseball to town by coaxing a Double-A team from Lynn, MA; that team moved to Ohio in 1989.

Three Minor League teams play in a city named Burlington, more than any other; North Carolina's Burlington has Royals and Iowa's has Bees.

Visalia Rawhide
Recreation Ballpark, Visalia, CA
Class A-Advanced California League
Arizona Diamondbacks
Got: **May 16, 2013; Visalia Rawhide 6, Lancaster JetHawks 5**

The 2019-20 renewal of these two affiliates brings their partnership within one cycle of the farm franchise's longest – Minnesota Twins, 1977-92. Its 2,700 capacity, including "pasture" seating, is full-season affiliated baseball's smallest. They evoke TV's *Rawhide* with its theme song, a brand-like logo, and some apparently hand-painted false fronts.

A seven-year renovation justified a ten-year lease – longest in team history. More third-base seats, new seating off right field, a grass picnic area, party suites and a new grandstand jumped attendance seventy percent 2006-09. That upgrade turned a no-frills 1946 facility into a modern brick beauty.

The team website refers to Rawhide Ballpark but the city-owned facility's signage says Recreation Ballpark. (Have you noticed that the California League seems to have more of these what-shall-we-call-this-place disputes than any other circuit? Here ... Stockton, where I first learned this even happens ... Adelanto Stadium, whose name was disputed back when it had a Minor League team (see **Down East Wood Ducks [CURRENT]**) ... Lancaster Municipal Stadium, whose team calls it [with signage, which is not cheap!] The Hangar ...).

This team is changing hands, and I think the whole league is in trouble. It has more friction than any other I know between ballpark owners and tenants (see also **Stockton Ports [CURRENT]** and **Adelanto, CA [LEGACY]**), and the state has made it just about impossible to build or renovate stadiums (see **El Paso Chihuahuas [CURRENT]**). Am I overreacting? We'll see; the Cali league has lost two franchises *since* I first had that thought.

West Michigan Whitecaps
Fifth Third Ballpark, Comstock Park, MI
Class A Midwest League
Detroit Tigers
Got: **June 26, 2012; West Michigan Whitecaps 13, Bowling Green Hot Rods 11**

Old Kent Park was built with private funds, and branded under a naming rights deal with a local bank, to bring the Madison Muskies to the Grand Rapids suburb in 1994. Ohio-based Fifth Third Bank bought Old Kent Bank in 2000, honoring the contract but changing the name of the ballpark. Several expansions later, the stadium seats more than 10,000 – *huge* for low-A ball. The Tigers themselves drew its top crowd, 11,006, to a 1999 exhibition.

A January 2014 fire destroyed much of its right half, but it made like a phoenix – after a lightning-speed rebuild, opening on time three months later and hosting that year's Midwest League All-Star Game as scheduled. The club used the forced rebuild to make improvements, including a much larger souvenir shop called CapSized. It has one of six manual scoreboards in the Minors.

Its legendary Fifth Third Burger, which created a media sensation in 2009 and was retired after the 2018 season, contained five one-third pound beef patties, five slices of American cheese, a cup of chili plus Fritos, salsa, sour cream, lettuce, tomatoes, and 4,800 calories. The bun alone weighed a whole pound. What did such a massive meal cost? Twenty bucks the first season, twenty-seven the last! Why was it retired? The news release was appropriately vague, but what I saw between those lines was concern about its decadence.

West Virginia Black Bears
Monongalia County Ballpark, Granville, WV

Class A-Short Season New York-Pennsylvania League
Pittsburgh Pirates
Got: **June 18, 2015; Hudson Valley Renegades 11, West Virginia Black Bears 5**

One of several university-built ballparks that defrays costs by sharing with a short-season professional club, this one happened because the school changed sports conferences. When the West Virginia University Mountaineers left the Big East for the Big 12, the school declared it needed a new stadium to compete in its new circuit. With state and local help, WVU pieced together a deal to build one.

Oddly, at least to me, the New York-Penn League quickly held a news conference to announce it would put a team in the stadium when it was ready. This obvious move really didn't need to be announced, making me think of dogs marking territories. A higher level team could have bigfooted the NYPL – and there's only one lower level nearby. Perhaps WVU wanted to head that off; any higher team would mean a full-season that would have schedule overlaps with the collegiate club.

The Jamestown Jammers were a logical choice: within 220 miles of a dozen affiliated teams, four of them Triple-A, in a seventy-three-year-old-ballpark with neither replacement nor renovation in sight – and an affiliate of the locally favorite Pirates. Their 1994 move *to* Jamestown was one of *five* in the fourteen-team NYPL that summer.

The beautifully modern facility literally nestles on a hillside in a very developed area near the campus. The address is in Granville, not Morgantown, but it's hard to tell the difference from behind the wheel. WVU opened its new playpen to a campus then-baseball record 3,110 April 10, 2015.

West Virginia Power
Appalachian Power Park, Charleston, WV
Class A South Atlantic League
Seattle Mariners

Got: **May 12, 2012; Charleston RiverDogs 14, West Virginia Power 2**

The long-time Pirate farm team hooked up with the M's effective with the 2019 season, after the Power lost the Bucs to the Greensboro Grasshoppers. Appalachian Power Park has a very industrial feel, what with the name of a utility on it and wrought-iron gates and railings within it.

Although its listed capacity is only 4,500, it has held more than twice that – reporting more than 10,400 at a first-season game. This is not as incredible as it sounds; most post-1990 ballparks have more open space, and so fewer seats but much more standing room.

The postwar baseball boom brought Watt Powell Park, reviving Charleston's sporadic professional baseball history through 1983. A 1987 SAL expansion created the Charleston Wheelers. This park opened in 2005, bringing another new nickname *and* location identifier.

From Watt Powell, only Wheeler Bob, the Toastman, and Rowdy Alley remain: Bob hawks souvenirs (for more than forty years now!) the old-fashioned way; Toastman – who is by day city official Rod Blackstone – highlights opponents' failures by shouting "You're toast!" as he toasts bread and tosses it to the crowd; Rowdy Alley is occupied by a group of fans led by one "Billy Bob" who live up to the name.

Speaking of names, can you guess the name of the souvenir store? The Power Outlet!

Williamsport Crosscutters
BB&T Ballpark at Historic Bowman Field, Williamsport, PA
Class A-Short Season New York-Pennsylvania League
Philadelphia Phillies
Got: **July 8, 2013; Auburn Doubledays 4, Williamsport Crosscutters 1**

Different in 2020: stadium name (name sponsor BB&T Bank merging with SunTrust to become Truist)

Memorial Field, opened in 1926, was renamed in 1929 for J. Walton Bowman – who raised the $75,000 that built it. "The Bow" is fifteen years older than Little League Baseball, which declined its 1957 offer to host its World Series.

After the city lost its short-lived Double-A Bills (1987-91) to Binghamton, NY, this franchise moved from Geneva, NY, in 1994 – one of *five* members of the fourteen-team NYPL that moved that year.

Susquehanna Bank bought naming rights in 2013, funding a renovation of the then-deteriorating facility. BB&T bought Susquehanna Bank in 2015, reworking the stadium name. A different, mostly field-level, renovation soon followed so Major League Baseball could start the MLB Little League Classic in 2017. MLB sank $4 million into that renovation for what is now an annual event.

This ballpark proved tough for me. It was one of my two unsuccessful tries at getting two ballparks in one day; a night game I paired with a Harrisburg Senators day game, it had been moved up an hour for a double-header because the 'Cutters had been rained out the day before (lesson learned: *confirm* time *on* game day). I called it a *Go-Back* because I didn't see all the action played there that day; I was almost there for my first re-try when they declared a rainout. Finally, I got in a full nine-inning game in on the last day of my 2015 vacation. I've even been back once since, to see if the MLB renovation was a *Rebuilt*. It wasn't.

Wilmington Blue Rocks

Judy Johnson Field at Daniel S. Frawley Stadium, Wilmington, DE

Class A-Advanced Carolina League

Kansas City Royals

Got: **June 30, 2012; Lynchburg Hillcats 1, Wilmington Blue Rocks 0**

Opened as Legends Stadium in 1993, it was renamed a year later for the Wilmington mayor who brought baseball back. The field is separately named for local Negro Leaguer William Julius "Judy" Johnson, captain of a team that included the legendary players Satchel Paige *and* Josh Gibson. Frawley also hosts the Delaware Sports Museum and Hall of Fame, which includes a "conversation" with Johnson.

The "Blue Rocks" nickname, dating to 1940, was the result of a contest whose winner said he was thinking of the blue granite along the Brandywine River; a chunk decorates the entrance. (I believe that particular Blue Rock must play first base; it doesn't look mobile enough to play anywhere else.)

Wilmington lost the original Rocks to poor attendance in 1952. Their replacement christened Legends by beating Winston-Salem 6-5 with a four-run ninth inning.

In 2014, Rocks' ownership bought the Binghamton Mets to bring Double-A ball to Wilmington – but the seller reneged and later sold to a different buyer who kept them in Binghamton. Had that sale gone through, the existing Rocks would have moved to Kinston, NC.

Frawley Stadium is located in a waterfront area and is one of many ballparks local media have reported turned their surrounding areas around.

Winston-Salem Dash
BB&T Ballpark, Winston-Salem, NC
Class A-Advanced Carolina League
Chicago White Sox
Got: **Aug. 27, 2011; Myrtle Beach Pelicans 3, Winston-Salem Dash 1**
Different in 2020: stadium name (name sponsor BB&T Bank merging with SunTrust to become Truist)

As Winston and Salem grew together into a "Twin City," the professional baseball team took the nickname Twins in 1908. The cities merged, administratively and complete with hyphen, in 1913. In 2009, about to move to BB&T, the Winston-Salem Warthogs misappropriated "Dash" from that hyphen.

Wake Forest University had acquired Ernie Shore Field, the Warthogs' home since 1956, but leased it back to the Dash when the new park was delayed into 2010. Shortly before it finally opened, locally based BB&T Bank bought naming rights. Expect the name to change, as BB&T and SunTrust merge into Truist.

Before Shore, South Side Park – which as you may guess was located south of downtown – was the home of Winston-Salem baseball until it burned down in 1955. Its replacement was named for then-Forsyth County Sheriff Ernie Shore, who led the drive to raise the money to replace it. Shore pitched 1912-22 in the big leagues, in '17 famously retiring twenty-six straight batters to finish a game started by a quickly ejected then-pitcher named Babe Ruth. Shore served as sheriff 1934-70.

The ChiSox bought a majority interest in their longtime affiliate in 2014. The two originally paired up in 1997 as the Sox implemented their Southeastern strategy. Today, and for decades now, all ChiSox farm teams in the affiliated levels are in either North Carolina or Alabama.

Bull Durham (1988) featured the then-Winston-Salem Spirits as an opponent of Crash, Nuke, and Annie's Durham Bulls.

Wisconsin Timber Rattlers
Neuroscience Group Field at Fox Cities Stadium, Grand Chute, WI
Class A Midwest League
Milwaukee Brewers

Got: **Aug. 3, 2014; Wisconsin Timber Rattlers 1, Peoria Chiefs 1, 9 inns., spnd, rain**

When Fox Cities Stadium opened in 1995, the Appleton Foxes changed their long-time name – at least on the field – as they left Goodland Field behind. The corporate name was and at this writing remains Appleton Baseball Club, Inc. "Fox Cities" includes several communities; the stadium has an Appleton ZIP code, but maps and Grand Chanute's website show it there.

The area has had professional baseball continually since 1891. Its first affiliated team, and the first affiliated team called Foxes, was a Washington Senators' farm club that joined the Illinois-Indiana-Iowa League in 1958. The Three-I folded in 1962, but its Appleton Foxes along with the Burlington Bees and Cedar Rapids Braves survived by joining the Midwest League. A 2019 alternate nickname took over social media for a time: "Udder Tuggers," saluting Wisconsin dairies.

This isn't the northernmost stadium in affiliated baseball – that would be Nat Bailey Stadium in Vancouver, BC – but it is the northernmost in the US interior. Weather can be a problem, but April 2018 took the cake ... or at least the icing and the snow. The Rattlers had to move an entire home series with Kane County to Peoria's Dozer Park after a snowstorm whited out most of the Midwest League schedule the preceding weekend. My only visit here so far was on an August weeknight, when it was idyllically pleasant.

II. LEGACY (Ballparks That Have Been a Regular Host of MiLB in Which I Have Seen MiLB Action)

Adelanto, CA

Stadium name today: Adelanto Stadium

Last stadium name while home to an affiliated team: Stater Bros. Stadium

Organized Baseball teams: High Desert Mavericks, California League, 1991-2016

Got: **May 22, 2013; High Desert Mavericks 11, San Jose Giants 6**

How I got it: during my project, on a baseball vacation before the Mavs left

After the 2016 season, the High Desert Mavericks and Bakersfield Blaze franchises changed Class A-Advanced circuits from the California League to the Carolina League (see **Down East Wood Ducks [CURRENT]**). Both extended their last campaigns by making the playoffs, and the Mavs won the crown – leaving the Cali without a defending champion, and the Caro sort of with two, in 2017.

Opened in 1991 in one of the world's windiest spots, then-Mavericks Stadium drew the Riverside Red Wave north into the Mojave Desert. The first Cali team to draw more than 200,000 in one season nevertheless had a troubled stay. The ballpark's steep stands and open-girder design make it feel space-age, but it repelled big-league parent clubs because the windy conditions are so hard on pitchers. The ball club never recognized the city's 2006 naming-rights deal with Stater Bros. Markets, later selling *field* naming rights to Heritage Victor Valley Medical Group. In 2016, Adelanto

City Council terminated the lease over its dollar-a-year price – but an injunction left lease and team intact for what proved to be one last season. The departure ended both naming contracts.

It remains a baseball facility, hosting a team in the independent Pecos League.

Augusta, GA

Stadium name today: Lake Olmstead Stadium

Last stadium name while home to an affiliated team: Lake Olmstead Stadium

Organized Baseball teams: Augusta GreenJackets, South Atlantic League, 1995-2017

Got: **Aug. 22, 2009; Augusta GreenJackets 4, Charleston RiverDogs 2**

How I got it: before my project, on a weekend trip

The Class A GreenJackets left Olmstead for a new ballpark in North Augusta, SC, for the 2018 season (see **Augusta GreenJackets [CURRENT]**).

The city is redeveloping the "Lake O" into an amphitheater.

The brick-exterior ballpark is nice-looking from the outside but small and not very functional. With 4,822 seats, it never managed to hold even 6,000 fans for a game. Hot summer nights led the city to install six industrial fans. This was this piece of ground's second shot at baseball, having also been the site of Heaton Stadium 1988-94 (see **Augusta, GA [VISITED]**).

The move, which was actually east rather than north and less than four driving miles, ended – albeit nominally – an Augusta professional baseball history that dated to 1885 and included the legendary Ty Cobb's 1904 pro debut.

Not a golf fan? The team nickname refers to the fact that the winner of the Masters Tournament at the nearby Augusta National Golf Club gets a green blazer as well as a pile of green paper.

Bakersfield, CA

Stadium name today: Sam Lynn Ballpark

Last stadium name while home to an affiliated team: Sam Lynn Ballpark

Organized Baseball teams: Bakersfield Badgers, California League, 1941-42; Bakersfield Indians, California League, 1946-55; Bakersfield Boosters, California League, 1956; Bakersfield Bears, California League, 1957-67; Bakersfield Dodgers, California League, 1968-75; Bakersfield Outlaws, California League, 1978-79; Bakersfield Mariners, California League, 1982-83; Bakersfield Dodgers, California League, 1984-94; Bakersfield Blaze, California League, 1995-2016

Got: **May 20, 2013; Bakersfield Blaze 5, High Desert Mavericks 3**

How I got it: during my project, on a baseball vacation before the Blaze left

The Bakersfield Blaze franchise, with that of the High Desert Mavericks, moved from the Class A-Advanced California League to the also high-A Carolina League before the 2017 season (see **Fayetteville Woodpeckers [CURRENT]** and **Buies Creek, NC [LEGACY]**). Both teams extended their last Cali season by making the playoffs.

Opened in 1941 for the Bakersfield Badgers, the park once reported 8,175 – more than twice its seat count. Lynn, the local Coca-Cola bottler who popularized semi-pro and youth baseball in the San Joaquin Valley, joined San Francisco Seals President Charlie Graham to form a new league. Its April 1941 debut was bittersweet; Lynn died Dec. 1, 1940.

Its centerfield wall is just 354 feet from home, and it was the last affiliated ballpark where batters faced the setting sun. A sun-wall flopped because measurements taken in November weren't adjusted for that; the summer sun sets beside rather than behind it. Its last season was its 75th – 68th with a Cali team. My 100th *Get* remains a baseball facility, hosting a team in the independent Pecos League.

Birmingham, AL

Stadium name today: Rickwood Field

Last stadium name while home to an affiliated team: Rickwood Field

History in affiliated baseball: Birmingham Barons, Southern Association, 1910-61; Birmingham Barons, Southern League, 1964-65; Birmingham Athletics, Southern League, 1967-75; Birmingham Barons, Southern League, 1981-87

History in Negro League baseball:* Birmingham Stars, Negro Southern League, 1920 (probably partial); Birmingham Black Barons, Negro Southern League, 1920 (possibly 1921)-23; Birmingham Black Barons, Negro National League, 1924-25; Birmingham Black Barons, Negro Southern League, 1926; Birmingham Black Barons, Negro National League, 1927-1930; Birmingham Black Barons, Negro Southern League, 1931-36; Birmingham Black Barons, Negro American League, 1937-38, 1940-1955; Birmingham Giants, Negro American League, 1956; Birmingham Black Barons, Negro American League, 1957 (possibly during 1956 season)-60; Birmingham Black Barons, barnstorming, 1961-63

Got: May 29, 2013; Chattanooga Lookouts 7, Birmingham Barons 6

How I got it: my first *Get* of a park that was not then the home of an MiLB team; I began the project after hearing about this ballpark but before I could get to a "Rickwood Classic"

The Class Double-A Barons left Rickwood for a new ballpark in suburban Hoover, AL, for the 1988 season.

When I heard about the ballpark (see Chapter 10, **Rickwood Field**) and its annual Rickwood Classic – a Barons' regular-season game played there – I decided to go for the history of it. By the time I did, I had started this project; it was a while before I realized

---

*Years must be considered approximate. Negro Leagues history and records are sketchy and sometimes conflicting. For instance, after running across a newspaper article announcing that the Black Barons' new owner was changing their name to Giants in the 1956 season, I found no later references to Birmingham Giants. Birmingham's Negro

it should count. Was Rickwood ever the home of a Minor League team? Yes. Did I see a Minor League game there? Yes. Put it in the scorebook!

Industrialist A.H. "Rick" Woodward bought the Birmingham Coal Barons in February 1910, broke ground in April, and christened the park Aug. 18. The oldest existing stadium that ever housed professional ball joined the National Register of Historic Places in 1992. Arguably, it's the only one that ever hosted Negro leagues ball; Asheville's McCormick Field did as late as 1949 but was completely rebuilt in 1992. The Birmingham Black Barons played at Rickwood 1920-63; seventeen-year-old Willie Mays of nearby Westfield played his first games under contract with them in 1948.

Now also a museum, Rickwood appears in the films *Cobb* (1994), *Soul of the Game* (1996) and *42* (2013).

Buies Creek, NC
Stadium name today: Jim Perry Stadium
Last stadium name while home to an affiliated team: Jim Perry Stadium
Organized Baseball teams: Buies Creek Astros, 2017-18
Got: **July 3, 2017; Buies Creek Astros 6, Potomac Nationals 0**
How I got it: during my project, I included it in a baseball vacation because it was serving as the temporary home of the future Fayetteville Woodpeckers

An existing collegiate ballpark opened in the 1940s as Taylor Field, the home of Campbell University Fighting Camels baseball hosted the Buies (BOO-eez) Creek Astros of the Class A-Advanced Carolina League – a temporary team that bridged the two-year gap between the Bakersfield Blaze (see **Bakersfield, CA [LEGACY]**) of the same level's California League and the **Fayetteville Woodpeckers (CURRENT)** of the Carolina.

Southern League Museum's timeline shows gaps including the Black Barons folding during the 1932 season but nothing about when or how they resumed. There are also references to other nicknames, including Monarchs. Even exactly what year the leagues and/or teams ended varies from one source to another.

To get their high-A players out of a windy pitcher-killing ballpark, the Texas Rangers engineered moving the two teams from the Cali to the Caro for 2017. They bought their affiliate, and the Astros helped by buying another. The Rangers moved theirs into existing Grainger Stadium in Kinston, NC, but building a new ballpark for the Astros' team in Fayetteville took time.

Later renamed for its most baseball-famous alumnus, the stadium benefits from the Astros' visit because of improvements they made to it. The ball club made the playoffs in 2018, advancing to the championship and then winning a "series" that was shortened to one game by Hurricane Florence.

Charleston, WV

Stadium name today: None (redeveloped)

Last stadium name while home to an affiliated team: Watt Powell Park

Organized Baseball teams: Charleston Senators, Central League, 1949-51; Charleston Senators, American Association, 1952 (partial)-60; Charleston Marlins, International League, 1961 (partial); Charleston Indians, Eastern League, 1962-64; Charleston Charlies, International League, 1971-83; Charleston Wheelers, South Atlantic League, 1987-94; Charleston AlleyCats, South Atlantic League, 1995-2004

Got: **April 1990**

How I got it: before my project, I worked there

The Class A AlleyCats left Watt Powell for a new ballpark in Charleston (see **West Virginia Power [CURRENT]**) for the 2005 season. The railroad beyond right field now passes a cancer clinic and a community center.

Opened in 1948, its history was sporadic and colorful: The Central League collapsed in 1951; a club arrived *during* the 1952 season after the Class Triple-A Toledo Mud Hens flew their coop; 1960 was the only season the Washington Senators had a farm team named Senators; they didn't move in 1961 – they folded; the Marlins, flitting across four cities in three seasons, played most of 1961 here; the Indians moved to Reading, PA, as Reading's Red

Sox moved to Pittsfield, MA; the Charlies were named not for the city but for their owner's father.

In 1987, the SAL-expanding Wheelers resumed Charleston baseball history. I worked for them, and still get a kick out of two orientation day stories – a hurricane drove the 1961 franchise there from Puerto Rico (two months before that year's first); the New York Yankees' southern popularity results from their being the last MLB team to integrate (they did so *before* the Philadelphia Phillies, Detroit Tigers, and Boston Red Sox).

Charlotte, NC (see Fort Mill, SC [LEGACY])

Clearwater, FL
Stadium name today: Jack Russell Memorial Stadium
Last stadium name while home to an affiliated team: Jack Russell Memorial Stadium
Organized Baseball teams: Clearwater Phillies, Florida State League, 1985-2003; Dunedin Blue Jays, Florida State League, 2019
Got: **Aug. 3, 2019; Bradenton Marauders 5, Dunedin Blue Jays 1**
How I got it: while the Dunedin Blue Jays played here during their ballpark's renovation

The Class A-Advanced Phillies left Russell for a new nearby ballpark for the 2004 season (see **Clearwater Phillies [CURRENT]**).

Opened in 1955, it was named for the retired Major Leaguer who got it built, with "Memorial" added after he died in 1990.

Much of it was later torn down. It appears to have since been renovated, but it's unlikely to host MiLB permanently again. Not only would the now Clearwater Threshers have to allow it, what's left of the grandstand has no cover except the shade of the press box – which would be small for a high school field.

Long-time fans will enjoy the plaques honoring famous big-leaguers who played here – including, of course, Jack Russell.

I took advantage of the Jays' temporary usage to collect Russell as I did Rickwood Field, Henley Field, and Holman Stadium (see, respectively, **Birmingham, AL**, **Lakeland, FL**, and **Vero Beach, FL [all LEGACY]**), but rain forced three tries – the last not on a vacation but a weekend 2,000-mile round trip. It was worth it: this was my 200th professional (Majors and Minors) ballpark. Too bad it was a one-time thing – it also had the best bratwurst I've ever had at a baseball game.

Fort Mill, SC

Stadium name today: None (being redeveloped)

Last stadium name while home to an affiliated team: Knights Stadium

Organized Baseball teams: Charlotte Knights, Southern League, 1990-92; Charlotte Knights, International League, 1993-2013

Got: **May 28, 2012; Charlotte Knights 2, Rochester Red Wings 1**

How I got it: during my project

The Class Triple-A Knights left Knights for a new ballpark in Charlotte, NC, for the 2014 season (see **Charlotte Knights [CURRENT]**).

Just before the 1985 season, the Double-A Charlotte Orioles of the Southern League lost Jim Crockett Memorial Park to arson. Five seasons followed in temporary parks – the first on the Crockett site, then in 1989 in Fort Mill in the under-construction shadow of what would open in 1990 as Knights Castle.

Three seasons later, the International League expanded and Charlotte won a slot. Triple-A bumping Double-A, ironically, took Charlotte fans from watching future Cubs to future White Sox. They drew well only briefly, soon languishing in the league's bottom two in attendance, and finally abandoned their suburb when Charlotte opened a new Uptown stadium in 2014.

Cato Corporation bought and demolished the old park – originally for a distribution center, later changed to a mixed-use development.

Helena, MT

Stadium name today: Kindrick Legion Field

Last stadium name while home to an affiliated team: Kindrick Legion Field

Organized Baseball teams: Helena Brewers, Pioneer League, 1978-2000; Helena Brewers, Pioneer League, 2003-18

Got: **Aug. 17, 2014; Ogden Raptors 3, Helena Brewers 2**

How I got it: during my project, on the longest baseball trip I ever took – as far east as Portland, ME; as far west as Hillsboro, OR, as far north as Spokane, WA, and as far south as Colorado Springs, CO

The Rookie-Advanced Brewers left Kindrick for an existing ballpark in Colorado Springs, CO, for the 2019 season (see **Rocky Mountain Vibes, San Antonio Missions,** and **Amarillo Sod Poodles [CURRENT]**).

Kindrick remains a baseball facility, now primarily for American Legion baseball. On the National Register of Historic Places since 1988, the wooden ballpark is a time warp to 1932 Americana on a diamond. Its debut was a major media event. Then-Legion Field cost little, even in the Depression: American Legion Post 2 contributed $650, securing the original name and Legion ball use; promoters collected $900; businesses donated labor and materials; players bought the materials for Helena's first outfield fence. Its name at some point morphed into Memorial Park Field, before it was renamed in 1973 for Legion *and* baseball booster Ace Kindrick.

It first landed a professional club in 1978, but that team moved to Utah after the 1999 season. The second iteration of the H-Brewers happened when the Medicine Hat Blue Jays moved to the Montana city in 2003.

Hoover, AL

Stadium name today: Hoover Metropolitan Stadium

Last stadium name while home to an affiliated team: Regions Park

Organized Baseball teams: Birmingham Barons, 1988-2012

Got: **May 31, 2011; Birmingham Barons 4, Chattanooga Lookouts 1**

How I got it: before my project, while I was temporarily in the area

The Class Double-A Barons left the Hoover Met for a new ballpark in Birmingham for the 2013 season (see **Birmingham Barons [CURRENT]**). Hoover, a Birmingham suburb located about twenty miles to the south, was the home of Birmingham affiliated baseball 1988-2012.

The Met has hosted the collegiate Southeastern Conference baseball tournament every year but one since 1996 and through at least 2021. With New Orleans, Nashville, Jacksonville, and Memphis also in the bidding when the last contract expired in 2016, Hoover saved the seemingly lost event by announcing a plan to build the Hoover Metropolitan Complex – later renamed the

Finley Center – around it. The SEC members voted unanimously to keep the tourney in Hoover.

Helped by a White Sox non-prospect named Michael Jordan, it drew 467,868 in 1994 – still the most ever among current Southern League cities.

Regions Bank bought naming rights in 2007, calling it Regions Park until the Barons left and the city resumed the Hoover Met name.

Huntington, WV

Stadium name today: None (demolished)

Last stadium name while home to an affiliated team: St. Cloud Commons

Organized Baseball teams: Huntington Cubs, Appalachian League, 1990-94; River City Rumblers, Appalachian League, 1995

Got: **June 19, 1990; Princeton Patriots 1, Huntington Cubs 0**

How I got it: before my project, doing my first play-by-play of a professional game

The Rookie-Advanced Rumblers folded after one unaffiliated season following the loss of the Chicago Cubs as their parent club. They were the last Appy team that did not use a Major League nickname.

The Cubs had moved their Appy club from Wytheville, VA, into this eighty-year-old wooden ballpark with the expectation of a new stadium soon. When none materialized by 1994, they moved their rookie players to another league and the Appy league club played that one more Rumblin' season.

The early days of the 1990 inaugural season were electric, but the grandstand had terrible sight lines even from the press box and a white façade directly behind the plate made fielders lose sight of fly balls on the way up. The frustration was palpable – the Commons was never really ready for professional ball and had been passed up right along by the sporadic teams that did play in Huntington during some of those eighty years. Meanwhile,

Marshall University Thundering Herd baseball didn't have a serviceable home field either. It still doesn't, but in 2019 MU acquired a site on which to build one by 2021.

Huntsville, AL
Stadium name today: Joe W. Davis Municipal Stadium
Last stadium name while home to an affiliated team: Joe W. Davis Municipal Stadium
Organized Baseball teams: Huntsville Stars, 1985-2014
Got: **2005 or 2006**
How I got it: before my project, on a weekend trip

The Class Double-A Stars officially left Davis for a new ballpark in Biloxi, MS, after the 2014 season – but it took them half of 2015 to get there (see **Biloxi Shuckers [CURRENT]**).

Huntsville City Council is working on renovating it into a multi-use entertainment venue.

Once the "Crown Jewel of the Southern League," "The Joe" ended as the SL's oldest venue. Named for the longtime mayor who had it built, its demise was twice delayed. The Stars made the 2014 playoffs, then construction delays forced the 2015 Biloxi Shuckers to play their first twenty-five "home" games on the road – ten at their opponents' parks and fifteen at Davis. Only 224 fans attended its 2,226th and final professional baseball game.

"Stars" referred to Huntsville's place in the aerospace industry and the jazz classic whose title appears on Alabama license plates. The former Nashville Sounds moved into it when the Music City landed Triple-A ball in 1985. Meanwhile, Greater Huntsville's run without MiLB proved short: The Mobile BayBears were sold to a firm that is moving them to a ballpark in suburban Madison in 2020. Ground was broken June 9, 2018.

Jamestown, NY
Stadium name today: Russell E. Diethrick, Jr. Park

Last stadium name while home to an affiliated team: Russell E. Diethrick, Jr. Park

Organized Baseball teams: Jamestown Falcons, Pennsylvania-Ontario-New York League, 1941-57; Jamestown Tigers, New York-Pennsylvania League, 1961-65; Jamestown Dodgers, New York-Pennsylvania League, 1966; Jamestown Braves, New York-Pennsylvania League, 1967; Jamestown Falcons, New York-Pennsylvania League, 1968-72; Jamestown Expos, New York-Pennsylvania League, 1973; Jamestown Expos, New York-Pennsylvania League, 1977-93; Jamestown Jammers, New York-Pennsylvania League, 1994-2014

Got: **July 9, 2013; Jamestown Jammers 5, Batavia Muckdogs 2**

How I got it: during my project, before the Jammers left

The Class A-Short Season Jammers left Diethrick for a new ballpark in Granville, WV, for the 2015 season (see **West Virginia Black Bears [CURRENT]**).

Diethrick remains home to the Jamestown Community College Jayhawks, on whose campus it sits, and is a past and future Babe Ruth World Series site.

Opened in 1941, then-Jamestown Municipal Stadium's first professional team was the Jamestown Falcons of the Pennsylvania-Ontario-New York (PONY) League. That franchise folded in 1957, the same year the PONY League changed its name to the New York-Penn League after losing its last Ontario-based team. Another Jamestown gap, 1974-76, was filled by a team that moved to Vermont in 1994, but the Niagara Falls Rapids immediately stepped in as the Jammers. Five of the league's teams – more than a third – moved that year, but Jamestown was the only city to both lose and gain one.

In 1997, the city renamed the ballpark for a local banker who helped land the Rapids team and also made the place a Babe Ruth stalwart.

Kingsport, TN
Stadium name today: J. Fred Johnson Stadium

Last stadium name while home to an affiliated team: J. Fred Johnson Stadium

Organized Baseball teams: Kingsport Mets, Appalachian League, 1969-82; Kingsport Mets, Appalachian League, 1984-94

Got: June 29, 1990; Kingsport Mets 4, Huntington Cubs 0

How I got it: before my project, doing play-by-play

The Rookie-Advanced Mets left J-Fred for a new ballpark in Kingsport for the 1995 season (see **Kingsport Mets [CURRENT]**).

My working-broadcaster memory of J-Fred: a very impressive ballpark for an entry-level professional league – except for right field. The double-duty playpen hosted Kingsport's Dobyns-Bennett High School football and baseball as well as the K-Mets, which carried a big plus and a big minus. The plus was a Tennessee-high-school-football-quality facility from field to grandstands and press box, but – as often happens when squeezing baseball into a football stadium – the minus was a close outfield wall. At 301 feet, it was very short for professional ball.

It was a distraction to me as a broadcaster and probably to fans in the stands, and certainly made any left-handed hitter a home-run threat. Yet it was a very enjoyable place to work, or take in, a game.

Lakeland, FL

Stadium name today: Henley Field

Last stadium name while home to an affiliated team: Henley Field

Organized Baseball teams: Lakeland Highlanders, Florida State League, 1923-26; Lakeland Pilots, Florida International League, 1946-52; Lakeland Pilots, Florida State League, 1954-55; Lakeland Indians, Florida State League, 1960; Lakeland Giants, Florida State League, 1962; Lakeland Tigers, Florida State League, 1963-64; Lakeland Flying Tigers, Florida State League, 2002; Lakeland Flying Tigers, Florida State League, 2016

Got: Aug. 11, 2016; Lakeland Flying Tigers 12, Clearwater Threshers 2; Clearwater Threshers 1, Lakeland Flying Tigers 0

How I got it: during my project, included in a baseball vacation because the Flying Tigers played the 2016 season at Henley while Marchant was being renovated

The Class A-Advanced Tigers left the FSL after the 1964 season, but returned for the 1967 campaign in the Tigers' new Joker Marchant Stadium (see **Lakeland Flying Tigers [CURRENT]**).

Henley has also hosted Florida Southern College Moccasins baseball for decades. In late 2015, the city offered to sell it to the school for $1 million. The agreement came quickly but the closing was delayed until after the 2016 season so the Flying Tigers could use it during renovations to Marchant – repeating a 2002 arrangement.

Originally Athletic Field, it was renamed in 1942 for the man whose vision got it built in 1922. In addition to the Minors, it hosted spring training for the Cleveland Indians 1923-25 and the Tigers 1934-65. A 1962 Tigers-Yankees spring game packed 4,022 fans into a ballpark with a stated capacity of 1,000.

In 1966, the Tigers moved their spring games into just-opened Marchant. With their FSL club's return the next season, they became the first Major/Minor clubs to share a stadium – now a common practice.

Henley "plays" the home of the Tampigo Stogies in the film *Long Gone* (1987) and joined the National Register of Historic Places in 1997.

Las Vegas, NV

Stadium name today: Cashman Stadium

Last stadium name while home to an affiliated team: Cashman Stadium

Organized Baseball teams: Las Vegas Stars, Pacific Coast League, 1983-2000; Las Vegas 51s, 2001-18

Got: May 13, 2013; Albuquerque Isotopes 5, Las Vegas 51s 2

How I got it: during my project (the swing included eleven of the twelve California stadiums [already had Stockton], Arizona's only, and Nevada's only other)

The Class Triple-A 51s left "The Cash" for a new ballpark after the 2018 season (see **Las Vegas Aviators [CURRENT]**), simultaneously changing their nickname. Their new ballpark is in the Howard Hughes Corporation-planned community of Summerlin, technically part of Vegas. Summerlin was the famed recluse's mother's maiden name.

Cashman served double duty in 2018, also hosting the United Soccer League USL Championship's Las Vegas Lights FC – now the primary tenant. When the 51s left, its future held a renovation into a minor-league soccer-specific facility. A new idea has emerged: Las Vegas city council will rebuild Cashman if that will help the National Hockey League's Golden Knights' owner to land a Major League Soccer expansion club.

Cashman's baseball history includes Big League Weekend, which starting in 1993 brought two major-league teams to town from spring training for two games. The first BLW drew Cashman's baseball record 15,025. Cashman is also the first Minor League field to host a big-league opener: The Raiders' return to the Oakland Coliseum from Los Angeles forced renovations into the gap between the 1995 National Football League season and the 1996 MLB campaign. They didn't quite make it, running six games into baseball season.

Martinsville, VA

Stadium name today: Hooker Field

Last stadium name while home to an affiliated team: Hooker Field

Organized Baseball teams: Martinsville Phillies, Appalachian League, 1988-2000; Martinsville Astros, Appalachian League, 2001-03

Got: **July 23, 1990; Huntington Cubs 9, Martinsville Phillies 6**

How I got it: before my project, doing play-by-play

The Rookie-Advanced Astros left Hooker for a new ballpark in Greeneville, TN, for the 2004 season (see **Greeneville Reds [CURRENT]**).

Opened as English Field in the 1930s, it underwent what is variously reported as a renovation or a replacement five decades later. Martinsville-based Hooker Furniture helped finance that, and the ballpark was renamed Hooker Field. It landed Appy ball for 1988. Even after the renovation, folks around town and the league called it English Field – I didn't know the official name was Hooker Field until the team owner called it that in my pre-game show. (Which suggests, although I don't remember it, the signage wasn't very sign-ificant.)

I don't know what it was like before, of course, but even after the renovation it was a very basic ballpark even for a small-town low-Minors league – including the press box. It was as authentic a ballpark as I've worked in, though – even if I did feel like donning a 1940s felt hat with a "PRESS" card in the hatband.

Maumee, OH
Stadium name today: Ned Skeldon Stadium
Last stadium name while home to an affiliated team: Ned Skeldon Stadium
Organized Baseball teams: Toledo Mud Hens, International League, 1965-2001
Got: **May 14, 1989; Toledo Mud Hens 10, Syracuse Chiefs 6**
How I got it: before my project, during spare time on a weekend golf trip

The Class Triple-A Mud Hens left "The Ned" for a new ballpark in downtown Toledo for the 2002 season (see **Toledo Mud Hens [CURRENT]**). Their former diamond still hosts amateur baseball games, but much of the seating area is closed off and deteriorating.

This is where I saw my first Minor League game, in 1989. The county is actively considering its future. Opened as Lucas County Stadium, it was converted from its previous use as a racetrack at the county fairgrounds. In 1988, it was renamed for the Toledo vice mayor and Lucas County Commission president who sold that idea to local businesses in the hope of putting Toledo back into Minor League baseball after a nine-season absence. It worked, as the Richmond Virginians abandoned the commonwealth for Maumee and adopted the Mud Hen moniker that dated to the 1890s.

The nickname gained national fame during this team's run here, after TV's *M*A*S*H* (1972-83) made Cpl. Max Klinger a big fan.

Melbourne, FL (see Viera, FL [LEGACY])

Nashville, TN
Stadium name today: None (demolished)
Last stadium name while home to an affiliated team: Herschel Greer Stadium
Organized Baseball teams: Nashville Sounds, Southern League, 1978-84; Nashville Sounds, American Association, 1985-97; Nashville Sounds, Pacific Coast League, 1998-2014
Got: **1995 or 1996**
How I got it: before my project, while living there

The Class Triple-A Sounds left Greer for a new ballpark in Nashville for the 2015 season (see **Nashville Sounds [CURRENT]**). FTP is on mostly the same land as historic Sulphur Dell Ballpark (1870-1969).

After a failed redevelopment effort, Greer was demolished in 2019. Built for just $1 million in private funds on city land and named for the founder of Nashville's last previous professional baseball club, Greer opened in 1978 as two Double-A franchises moved from the Eastern League to the Southern. The famous guitar scoreboard was actually just a wooden frame around a regular scoreboard – much improved at FTP.

Greer saw more than its share of history: top Southern League attendance, 1978-84; led all Minors in attendance, 380,159,

1979; Southern League all-time record attendance, 575,676, 1980; largest crowd, 22,315, 1982; Triple-A arrives, as Evansville Triplets move to Nashville, 1985; back-to-back no-hitters by Randy Johnson of Indianapolis and Jack Armstrong of Nashville, 1987; guitar-shaped scoreboard, 1993; a second team, the displaced Double-A Charlotte Knights, 1993-94; perfect game by John Wasdin, 2003; and a unique cross-affiliation as the Sounds served as the Brewers' top affiliate even as the Milwaukee Admirals did so for the National Hockey League's Nashville Predators, 2005-14.

New Britain, CT

Stadium name today: New Britain Stadium

Last stadium name while home to an affiliated team: New Britain Stadium

Organized Baseball teams: Hardware City Rock Cats, Eastern League, 1996; New Britain Rock Cats, Eastern League, 1997-2015

Got: **July 24, 2014; New Britain Rock Cats 7, Portland Sea Dogs 1**

How I got it: during my project, on a baseball vacation before the Rock Cats left

The Class Double-A Red Sox left New Britain for a new ballpark in Hartford, CT, after the 2015 season – but didn't get into the place until the 2017 campaign (see **Hartford Yard Goats [CURRENT]**).

After Hartford announced the ballpark in 2014, the Minnesota Twins promptly dropped the Cats. Did they see something coming? Construction problems pushed the re-christened Yard Goats to the road for the entire 2016 campaign. Their territorial rights prevent affiliated ball in NBS, but it quickly landed the independent Bees. That and hard feelings kept it from being the Goats' stopgap. Their last Friday game at NBS drew a stadium record 8,672 and the Sunday finale ended on a fifteenth-inning walk-off home run.

"Rock Cats" long pre-dated the Rockies and was probably for Rockwell Park, next to the then-Bristol Red Sox' 1973-82 home.

Bristol was the franchise's seventh city in nineteen years; the next forty-three saw just two cities, three stadiums, two parent clubs and two nicknames. Beehive Stadium hosted the first thirteen NB seasons; NBS was built next door to comply with Minor League standards enacted in 1990.

Oneonta, NY

Stadium name today: Damaschke Field

Last stadium name while home to an affiliated team: Damaschke Field

Organized Baseball teams: Oneonta Red Sox, New York-Pennsylvania League, 1966; Oneonta Yankees, New York-Pennsylvania League, 1967-98; Oneonta Tigers, New York-Pennsylvania League, 1999-2009

Got: **between June 22-28, 2002**

How I got it: before my project, while on an umpiring assignment

The Class A-Short Season Tigers left Damaschke for an existing ballpark in Norwich, CT, for the 2010 season (see **Norwich Sea Unicorns [CURRENT]**).

Elm Park opened on the Damaschke site in 1905, with the current grandstand erected in 1938 and the new name – for long-time Oneonta sports and recreation figure E.C. "Dutch" Damaschke – following in 1969.

In 1991, the then-Yankees started playing one game per season at nearby Cooperstown's Doubleday Field but ended the series after their first season in Connecticut. That move was the last domino of a series triggered by the Richmond Braves' 2009 shift to suburban Atlanta. In 2010, the Connecticut Defenders moved to Richmond and the O-Tigers went to Norwich.

Damaschke's Minor League era included a few Triple-A games in 1969, pinch hitting after a fire damaged the Syracuse Chiefs' home.

Princeton, WV

Stadium name today: None (replaced)

Last stadium name while home to an affiliated team: H.P. Hunnicutt Stadium

Organized Baseball teams: Princeton Pirates, Appalachian League, 1988-89; Princeton Patriots, Appalachian League, 1990; Princeton Reds, Appalachian League, 1991-96; Princeton Devil Rays, Appalachian League, 1997-99

Got: **July 27, 1990; Princeton Patriots 8, Huntington Cubs 3**

How I got it: before my project, doing play-by-play

The Rookie-Advanced Devil Rays stayed on the same site when their ballpark was rebuilt in 1999. The entire wooden structure except for the four outfield light poles was replaced in concrete and steel. If you've been to the current ballpark, you've been to the site of this one.

Princeton and nearby league-mate Bluefield are two of the smallest cities in the minors. Wondering what attracted *two* professional teams? I'll offer some educated speculation:

The Appy won two expansion franchises in 1988. (Leagues whose teams play almost every day in series must have an even number. That's not a rule; it's a practicality.) Martinsville had hosted Appy teams with varying levels of success and added a sixth city of 15,000+ in an area that has lots of little cities and few big ones. Princeton, on the other hand, was smaller than any in the circuit except Wytheville, VA – which would lose that franchise in 1990. The league had recently stretched its footprint, increasing everybody's travel expenses, with the 1986 entry of Burlington, NC. Also, of logically possible places, only Princeton had never failed in the Appy League. Of course, it had never been in it. Finally, it built a stadium.

Savannah, GA

Stadium name today: William L. Grayson Stadium

Last stadium name while home to an affiliated team: William L. Grayson Stadium

Organized Baseball teams: Savannah Indians, South Atlantic League, 1941-42, 1946-53; Savannah Athletics, South Atlantic League, 1954-55; Savannah Redlegs, South Atlantic League, 1956-58; Savannah Reds, South Atlantic League, 1959; Savannah Pirates, South Atlantic League, 1960; Savannah White Sox, South Atlantic League, 1962; Savannah Senators, Southern League, 1968-69; Savannah Indians, Southern League, 1970; Savannah Braves, Southern League/Dixie Association, 1971; Savannah Braves, Southern League, 1983; Savannah Cardinals, South Atlantic League, 1984-95; Savannah Sand Gnats, South Atlantic League, 1996-2015

Got: Aug. 27, 2011; Savannah Sand Gnats 5, Charleston RiverDogs 3

How I got it: before my project, on a weekend trip

The Class A Sand Gnats left Grayson for a new ballpark in Columbia, SC, for the 2016 season (see **Columbia Fireflies [CURRENT]**).

Municipal Stadium opened on the site in 1926, but a 1940 hurricane left just two sections of bleachers and the concrete outfield wall standing. Can a ballpark that had been rebuilt from that be considered the same ballpark, repaired?

City Council named the rebuild for the Georgia National Guard General, Spanish-American War veteran and national Fraternal Order of Eagles president who led it. World War II suspended the project, and Grayson died before it resumed; some brickwork sat unfinished for seventy years.

With its neighborhood, it joined the National Register of Historic Places in 1999. Savannah High School and Benedictine Academy played an annual Thanksgiving Day game there 1927-59.

Savannah professional baseball dates to 1904, continuously since 1968. Late in the 1962 season, racial tensions drove that franchise to Lynchburg, VA.

Toledo, OH (see Maumee, OH)

Tucson, AZ

Stadium name today: Kino Veterans Memorial Stadium

Last stadium name while home to an affiliated team: Kino Veterans Memorial Stadium

Organized Baseball teams: Tucson Sidewinders, Pacific Coast League, 1998-2008; Tucson Padres, Pacific Coast League, 2011-13

Got: **May 14, 2013; Tucson Padres 12, Round Rock Express 1**

How I got it: during my project, with a great deal of luck: the Tucson Sidewinders moved to Reno three years before I started the project, but the Padres' temporary stay provided a second chance

The Class Triple-A Padres left Kino for a new ballpark in El Paso, TX, for the 2014 season (see **El Paso Chihuahuas [CURRENT]**).

They never intended to be a permanent Tucson team, but they were a good fit for an empty stadium. Kino had lost the Tucson Sidewinders to Reno, NV, after the 2008 campaign (see **Reno Aces [CURRENT]**), and the Padres needed a temporary home because of a kerfuffle in Oregon – but they didn't end up where they intended. When the Portland Beavers lost their ballpark, their parent Padres bought them to move them to suburban San Diego – via Tucson, starting in 2011, while Escondido built a stadium. When that playpen fell through, the Padres sold the club to a group that moved it to El Paso – which had lost its Double-A Diablos to Springfield, MO, in 2005.

Yet Kino had one last hurrah: The new El Paso stadium wasn't ready at the start of the 2014 season, so Kino hosted the Chihuahuas' season-opening four-game homestand that April.

Vero Beach, FL

Stadium name today: Holman Stadium

Last stadium name while home to an affiliated team: Holman Stadium

Organized Baseball teams: Vero Beach Dodgers, Florida State League, 1980-2006; Vero Beach Devil Rays, Florida State League, 2007-08

Got: April 15, 2016; St. Lucie Mets 4, Brevard County Manatees 0

How I got it: during my project, the stadium began hosting a regular-season Florida State League game each April 15 as the Jackie Robinson Celebration Game; I'm embarrassed to admit I didn't recognize this was an opportunity under my own rules until its second year

The Class A-Advanced Devil Rays left Holman for a just-rebuilt ballpark in Port Charlotte, FL, for the 2009 season (see **Charlotte Stone Crabs [CURRENT]**).

Holman had been their home for only two seasons. The Vero Beach Dodgers played at Holman from 1980 until the Los Angeles Dodgers moved their spring- and Minor League operations from Florida to Arizona. The Dodgers' roots go back even further, to 1951, when Holman and its complex became the Dodgers' spring-training home. Bud Holman convinced Dodgers' owner Walter O'Malley to build Dodgertown on an old naval base in 1951, three years after he made Vero Beach the Dodgers' spring home.

After losing the Rays, it hosted camps, tournaments including the collegiate Dodgertown Classic, and since 2014 the Jackie Robinson Celebration Game. Peter O'Malley, Walter's son, saved it in 2012 – expanding it, renaming it Historic Dodgertown-Vero Beach and landing the Minor League Baseball Umpire Training Academy.

Major League Baseball leased and now operates Holman and Dodgertown. MLB renamed the latter The Jackie Robinson Training Complex.

Viera, FL

Stadium name today: USSSA Space Coast Stadium and Athletic Complex

Last stadium name while home to an affiliated team: Space Coast Stadium

Organized Baseball teams: Brevard County Manatees, Florida State League, 1994-2016

Got: July 6, 2012; Brevard County Manatees 10, Tampa Yankees 2

How I got it: during my project, on a baseball vacation before the Manatees left

A classic game of musical ballparks turned Space Coast Stadium from hosting professional to amateur baseball.

The Brewer-affiliated Class A-Advanced Manatees shared it with Washington Nationals spring and rookie Gulf Coast League operations until the latter moved into a new shared complex in West Palm Beach, FL. Brevard County promptly leased the then-Carl Barger Baseball Complex to the United States Sports Specialty Association, and the Manatees moved to the very Kissimmee venue the USSSA had vacated. The USSSA and the county renovated the Barger complex into not only an amateur sports facility but also USSSA headquarters.

Originally just Space Coast Stadium, it opened in 1994 as the spring home of the then-Florida Marlins – who later swapped sites with the Montreal Expos, now the Nats. It was the only one hosting FSL and spring games of different organizations. The name and model space shuttle out front salute Cape Canaveral, whose launch pad is just thirteen air miles away.

Winston-Salem, NC

Stadium name today: Gene Hooks Field at David F. Couch Ballpark

Last stadium name while home to an affiliated team: Ernie Shore Field

Organized Baseball teams: Winston-Salem Twins, Carolina League, 1956; Winston-Salem Red Birds, Carolina League, 1957-60; Winston-Salem Red Sox, Carolina League, 1961-83; Winston-Salem Spirits, Carolina League, 1984-94; Winston-Salem Warthogs, Carolina League, 1995-2008; Winston-Salem Dash, Carolina League, 2009-10

Got: July 15, 1990; Kinston Indians 11, Winston-Salem Spirits 6

How I got it: before my project, while doing play-by-play, we got rained out of a road game; our manager arranged for our players to work out here (two hours by car, more of course by bus) after Winston-Salem's home game, and some of the coaches and us media folks saw the last few innings of the Spirits vs. the Kinston Indians; unless the Dash play a throwback game here or one of the many teams in the area uses it during a renovation, this is the *Go-Back* I can never complete

The Class A-Advanced Dash left then-Ernie Shore Field for a new ballpark in Winston-Salem during the 2010 season (see **Winston-Salem Dash [CURRENT]**). Their former home – known as Ernie Shore Field during its professional era – replaced South Side Park after it burned down in 1955.

In 2008, in conjunction with the originally planned moving date, Wake Forest University bought Shore and renamed it Gene Hooks Field at Wake Forest Baseball Park. Hooks was a former Demon Deacons' athletics director. During a subsequent renovation, the school renamed the ballpark again, for a key donor to the project. Ernie Shore played with Babe Ruth, served as Forsyth County sheriff, and led the effort to replace South Side Park after it burned down. In fact, because construction of the new park ran late, WFU hosted the Dash in their old playpen for the 2009 season and most of the first half of the 2010.

It was a filming location for the movie *Mr. Destiny* (1990).

Yakima, WA

Stadium name today: Yakima County Stadium

Last stadium name while home to an affiliated team: Yakima County Stadium

Organized Baseball teams: Yakima Bears, Northwest League, 1990-2012

Got: **Aug. 17, 2012; Yakima Bears 6, Spokane Indians 1**

How I got it: during my project, I read that the Bears had signed to move to Hillsboro, OR, and I decided to see a game there while I could – so I used a long weekend to fly to Seattle to see not only Yakima but also the Everett AquaSox, Vancouver Canadians, and Tacoma Rainiers

The Class A-Short Season Bears left Yakima for a new ballpark in Hillsboro, OR, for the 2012 season (see **Hillsboro Hops [CURRENT]**). That was something of a homecoming; nearby Salem, OR, was the original home of the franchise – then the Senators – that moved into "The Yak" and became the Bears.

They were in their fourth season in Yakima when the stadium opened in 1993, having played those early seasons at Parker Field, which opened in 1937. A stadium that looks better from the outside than on the inside, The Yak's seating area reminded me of the county fair grandstands where I grew up. The 2012 move was a long time coming: The club spent several years calling for either major renovations or a new ballpark while simultaneously scouring the league landscape for places willing to build one. Yakima County Stadium had the smallest capacity in the league and was seen as the reason the Bears were reportedly losing money.

During the first year of my project, I learned this stadium was in its last season – so I hopped a jet over Labor Day weekend and knocked off four Pacific Northwest ballparks.

III. VISITED (Ballparks That Have Been a Regular Host Of MiLB Which I Have Visited But NOT Seen MiLB Action)

Albuquerque, NM

Stadium name today: None (redeveloped)

Last stadium name while home to an affiliated team: Albuquerque Sports Stadium

Organized Baseball teams: Albuquerque Dodgers, Texas League, 1969-70; Albuquerque Dodgers, Dixie Association, 1971; Albuquerque Dukes, Pacific Coast League, 1972-2000

How I got it: during my project, seeing a game in its replacement

This ballpark was replaced on the same site for the 2003 season (see **Albuquerque Isotopes [CURRENT]**). If you've been to the current ballpark, you've been to the site of this one.

Opened in 1969, it hosted Los Angeles Dodgers' prospects: Every 1963-2000 Albuquerque team was a Dodgers' farm club, and again in Isotopes Park 2010-15.

Despite the above team listings, Albuquerque didn't change leagues in three straight seasons. After the 1970 campaign, coincidentally and luckily, both the Texas and Southern leagues found themselves with an odd number of teams – making tough scheduling in leagues where all teams play most days. Odd + odd = even, so the leagues – whose champions sometimes held a "Dixie World Series" – played an interlocutory schedule as the Dixie Association in 1971. Another coincidence explains 1972, when Albuquerque landed a Pacific Coast League team and its Texas League franchise moved to El Paso.

Alexandria, LA

Stadium name today: None (demolished)

Last stadium name while home to an affiliated team: Bringhurst Field

Organized Baseball teams: Alexandria Aces, Evangeline League, 1934-42; Alexandria Aces, Evangeline League, 1946-57; Alexandria Aces, Texas League, 1972-75

How I got it: during my project, while passing through on a work assignment

The Class Double-A Aces left Bringhurst for an existing ballpark in Amarillo, TX, for the 1976 season (see **Northwest Arkansas Naturals [CURRENT]**).

As the above history shows, the four-year Alexandria tour of the franchise that would become the NWA Naturals was Bringhurst's swan song of affiliated baseball.

I visited Bringhurst two years before its demolition, and it looked like a typical ballpark of its era – which is to say I thoroughly enjoyed seeing it but I wouldn't want to try to turn a profit in it. It did have independent teams trying to do so for many of its non-affiliated years, but despite much effort to repurpose it after the indy Alexandria Aces played their last game in 2014 – followed by a fire that burned down a clubhouse and the office – it was finally torn down in 2017.

Asheville, NC

Stadium name today: None (redeveloped)

Last stadium name while home to an affiliated team: McCormick Field

Organized Baseball teams: Asheville Tourists, South Atlantic League, 1924-30; Asheville Tourists, Piedmont League, 1931-42; Asheville Tourists, Tri-State League, 1946-49; Asheville Tourists, Tri-State League, 1950-55; Asheville Tourists, South Atlantic League, 1959-63; Asheville Tourists, Southern League, 1964-66; Asheville Tourists, Carolina League, 1967; Asheville Tourists, Southern League, 1968-70; Asheville Tourists, Dixie Association, 1971; Asheville Orioles, South Atlantic League, 1972-75; Asheville Tourists, Western Carolinas League, 1976-79; Asheville Tourists, South Atlantic League, 1980-91

How I got it: during my project, seeing games in its replacement

This ballpark was replaced on the same site for the 1992 season (see **Asheville Tourists [CURRENT]**). If you've been to the current ballpark, you've been to the site of this one.

Two items in the above history that appear to be team moves are not, and one that may not is: In 1964, the Class Double-A South Atlantic League changed its name to the Southern League; in 1980, the Class A Western Carolinas League changed its name to the South Atlantic League; although Asheville had teams in both 1975 and '76, they were not the same franchise. When the Class Double-A Southern League club moved to Charlotte, NC, it was seamlessly replaced by moving the Class A SAL franchise that played in 1975 in Anderson, SC, to Asheville in '76 – same name both years, but different leagues and, for that matter, levels.

Auburn, NY

Stadium name today: None (redeveloped)

Last stadium name while home to an affiliated team: Falcon Park

Organized Baseball teams: Auburn Bouleys, Canadian-American League, 1938; Auburn Colts, Canadian-American League, 1940; Auburn Cuyugas, Border League, 1946-51; Auburn Yankees, New York-Pennsylvania League, 1958-61; Auburn Mets, New York-Pennsylvania League, 1962-66; Auburn Twins, New York-Pennsylvania League, 1967-71; Auburn Phillies, New York-Pennsylvania League, 1972-77; Auburn Sunsets, New York-Pennsylvania League, 1978; Auburn Red Stars, New York-Pennsylvania League, 1979; Auburn Americans, New York-Pennsylvania League, 1980; Auburn Astros, New York-Pennsylvania League, 1982-94

How I got it: during my project, seeing a game in its replacement

This ballpark was replaced on the same site for the 1995 season (see **Auburn Doubledays [CURRENT]**). If you've been to the current ballpark, you've been to the site of this one.

Augusta, GA

Stadium name today: None (redeveloped)

Last stadium name while home to an affiliated team: Heaton Field

Organized Baseball teams: Augusta Pirates, South Atlantic League, 1988-94

How I got it: during my project, seeing games in its replacement

This ballpark was replaced on the same site for the 1995 season (see **Augusta, GA [VISITED]**). If you've been to the current ballpark, you've been to the site of this one.

Batavia, NY

Stadium name today: None (redeveloped)

Last stadium name while home to an affiliated team: Dwyer Stadium

Organized Baseball teams: Batavia Clippers, Pennsylvania-Ontario-New York League, 1939-53; Batavia Indians, New York-Pennsylvania League, 1957-59; Batavia Pirates, New York-Pennsylvania League, 1961-65; Batavia Trojans, New York-Pennsylvania League, 1966-87; Batavia Clippers, New York-Pennsylvania League, 1988-95

How I got it: during my project, seeing a game in its replacement

This ballpark – opened as State Street Park, renamed for General Douglas MacArthur during World War II and renamed again for long-time team president Edward Dwyer in 1973 – was replaced on the same site for the 1996 season (see **Batavia Muckdogs [CURRENT]**). If you've been to the current ballpark, you've been to the site of this one.

Baton Rouge, LA

Stadium name today: Pete Goldsby Field

Last stadium name while home to an affiliated team: Pete Goldsby Field

Organized Baseball teams: Baton Rouge Rebels, Evangeline League, 1956-57

How I got it: during my project, while passing through on a work assignment

The Class C Rebels – in a level that hasn't existed since the Minors' 1964 reorganization – folded with the Evangeline League after the 1957 season.

Earlier Baton Rouge affiliated teams – most of them called Red Sticks, the pluralized English translation of the French *baton rouge* – played at City Park until Goldsby opened in 1956, but the team lasted just two more seasons there. Based on my 2015 visit, I would have to say Goldsby was a pretty rudimentary Minor League park even at its debut.

The city also had one season in Class A, 1976, in the Gulf States League that lasted only that one year – but it played at Louisiana State University's Alex Box Stadium. This may surprise non-Southerners, but Minor League ball would be a tough sell in the same city as the LSU Bulldogs.

Bradenton, FL

Stadium name today: None (redeveloped)

Last stadium name while home to an affiliated team: McKechnie Field

Organized Baseball teams: Bradenton Growers, Florida State League, 1923-24; Bradenton Growers, Florida State League, 1926

How I got it: during my project, seeing a game in its replacement

This ballpark was replaced on the same site with, originally, the same name for the 1993 season, although it wouldn't land a Minor League team for another few years (see **Bradenton**

Marauders [CURRENT]). If you've been to the current ballpark, you've been to the site of this one.

After losing the Growers of the then-Class D Florida State League, the site housed only spring-training, winter and rookie ball until the Sarasota Reds became the Bradenton Marauders in 2010. Along the way, it was renamed for "Deacon" Bill McKechnie in 1962.

Bristol, VA

Stadium name today: None (redeveloped)

Last stadium name while home to an affiliated team: Shaw Stadium

Organized Baseball teams: Bristol Twins, Appalachian League, 1940-55

How I got it: during my project, while go-backing Boyce Cox Field at DeVault Memorial Stadium in Bristol

The Class D Twins folded after the 1955 season.

A factory now occupies the land, but a plaque commemorates the ballpark – or, rather, an incredible accomplishment there. It is near but not on the actual site, probably either because of the factory or to put it roadside where the public can see it.

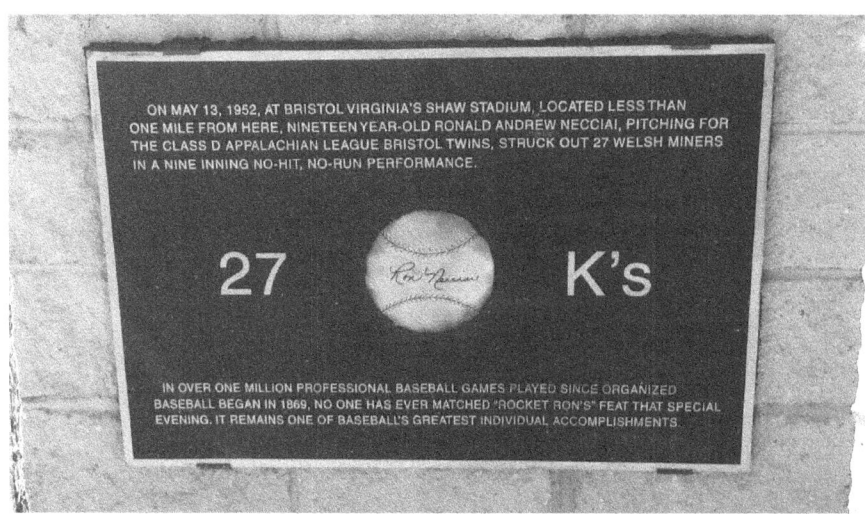

Ron Necciai, a kid with a history of stomach trouble, faced the Welch Miners May 13, 1952, and struck out twenty-seven batters while throwing a no-hitter. Four men reached base: one walk, one error – one of only two balls batted into fair territory in the entire nine innings – one hit batter, and one uncaught third strike. The last came in the ninth, allowing Necciai to record four Ks that inning.

In his next start, Necciai struck out twenty-four in a two-hitter. He lasted only six weeks in big-league baseball; his stomach problems stopped after he quit playing.

Burlington, IA

Stadium name today: None (redeveloped)

Last stadium name while home to an affiliated team: Community Field

Organized Baseball teams: Burlington Indians, Central Association, 1947-49; Burlington Flints, Illinois-Indiana-Iowa League, 1952-53; Burlington Bees, Illinois-Indiana-Iowa League, 1954-61; Burlington Bees, Midwest League, 1962-71

How I got it: during my project, seeing a game in its replacement

This ballpark was replaced on the same site for the 1973 season (see **Burlington Bees [CURRENT]**). If you've been to the current ballpark, you've been to the site of this one.

Canton, OH

Stadium name today: Thurman Munson Stadium

Last stadium name while home to an affiliated team: Thurman Munson Stadium

Organized Baseball teams: Canton-Akron Indians, Eastern League, 1989-96

How I got it: during my project, while seeking advice on getting into play-by-play

The Class Double-A Indians left Munson for a new ballpark in nearby Akron just eight seasons after it opened (see **Akron RubberDucks [CURRENT]**) – the shortest tenure I've found for a newly opened stadium that was not intended to be a temporary home.

The Canton ballpark was of course named for the Yankee great who, less than ten years before it opened, died when he crashed his private airplane while practicing landings at Akron-Canton Airport. It continues to host baseball in the form of independent professional, collegiate and high school games.

This was a harbinger of something now common in professional baseball: a farm team almost in the back yard of its major-league parent club. One advantage, aside from the obvious savings in travel time and costs, is the ability to have an injured big-leaguer rehabilitate nearby.

Casper, WY
Stadium name today: Mike Lansing Field
Last stadium name while home to an affiliated team: Mike Lansing Field
Organized Baseball teams: Casper Rockies, Pioneer League, 2002-07; Casper Ghosts, Pioneer League, 2008-11
How I got it: during my project, while passing by on a baseball trip

The Rookie-Advanced Ghosts left Lansing for a just-renovated ballpark in Grand Junction, CO, for the 2012 season (see **Grand Junction Rockies [CURRENT]**). Lansing had opened for them in 2002, placing it among the newly built ballparks that kept their professional team for the shortest time.

The season before Lansing opened, the Butte Copper Kings moved to Casper and joined the Rockies' farm system. They originally used the Rockies' nickname, but adopted "Ghosts" in 2008. The Rockies bought the Ghosts after the 2010 season and moved them to Grand Junction effective with the 2012 campaign.

Lansing remains a baseball facility, primarily hosting American Legion and summer collegiate games.

Charleston, WV

Stadium name today: None (redeveloped)

Last stadium name while home to an affiliated team: Kanawha Park

Organized Baseball teams: Charleston Senators, Middle Atlantic League, 1931-42

Got: **April 1990**

How I got it: before my project, I worked there

This ballpark was replaced on the same site in 1948 (see **Charleston, WV [LEGACY]**). If you've been to the site of since-demolished Watt Powell Park, you've been to the site of this one.

Opened in 1917, it replaced Wehrle Park in the East End but did not land a professional team until 1931. At some point, it became known as Exhibition Park. The wooden ballpark lost much of its grandstand to a 1939 fire, initially causing the team to play many more games away than home and in 1942 spelling another end to pro baseball in it and Charleston.

Former minor-league player and forever baseball enthusiast Watt Powell keyed building not only this ballpark but the successor that would open the year after his death and wear his name until it was torn down in 2005.

Columbia, SC

Stadium name today: Capital City Stadium

Last stadium name while home to an affiliated team: Capital City Stadium

Organized Baseball teams: Columbia Mets, South Atlantic League, 1991-92; Capital City Bombers, South Atlantic League, 1993-2004

How I got it: during my project, while passing through on a work assignment

The Class A Bombers left Cap-City for an existing ballpark in Greenville, SC, for the 2005 season (see **Greenville Drive [CURRENT]**).

Although the name as well as the land carried over, the 1927 ballpark was entirely rebuilt in 1991. The Shelby Mets moved into "The Cap" in 1983, returning affiliated baseball to town after a twenty-two-season absence. In 1993, the Columbia Mets changed their name to Capital City Bombers – for the Doolittle Raiders, the World War II bomber crew that trained in Columbia before its historic raid on Tokyo.

The ballpark was optioned to developers who were unable to develop anything and have since re-optioned it, but professional ball returned to town in a new downtown stadium opened in 2016.

Columbia, SC

Stadium name today: None (redeveloped)

Last stadium name while home to an affiliated team: Capital City Stadium

Organized Baseball teams: Columbia Comers, South Atlantic League, 1927-30; Columbia Senators, South Atlantic League, 1936-37; Columbia Reds, South Atlantic League, 1938-42; Columbia Reds, South Atlantic League, 1946-55; Columbia Gems, South Atlantic League, 1956-57; Columbia Reds, South Atlantic League, 1960-61; Columbia Mets, South Atlantic League, 1983-90;

How I got it: visited its replacement, while passing through on a work assignment

The Class A Bombers' home ground was the same in 1990 and '91, but its stadium was not.

The original Capital City Stadium, opened in 1927, was entirely rebuilt during the 1990-91 off-season. If you've been to its replacement, you've been to the site of this one.

The replacement, now abandoned in favor of a new downtown ballpark, is under contract for sale and redevelopment.

Duluth, MN

Stadium name today: Wade Municipal Stadium

Last stadium name while home to an affiliated team: Wade Municipal Stadium

Organized Baseball teams: Duluth Dukes, Northern League, 1941-42; Duluth Marine Iron, Twin Ports League, 1943; Duluth Dukes, Twin Ports League, 1943; Duluth Heralds, 1943; Duluth Dukes, Northern League, 1946-55; Duluth-Superior White Sox, Northern League, 1956-58; Duluth-Superior Dukes, Northern League, 1959-70

How I got it: before my project, while working public address

The Class A-Short Season Dukes' league was decertified by Minor League Baseball after the 1970 season.

Opened in 1941 as Duluth All-Sports Municipal Stadium, "The Wade" was renamed in 1955 for the owner of the Dukes two years after his death. I confess I'd forgotten about this park, until I remembered while editing that I provided stadium public address there during a Little League post-season tournament sometime in the late 1970s. I knew it had hosted professional ball, but had to confirm that its history ever included affiliated ball.

It was then somewhat in disrepair, but has since been renovated. It was fairly impressive to a kid just past twenty who had never been in a Minor League park, and in retrospect I think it must have been a class ballpark at one time – and may be again now.

Durham, NC

Stadium name today: Durham Athletic Park

Last stadium name while home to an affiliated team: Durham Athletic Park

Organized Baseball teams: Durham Bulls, Piedmont League, 1940-43; Durham Bulls, Carolina League, 1945-67; Raleigh-Durham Mets, Carolina League, 1968; Raleigh-Durham Phillies, Carolina League, 1969; Raleigh-Durham Triangles,

Carolina League, 1970-71; Durham Bulls, Carolina League, 1980-94

How I got it: during my project, while getting Durham Bulls Athletic Park in Durham

The Class A-Advanced Bulls left Durham Athletic Park for a new ballpark a few blocks away for the 1995 season (see **Myrtle Beach Pelicans, Durham Bulls [CURRENT]**).

El Toro Park, opened on the site of the DAP in 1926, was destroyed by a 1939 fire. The film *Bull Durham* (1988) gave its replacement fame – the first Class A ballpark to draw 300,000 – but the Bulls soon outgrew it. The city built Durham *Bulls* Athletic Park, which soon landed Triple-A ball.

The historic DAP remains a working field and museum. The Triple-A Bulls took a swing at nostalgia with a 2010 and 2011 DAP game, but no annual series like the Rickwood Classic (see **Birmingham, AL [LEGACY]**), resulted. The Foster and West Geer Streets Historic District, including the DAP, joined the National Register of Historic Places in 2013. It screened *Bull Durham* for the film's 30th anniversary in 2018.

Durham, NC

Stadium name today: None (redeveloped)

Last stadium name while home to an affiliated team: Durham Athletic Park

Organized Baseball teams: Durham Bulls, Piedmont League, 1926-33; Durham Bulls, Piedmont League, 1936-39

How I got it: during my project, seeing a game in its replacement

This ballpark, opened as El Toro Park in 1926 and renamed when the city of Durham acquired it in 1933, was replaced on the same site after it was destroyed by fire in June 1939. If you've been to the ballpark we saw in the film *Bull Durham* (1988), you've been to the site of this one. Its concrete and steel grandstand was thrown up in the two weeks after the fire, allowing the Bulls to continue their campaign, and the rest was built during the 1939-40 off-season.

Elmira, NY

Stadium name today: Dunn Field Municipal Stadium

Last stadium name while home to an affiliated team: Dunn Field Municipal Stadium

Organized Baseball teams: Elmira Pioneers, Eastern League, 1939-55; Elmira Pioneers, New York-Pennsylvania League, 1957-61; Elmira Pioneers, Eastern League, 1962-70; Elmira Royals, Eastern League, 1971; Elmira Pioneers, Eastern League, 1972; Elmira Pioneers, New York-Pennsylvania League, 1973-95

How I got it: during my project, while passing through on a baseball trip

The Class A-Short Season Pioneers left Dunn for just-renovated Stoklosa Alumni Field in Lowell, MA, in 1996 (see **Lowell Spinners [CURRENT]**) – a stop-gap while its new ballpark was built.

As the above history shows, Elmira baseball fans were quite used to a professional ball club named the Pioneers. Dunn, opened in 1939, is one of the few American ballparks that date pretty much as-is to the 1930s. It is at least the third sports playpen on the site, dating back to no later than the late nineteenth century. Among the events earlier incarnations hosted was the first night professional football game ever in 1902.

The stadium still stands and is used mostly for collegiate and other amateur baseball.

Eugene, OR

Stadium name today: None (under redevelopment)

Last stadium name while home to an affiliated team: Civic Stadium

Organized Baseball teams: Eugene Emeralds, Pacific Coast League, 1969-73; Eugene Emeralds, Northwest League, 1974-2009

How I got it: during my project, while getting PK Park in Eugene

The Class A-Short Season Emeralds left Civic for a year-old ballpark in Eugene for the 2010 season (see **Eugene Emeralds [CURRENT]**).

The Works Progress Administration, Chamber of Commerce and school district built Civic in 1938 for football or baseball. Baseball moved to Bethel Park before the Northwest League arrived in 1955. The 1969 MLB expansion returned professional baseball – the bumped Seattle Angels of the Pacific Coast League – but they deemed Bethel too small for Triple-A. The NwL, coincidentally expanding as the Triple-A team moved to Sacramento, returned to Eugene in 1974. In 2008, Civic joined the National Register of Historic Places.

The next year, deteriorating Civic lost the Ems to a new option: PK Park. In 2015, the city and a civic group bought it to create a youth recreational facility. A June fire destroyed the stadium, but the new "Civic Park" is arising from the ashes.

Honolulu, HI

Stadium name today: Aloha Stadium

Last stadium name while home to an affiliated team: Aloha Stadium

Organized Baseball teams: Hawai'i Islanders, Pacific Coast League, 1975-87

How I got it: during my project, while on vacation

The Class Triple-A Islanders left Aloha for an existing ballpark in Colorado Springs, CO, to start the 1988 season, moving into a new one when it opened (see **Rocky Mountain Vibes, San Antonio Missions [CURRENT]**).

The PCL's island experiment, begun in 1960, succeeded far too long to be the inevitable failure some called it when the former Sacramento Solons moved back to the mainland.

Long-standing concessions to logistics included visitors playing their Honolulu season series in one trip. The PCL forced the Islanders to play the entire 1976 championship series on the road – yet they won their second straight crown. Ironically, titles in their first two years at the Aloha marked the beginning of the franchise's decline toward the mainland.

Before the Aloha, the Islanders played at Honolulu Stadium – aka the Termite Palace. They played some 1986-87 games at the University of Hawai'i's Rainbow Stadium – now Les Murakami Stadium.

Idaho Falls, ID

Stadium name today: None (redeveloped)

Last stadium name while home to an affiliated team: McDermott Field

Organized Baseball teams: (then Highland Park) Idaho Falls Russets, Pioneer League, 1940-42; Idaho Falls Russets, Pioneer League, 1946-61; Idaho Falls Yankees, Pioneer League, 1962-63; Idaho Falls Angels, Pioneer League, 1964-75; (renamed McDermott Field) Idaho Falls Angels, Pioneer League, 1976-81; Idaho Falls A's, Pioneer League, 1982-84; Idaho Falls Nuggets, Pioneer League, 1985; Idaho Falls Braves, Pioneer League, 1986-91; Idaho Falls Gems, Pioneer League, 1992; Idaho Falls Braves, Pioneer League, 1993-99; Idaho Falls Padres, Pioneer League, 2000-03; Idaho Falls Chukars, Pioneer League, 2004-06

How I got it: during my project, seeing a game in its replacement

This ballpark was replaced on the same site for the 2006 season (see **Idaho Falls Chukars [CURRENT]**). If you've been to the current ballpark, you've been to the site of this one. In fact, depending how much difference you think makes a "different" ballpark, you may have been to the site of two.

The first stadium here, Highland Park, lost its grandstand to a 1975 fire. The rebuilt stadium opened with the 1976 season, still as Highland Park, but during the 1977 campaign it was renamed for newspaper publisher and baseball booster E.F. McDermott. That's the one that was torn down after the 2005 season.

Jackson, MS

Stadium name today: Smith-Wills Stadium

Last stadium name while home to an affiliated team: Smith-Wills Stadium

Organized Baseball teams: Jackson Mets, Texas League, 1975-90; Jackson Generals, Texas League, 1991-99

How I got it: during my project, while passing through on a work assignment

The Class Double-A Generals left Smith-Wills for a new ballpark in Round Rock, TX, for the 2000 season.

Hall-of-Fame pitcher Nolan Ryan's company bought the Generals to make that move (see **Round Rock Express [CURRENT]**). Five seasons later, the firm bought the Triple-A Edmonton Trappers to move them to the Austin suburb and the Double-A franchise to another new ballpark in Corpus Christi, TX (see **Corpus Christi Hooks [CURRENT]**).

Smith-Wills remains an active baseball field in the Mississippi capital, but the cake-box-style stadium's pro days will likely never return; the Jackson suburb of Pearl has since landed a Double-A team by building Trustmark Park (see **Mississippi Braves [CURRENT]**). I did see baseball here, but not pro ball – the day I stopped by, two American Legion teams happened to be playing.

Knoxville, TN

Stadium name today: None (redeveloped)

Last stadium name while home to an affiliated team: Bill Meyer Stadium

Organized Baseball teams: Knoxville Smokies, Tri-State League, 1954; Knoxville Smokies, South Atlantic League, 1957-63; Knoxville Smokies, Southern League, 1964-67; Knoxville Sox, Southern League, 1972-79; Knoxville Blue

Jays, Southern League, 1980-92; Knoxville Smokies, Southern League, 1993-99

How I got it: during my project, while job-hunting

The Class Double-A Smokies left Meyer for a new ballpark in nearby Kodak, TN, for the 2000 season (see **Tennessee Smokies [CURRENT]**).

Meyer, opened in 1953 as Knoxville Municipal Stadium, was renamed for former major-league catcher and manager Billy Meyer after he died in 1957. Perusing the nicknames in the above history, you won't be surprised to learn two colloquializations: Knox Sox for the Knoxville Sox and K-Jays for the Knoxville Blue Jays. Despite the listed history, Knoxville did have professional baseball in 1953 – but those Knoxville Smokies played at Chapman Highway Park.

Speaking of nicknames, the team has been an independently owned affiliated club most of its history but was owned and operated by the Toronto Blue Jays during their tenure together. The cake-box-style ballpark was demolished after the 1999 season and replaced by a recreational complex that includes amateur baseball fields.

Little Rock, AR

Stadium name today: None (redeveloped)

Last stadium name while home to an affiliated team: Ray Winder Field

Organized Baseball teams: Little Rock Travelers, Southern Association, 1932-55; Arkansas Travelers, Southern Association, 1957-58; Arkansas Travelers, Southern Association, 1960-61; Arkansas Travelers, International League, 1963; Arkansas Travelers, Pacific Coast League, 1964-65; Arkansas Travelers, Texas League, 1966-70; Arkansas Travelers, Southern League/Dixie Association, 1971; Arkansas Travelers, Texas League, 1972-2006

How I got it: during my project, while getting Dickey-Stephens Park

The Class Double-A Travelers left Winder for a new ballpark in North Little Rock for the 2007 season (see **Arkansas Travelers [CURRENT]**).

Opened as Travelers Field in 1932, Winder was originally named for the then-Little Rock Travelers and renamed in 1966 for Ray Winder – who became a ticket taker in 1915, part owner in 1944, and retired in 1965. He repeatedly saved or retrieved professional baseball for Little Rock. After the city lost three Double-A teams in six years, Winder landed Triple-A in 1963. The Travs' 1966 franchise swap with the Double-A Texas League's Tulsa Oilers finally brought stability.

The 12,246 at a 1991 Fernando Valenzuela rehabilitation start remains the state's largest baseball crowd ever.

"The Fenway Park of the South" was torn down in 2012 – except its scoreboard, which now overlooks a hospital parking lot. It had replaced Kavanaugh Field, which opened in 1901 as West End Park.

Louisville, KY

Stadium name today: None (demolished)

Last stadium name while home to an affiliated team: Cardinal Stadium

Organized Baseball teams: Louisville Colonels, American Association, 1957-62; Louisville Colonels, International League, 1968-72; Louisville Redbirds, International League, 1982-99

How I got it: before my project, while passing through

The Class Triple-A Redbirds left Cardinal Stadium for a new ballpark in Louisville for the 2000 season (see **Louisville Bats [CURRENT]**).

Cardinal, the University of Louisville *football* stadium, has an indelible place in Minor League *baseball* history: consecutive Minor League attendance records including a major watermark.

Louisville, without professional baseball since 1971, in 1982 landed the Springfield Redbirds – who had previously failed in Tulsa, OK, and New Orleans, LA. Under the slogan "Baseball – A Great Catch for Louisville!" the Redbirds broke the previous single-season Minor League attendance record, by far, with 868,418. The next season, they became the first Minor League team ever to draw one million in one year: 1,052,438!

Cardinal Stadium was demolished in 2019.

Macon, GA

Stadium name today: Luther Williams Field

Last stadium name while home to an affiliated team: Luther Williams Field

Organized Baseball teams: Macon Peaches, South Atlantic League, 1929-30; Macon Peaches, Southeastern League, 1932; Macon Peaches, South Atlantic League, 1936-42; Macon Peaches, South Atlantic League, 1946-55; Macon Dodgers, South Atlantic League, 1956-60; Macon Peaches, Southern Association, 1961; Macon Peaches, South Atlantic League, 1962-63; Macon Peaches, Southern League, 1964; Macon Peaches, Southern League, 1965-67; Macon Peaches, South Atlantic League, 1980-82; Macon Redbirds, South Atlantic League, 1983; Macon Pirates, South Atlantic League, 1984-87; Macon Braves, South Atlantic League, 1991-2002

How I got it: during my project, while passing through on a baseball vacation

The Class A Braves left Luther for a new ballpark in Rome, GA, for the 2003 season (see **Rome Braves [CURRENT]**).

A 2016 study said Macon *can* support professional baseball and identified eight sites for a new stadium – but didn't specify affiliated or independent ball. Williams was mayor when the ballpark opened in 1929, and it joined the National Register of Historic Places in 2004. A sign at one entrance reading "Macon Base Ball Park" shows not only its original name but its age – yet Macon pro baseball predates it by more than four decades.

Unlike its older sibling – Rickwood Field in Birmingham, AL – it hasn't hosted an affiliated game since losing its Braves. It *has* been a filming location: *The Bingo Long Traveling All-Stars & Motor Kings* (1976), *Trouble with the Curve* (2012), and *42* (2013), plus the first season of the TV series *Brockmire* (2017).

Moosic, PA

Stadium name today: None (redeveloped)

Last stadium name while home to an affiliated team: Lackawanna County Stadium

Organized Baseball teams: Scranton/Wilkes-Barre Red Barons, International League, 1989-2006; Scranton/Wilkes-Barre Yankees, International League, 2007-2011

How I got it: during my project, seeing games in its replacement

This ballpark was replaced on the same site for the 2013 season (see **Scranton/Wilkes Barre RailRiders [CURRENT]**). If you've been to the current ballpark, you've been to the site of this one.

SWB, seemingly a prime location for minor-league baseball, had none 1954-1988. Opened in 1989, this stadium lured the troubled Maine Guides from suburban Portland. The Guides had been sold in 1987 and changed affiliations in 1988. Their new parent was the Philadelphia Phillies, and the SWB Red Barons remained so through 2006. That off-season, the New York Yankees ended their nearly three-decade relationship with the Columbus Clippers and welcomed the Red Barons into their system. The team changed its nickname to Yankees that year and was sold to the Yankees and a partner in 2012.

Nashville, TN

Stadium name today: None (redeveloped)

Last stadium name while home to an affiliated team: Sulphur Dell

Organized Baseball teams: professional baseball was played here as early as 1885, but "affiliated" teams date only to the 1903 founding of Minor League Baseball; Nashville Volunteers, Southern Association, 1903-61; Nashville Volunteers, South Atlantic League, 1963

How I got it: during my project, seeing games in a new stadium on the same site

The Class Double-A Vols folded after the 1963 season, the second collapse of a Nashville Vols team in three years. If you've been to Nashville's current ballpark, you've been to the site of this one.

A marker off right field shows Sulphur Dell's home plate. Opened in 1870, its "Baseball's Most Historic Park" entrance sign was as famous as its short, sloping right field. Originally Athletic Park, it was renamed in 1908 when famed sportswriter Grantland Rice called it Sulphur Spring Dell because it lay in Sulphur Spring Bottom. A month later – in a day that nicknames were informal and fluid – the team began going by "Volunteers" or, more often, Vols.

That September, the Vols won their league crown in "The Greatest Game Ever Played in Dixie" – 1-0 over New Orleans before 10,700. In 1969, Nashville tore down what was then the oldest stadium that had ever housed professional baseball.

New Britain, CT

Stadium name today: Beehive Field

Last stadium name while home to an affiliated team: Beehive Field

Organized Baseball teams: New Britain Red Sox, Eastern League, 1983-94; Hardware City Rock Cats, Eastern League, 1995

How I got it: during my project, while getting New Britain Stadium

The Class Double-A Rock Cats left Beehive for a new ballpark, literally next-door, for the 1996 season (see **Hartford Yard Goats [CURRENT]**).

They played their first season at Beehive under the Hardware City location identifier before becoming the New Britain Rock Cats. The sole reason the Beehive lasted only a dozen seasons was that it didn't meet standards Organized Baseball enacted for its Minor League parks in 1990.

Between the two stadiums, the previously nomadic franchise found stability here before ultimately moving to Hartford. The Yard Goats seem stable there now, but only after losing their intended first season to a construction snafu that kept them on the road throughout the 2016 campaign.

New Orleans, LA

Stadium name today: Mercedes-Benz Superdome

Last stadium name while home to an affiliated team: Louisiana Superdome

Organized Baseball teams: New Orleans Pelicans, American Association, 1977

How I got it: before my project, during a nearby work assignment

The Class Triple-A Pelicans – the last of many New Orleans teams to use that nickname – left the Superdome for an existing ballpark in Springfield, IL.

A. Ray Smith's troubled club fled Tulsa, OK, for NOLA after the 1976 season but stayed only the one campaign – drawing less than 220,000 despite playing in the huge Superdome. After just four seasons in Springfield, it also left there – moving to Louisville, KY, and becoming one of Minor League baseball's most successful franchises (see **Louisville Bats [CURRENT]**.

Smith had acquired the Tulsa Oilers in 1961 and swapped franchises with the Double-A Arkansas Travelers in 1966. The resulting Travelers remain such, but the Oilers moved three times in six years.

Smith lived to see his franchise succeed (wildly) in Louisville, winning MiLB Executive of the Year in 1982 *and* '83. He died in 1999, the year before his team moved into Louisville Slugger Field.

Oakland, CA

Stadium name today: None (redeveloped)

Last stadium name while home to an affiliated team: Oakland Ball Park

Organized Baseball teams: Oakland Oaks, California League, 1913-55

How I got it: during my project, while passing through on a work assignment

The Class Triple-A Oaks left Oakland for an existing ballpark in Vancouver, BC, for the 1956 season (see **Vancouver Canadians [CURRENT]**) – unaware they would soon have been bumped by Major League Baseball's move to the West Coast.

The Oakland facility's actual name is somewhat vague. The commemorative plaque says Oakland Ball Park but various other sources refer to Oakland Baseball Park, Oaks Park, and Emeryville Park. Until the 1920s, the Oaks were commonly owned with the San Francisco Seals and – although this was their official home park – they played many of their home games across the Bay.

Attendance dropped after World War II as the ballpark fell into disrepair, leading to their move to Canada. In 1958, the New York Giants moved to San Francisco – which of course displaced the Seals and would have done so to the Oaks had they still been just across the Bay.

Old Orchard Beach, ME

Stadium name today: The Ballpark

Last stadium name while home to an affiliated team: The Ballpark

Organized Baseball teams: Maine Guides, International League, 1984-86; Maine Phillies, International League, 1987-88

How I got it: during my project, while getting Hadlock Field in Portland

The Class Triple-A Phillies left The Ballpark (yes, its official name) for a new playpen in Moosic, PA, for the 1989 season (see **Scranton/Wilkes-Barre RailRiders [CURRENT]**).

The Ballpark, a quaint suburban facility opened in 1984, was in trouble almost from the first. Its team's unusual business plan had its owner move his failing Charleston Charlies north into a stadium he built to attract summer tourist dollars. It drew well its first two seasons, but the usual the-novelty-wore-off downward arc was accelerated by non-fan ballpark visitors – mosquitoes and flies who feasted on fans.

In 1987, the Guides lost both their parent and their owner when the Indians dropped them for much-closer Buffalo and the team was sold. The new owner affiliated with the Philadelphia Phillies, agreeing to move to Moosic when its new stadium was finished. The Ballpark, renovated in 2010, still hosts semi-pro, college, and tournament baseball.

Omaha, NE

Stadium name today: None (redeveloped)

Last stadium name while home to an affiliated team: Johnny Rosenblatt Stadium

Organized Baseball teams: Omaha Cardinals, Western League, 1949-54; Omaha Cardinals, American Association, 1955-59; Omaha Dodgers, American Association, 1961-62; Omaha Royals, American Association, 1969-97; Omaha Golden Spikes, Pacific Coast League, 1998-2001; Omaha Royals, Pacific Coast League, 2002-10

How I got it: during my project, while getting Werner Park in Papillion

The O-Royals changed nicknames and left Rosenblatt for a new ballpark in suburban Papillion for the 2011 season (see **Omaha Storm Chasers [CURRENT]**), as the NCAA Division I College World Series and Creighton University Bluejays baseball moved into also-new TD Ameritrade Stadium downtown.

Rosenblatt hosted Omaha affiliated baseball 1949-2010 and the CWS 1950-2010 before its 2012 demolition. A colorful 1:1-scale Little League diamond overlaid on its infield – "Johnny Rosenblatt's Infield at the Zoo" – memorializes it within a parking lot for the Henry Doorly Zoo and Aquarium.

The Storm Chasers were the Omaha Royals from their 1969 founding through 2010, except for 1998-2001's "Golden Spikes." Rosenblatt's capacity, 23,100, was the largest in US Minor League baseball. Opened in 1948 as Omaha Municipal Stadium, it was renamed in 1964 for the man who got it built for professional baseball and then landed the CWS. Rosenblatt became mayor in 1954.

Orlando, FL
Stadium name today: None (redeveloped)
Last stadium name while home to an affiliated team: Tinker Field
Organized Baseball teams: Orlando Twins, Florida State League, 1963-72; Orlando Twins, Southern League, 1973-89; Orlando Sun Rays, Southern League, 1990-92; Orlando Cubs, Southern League, 1993-96; Orlando Rays, Southern League, 1997-99
How I got it: during my project, while passing through on a baseball vacation

The Rays left Tinker for an existing ballpark in nearby Kissimmee for the 2000 campaign, but stayed only four seasons (see **Montgomery Biscuits [CURRENT]**).

Tinker joined the National Register of Historic Places in 2004 but was demolished in 2015 to become Camping World Stadium Complex's outdoor concert venue. The stadium's history, commemorated by Tinker Field History Plaza, goes beyond baseball: Martin Luther King Jr. and Billy Graham both spoke here, the former 191 days after pronouncing his dream in Washington and the latter at a 1951 revival. Tinker appears in the film *Parenthood* (1989).

Basically new ballparks opened here in 1914, 1923 and 1963. Hall-of-Famer Joe Tinker – yes, as in "Tinker-to-Evers-to-Chance" – spent his post-baseball life as an Orlando real estate developer. He built the 1923 stadium, the first to take his name, and managed Orlando's first professional ball club.

Paintsville, KY

Stadium name today: None (demolished)

Last stadium name while home to an affiliated team: Johnson Central High School Field

Organized Baseball teams: Paintsville Tri-County Hilanders, Appalachian League, 1978-79; Paintsville Tri-County Yankees, Appalachian League, 1980-81; Paintsville Tri-County Brewers, Appalachian League, 1982-84

How I got it: before my project; I just missed pro ball here but later umpired and did high-school play-by-play at this field

The Brewers folded after the 1984 season.

Longtime WSIP radio owner Paul Pfyffe brought professional baseball to Paintsville in 1978. Originally a co-op team – using players under contract with a Major League parent but assigned outside its regular farm system, along with some free agents – it soon landed the New York Yankees, a true coup in Appalachia.

They left after four seasons, and Pfyffe took the Brewers affiliation from nearby Pikeville. The cities are less than forty miles apart; Pikeville's 1982 entry into the Appy League mitigated the other teams' long road trips to Paintsville. However, the loss of the Yankees hurt the Paintsville franchise, which folded after two more seasons.

Asked the three counties of the locale name, Pfyffe smiled wide and said, "Any three counties you want!"

The ball club played at Johnson Central High School's baseball field, later renamed Paul G. Pfyffe Field.

Pikeville, KY

Stadium name today: Pikeville Athletic Field Complex

Last stadium name while home to an affiliated team: Pikeville Athletic Field Complex

Organized Baseball teams: Pikeville Brewers, Appalachian League, 1982; Pikeville Cubs, Appalachian League, 1983-84

How I got it: before my project, I just missed pro ball here but later did high-school play-by-play at this field

The Cubs left Pikeville Athletic for an existing stadium in Wytheville, VA, after the 1984 season.

Pikeville and Paintsville – less than forty miles apart – have a close, competitive and ironic relationship. Paintsville landed Minor League ball in 1978 but was problematically far from its league mates, which led to Pikeville getting a team in 1982. The Milwaukee affiliate remained so just one season; the Brewers signed with none other than Paintsville after the Yankees left there.

The irony didn't stop there. Yankee-less Paintsville attendance plummeted, and the club folded after the 1984 campaign. Pikeville had joined the Chicago Cubs, who were happy with Pikeville and its fine high school field – but with Paintsville gone Pikeville was well over 100 miles from anywhere else in the league. League directors pressured the Cubs to move, and they were in Wytheville by the first pitch of 1985.

Pittsfield, MA

Stadium name today: Wahconah Park

Last stadium name while home to an affiliated team: Wahconah Park

Organized Baseball teams: Pittsfield Indians, Canadian-American League, 1950; Pittsfield Phillies, Canadian-American League, 1951; Pittsfield Senators, Eastern League, 1970-71; Pittsfield Rangers, Eastern League, 1972-75; Pittsfield Cubs, Eastern League, 1985-88; Pittsfield Red Sox, Eastern League, 1965-67; Pittsfield Mets, New York-Pennsylvania League, 1989-2000; Pittsfield Astros, New York-Pennsylvania League, 2001

How I got it: during my project, while on a baseball vacation

The Class A-Short Season Astros left Wahconah for a new ballpark in Troy, NY, for the 2002 season (see **Hudson Valley Renegades [CURRENT]**).

Wahconah baseball dates to 1892, professional ball to '94. Its wooden grandstand went up in 1919 and was renovated to its current look in 1950. Until the P-Astros left, it was one of only two affiliated ballparks in which batters faced the setting sun. Wahconah and Bakersfield's Sam Lynn Ballpark were built before lights made sunsets a game issue; the California League's 2016 contraction of the Bakersfield Blaze took that number to zero.

A 2004 "vintage" game drew Wahconah's record crowd, about 6,000. It joined the National Register of Historic Places in 2005.

Decades before the original Wahconah, another piece of Pittsfield land was the neutral site of the first intercollegiate baseball game ever: July 1, 1859, Amherst College whipped Williams College 73-32. *That's* old-time baseball!

Pocatello, ID

Stadium name today: Halliwell Park

Last stadium name while home to an affiliated team: Halliwell Park

Organized Baseball teams: Pocatello Gems, Pioneer League, 1984-85; Pocatello Giants, Pioneer League, 1987-89; Gate City Pioneers, Pioneer League, 1990; Pocatello Pioneers, Pioneer League, 1991; Pocatello Posse, Pioneer League, 1993

How I got it: during my project, while passing by on a baseball trip

The Advanced-Rookie Posse left Halliwell for an existing ballpark in Lethbridge, AB, after a single season in Pocatello, ID (see **Missoula PaddleHeads [CURRENT]**).

A new ballpark with the same name but a different site, Halliwell opened in the late 1960s.

Pocatello had professional baseball intermittently 1926-65. In 1987, the Pocatello Giants were, depending on the source, founded or resurrected. While still affiliated with the San Francisco Giants, its owners sold without paying off sizable local debt. The new owners tried to move it to Utah, then lost the Giants' affiliation. The team survived 1990-91 as a "co-op" – an unaffiliated team in an affiliated league – rebranded in 1991 to Gate City Pioneers, changed back in 1992, and folded.

The city got a final season of affiliated baseball in 1993, as the Pocatello Posse, when a Triple-A Pacific Coast League team bumped the Pioneer League's Salt Lake City Trappers to Pocatello.

Port Charlotte, FL

Stadium name today: None (redeveloped)

Last stadium name while home to an affiliated team: Charlotte Sports Park

Organized Baseball teams: Port Charlotte Rangers, Florida State League, 1987-2002

How I got it: during my project, seeing a game in its replacement

This ballpark was replaced on the same site with the same name for the 2009 season (see **Charlotte Stone Crabs [CURRENT]**). If you've been to the current ballpark, you've been to the site of this one.

Over the two spans, its teams have used both Charlotte and Port Charlotte as locale names. This is perhaps not confusing to locals, who know both the city of Port Charlotte and Charlotte

County, but nomads like me must take care not to conflate this Charlotte with Charlotte, NC, baseball. (Yes, I did that once – but I caught it in time.)

Provo, UT

Stadium name today: Larry H. Miller Field

Last stadium name while home to an affiliated team: Larry H. Miller Field

Organized Baseball teams: Provo Angels, Pioneer League, 2002-04

How I got it: during my project, while getting UCCU Ballpark in Orem

The Rookie-Advanced Angels left Miller for a new ballpark in Orem, UT, for the 2005 season (see **Orem Owlz [CURRENT]**).

Miller hosted them for only four seasons, as the Provo Angels, and was never intended to be their permanent home. The Helena Brewers had been trying to move to Provo since 1999, but the Utah city had been unable to build a ballpark. LHM became a small but temporary option when the H-Brewers agreed not to sell beer, allow tobacco or play at home on Sundays in the heavily Mormon state.

Provo never got a ballpark deal done, leading the Angels to move to Orem when Utah Valley University built and shared a bigger collegiate ballpark.

Rockford, IL

Stadium name today: Marinelli Field

Last stadium name while home to an affiliated team: Marinelli Field

Organized Baseball teams: Rockford Expos, Midwest League, 1988-92; Rockford Royals, Midwest League, 1993-94; Rockford Cubbies, Midwest League, 1995-98; Rockford Reds, Midwest League, 1999

How I got it: during my project, while passing through on a baseball vacation

The Class A Reds left Marinelli for a new ballpark in Dayton, OH, for the 2000 season (see **Dayton Dragons [CURRENT]**).

Marinelli opened in 1988, but when I visited there in 2014 I guessed the cake-box-like ballpark to be considerably older. It's also misaligned by about forty-five degrees, putting the setting sun in the eyes of some of the fans.

Perhaps I should say *some* of the fans; its teams never met attendance expectations. Even the first two seasons that were, as usual, the highest of its run were well short of projections. After the 1997 season, the franchise was sold to buyers who affiliated it with the Cincinnati Reds in 1999. They planned to move the team to Ohio that off-season, but construction delays pushed the move into the 2000 campaign.

Salem, VA

Stadium name today: Kiwanis Field

Last stadium name while home to an affiliated team: Municipal Field

Organized Baseball teams: Salem Rebels, Appalachian League, 1955-67; Salem Rebels, Carolina League, 1968-71; Salem Pirates, Carolina League, 1972-80; Salem Redbirds, Carolina League, 1981-86; Salem Buccaneers, Carolina League, 1987-95 (partial)

How I got it: before my project, while seeking advice on getting into play-by-play

The Advanced-A Avalanche left Municipal for a new ballpark, less than a mile away, in August 1995 (see **Salem Red Sox [CURRENT]**).

Kiwanis opened as Salem Municipal Field in 1932. I visited it during a 1980s off-season. Talking with a staffer, I remember resting my foot on a low wall with crumbling and even missing bricks.

Kiwanis Field hosts college, high school and other amateur games. It doesn't look renovated, just repaired. Municipal had been around over twenty years when it drew its first professional team, the Rebels of the Appalachian League. They joined that circuit with no parent club – just in time to miss their sophomore campaign as the league took a year off before going short-season. Remaining "Rebels" through Giants' and Pirates' partnerships, the last affiliated Appy team that didn't use its parent's nickname folded to make way for the current Carolina League club.

Salt Lake City, UT

Stadium name today: None (redeveloped)

Last stadium name while home to an affiliated team: Derks Park

Salt Lake City Bees, Pioneer League, 1940-42; Salt Lake City Bees, Pioneer League, 1946-57; Salt Lake City Bees, Pacific Coast League, 1958-65; Salt Lake City Giants, Pioneer League, 1967-68; Salt Lake City Bees, Pioneer League, 1969; Salt Lake City Bees, Pacific Coast League, 1970; Salt Lake City Angels, Pacific Coast League, 1971-74; Salt Lake City Gulls, Pacific Coast League, 1975-84; Salt Lake City Trappers, Pioneer League, 1985-92

How I got it: during my project, seeing a game in its replacement

This ballpark was replaced on the same site for the 1994 season (see **Salt Lake Bees [CURRENT]**). If you've been to the current ballpark, you've been to the site of this one.

Opened in 1940, it replaced a nearby ballpark that fell to an arsonist. *Salt Lake Tribune* Sports Editor John C. Derks was not only the driving force in getting it built but was himself a local sports icon. Originally Community Park, it was renamed for Derks in 1946.

This stadium hosted the home games of the longest winning streak in professional baseball history: The unaffiliated 1987 Salt Lake City Trappers won twenty-nine consecutive games, longer than even the longest MLB streak of twenty-six by the 1916 New York Giants.

San Francisco, CA

Stadium name today: None (redeveloped)

Last stadium name while home to an affiliated team: Seals Stadium

Organized Baseball teams: San Francisco Seals, Pacific Coast League, 1931-57; Mission Reds, Pacific Coast League, 1931-37

How I got it: during my project, while passing through on a work assignment

The Class Triple-A Seals left their namesake for an existing ballpark in Phoenix, AZ, for the 1958 season (see **Tacoma Rainiers [CURRENT]**). (Today's Phoenix Municipal Stadium, opened in 1964, is a same-site replacement of that park, a 1937 Works Progress Administration project.) MLB's move west bumped them, but Seals hosted the San Francisco Giants 1958-59 while they awaited Candlestick Park.

The Mission Reds also played at Seals 1931-37 before becoming the Hollywood Stars. The site is now a shopping center, but the Double Play Bar & Grill dates to the stadium days. The Seals having been a dynasty, it has much history – but probably the biggest belongs to an individual: Joe DiMaggio's less famous hitting streak, sixty-one straight PCL games in 1933.

If you decide to take a picture of the spot, don't park in the shopping center lot without wasting ten minutes reading the verbose signage.

San Juan, PR

Stadium name today: Sixto Escobar Stadium

Last stadium name while home to an affiliated team: Sixto Escobar Stadium

Organized Baseball teams: San Juan Marlins, International League, 1961 (partial)

How I got it: during my project, while on vacation

The Class Triple-A Marlins left Escobar for an existing ballpark in Charleston, WV, during the 1961 season (see **Charleston, WV [LEGACY]**).

This franchise had an amazing four different homes in three years, partly because of the Cuban Revolution. US interests leaving the island included the Havana Sugar Kings baseball team, and IL team owners initially thought keeping a team in the Caribbean was a good idea. The Miami Marlins obliged by moving to San Juan, but bookkeeping changed the other owners' minds. Forced back to the mainland, the Marlins played the rest of that season in Charleston, WV, before moving to Atlanta as the Crackers in 1962.

The ballpark was later converted to soccer, with baseball moving to Roberto Clemente Stadium. I've also visited that, but of course it never hosted any US affiliated team.

Scranton, PA (see Moosic, PA)

Spartanburg, SC

Stadium name today: Duncan Park

Last stadium name while home to an affiliated team: Duncan Park

Organized Baseball teams: Spartanburg Spartans, South Atlantic League, 1926-29; Spartanburg Spartans, South Atlantic League, 1938-39; Spartanburg Peaches, Tri-State League, 1946-55; Spartanburg Phillies, Western Carolinas League, 1963-79; Spartanburg Phillies, South Atlantic League, 1980-81; Spartanburg Traders, South Atlantic League, 1982; Spartanburg Spinners, South Atlantic League, 1983; Spartanburg Suns, South Atlantic League, 1984-85; Spartanburg Phillies, South Atlantic League, 1986-94

How I got it: during my project, while passing through on a work assignment

The Class A Phillies left Duncan for a new – in fact, partially finished – ballpark in Kannapolis, NC, for the 1995 season (see **Kannapolis Intimidators [CURRENT]**).

If Duncan Park still had full-season affiliated baseball, it might be the oldest able to say that. It opened in 1926, and although it's been renovated nearly a dozen times over the decades – that's why I say "might" – when I visited it in 2015, it still looked like both a ballpark of its era and a ballpark that could host Minor League play. Some of the 1990 standards would require upgrades, but it looks serviceable. If you like classic old ballparks, in fact, it looks wonderful.

Toledo, OH

Stadium name today: None (redeveloped)

Last stadium name while home to an affiliated team: Swayne Field

Organized Baseball teams: Toledo Mud Hens, American Association, 1909-13; Toledo Mud Hens, Southern Michigan League, 1914; Toledo Iron Men, American Association, 1916-18; Toledo Mud Hens, American Association, 1919-52; Toledo Sox, American Association, 1953-56

How I got it: during my project, while passing through on a work assignment

The Class Triple-A Sox left Swayne for an existing ballpark in Wichita, KS (q.v. **[VISITED]**), after the 1956 season.

The Milwaukee Brewers, bumped by the Boston Braves, had become the Toledo Sox in 1953. Swayne's more famous occupant, the Toledo Mud Hens, moved to Charleston, WV, during the 1952 season.

Swayne was demolished in 1955, but part of the left-field wall still stands at Swayne Field Shopping Center. More than just a monument to the old field, it remains the first *concrete* outfield wall ever erected for a US baseball field.

In 1914, the Cleveland Naps pulled their Swayne-based farm club to the other side of Lake Erie to block the Federal

League from using League Park when they were away. The Fed folded after the 1915 season, and the now-Indians sent their farm club home – as the Toledo Iron Men. They revived "Mud Hens" in 1919.

Victoria, TX

Stadium name today: Riverside Stadium

Last stadium name while home to an affiliated team: Riverside Stadium

Organized Baseball teams: Victoria Eagles, Big State League, 1956; Victoria Rosebuds, Big State League, 1957; Victoria Rosebuds, Texas League, 1958-60; Victoria Toros, Texas League, 1974; Victoria Cowboys, Gulf States League, 1976; Victoria Rosebuds, Lone Star League, 1977

How I got it: during my project, while passing through on a baseball vacation

The Class A Rosebuds folded with the Lone Star League, an effort to revive the Gulf States League that had failed a season before.

Victoria danced around the edge of affiliated ball throughout the twentieth century, fielding ten teams between 1910 and 1977. Riverside, which opened in 1947, hosted the last eight – starting with the 1956 Victoria Eagles of the Big State League.

When a transferring Triple-A club bumped the Memphis Blues, that Double-A Texas League club went to Riverside in 1974. However, a financially poor season plus a new stadium in Jackson, MS (q.v. **[VISITED]**), equaled a quick end to the Victoria Toros.

I've dropped by twice but haven't gotten inside; from its parking lot, it looks like a ramshackle joint that might be fun to play in but probably wouldn't be very serviceable for fans. It is also blue. Very blue.

Waterbury, CT

Stadium name today: Municipal Stadium

Last stadium name while home to an affiliated team: Municipal Stadium

Organized Baseball teams: Waterbury Timers, Colonial League, 1947-50; Waterbury Giants, Eastern League, 1966-67; Waterbury Indians, Eastern League, 1968-69; Waterbury Pirates, Eastern League, 1970-71; Waterbury Dodgers, Eastern League, 1973-76; Waterbury Giants, Eastern League, 1977-78; Waterbury Athletics, Eastern League, 1979; Waterbury Reds, Eastern League, 1980-83; Waterbury Angels, Eastern League, 1984; Waterbury Indians, Eastern League, 1985-86

How I got it: during my project, while passing through on a baseball weekend

The Class Double-A Indians left Municipal for an existing ballpark in Williamsport, PA, for the 1987 season (see **Williamsport Crosscutters [CURRENT]**).

Municipal opened in 1930 and first hosted an affiliated team in 1947. I passed by it in 2015 and am relieved to learn it has since hosted a Mickey Mantle World Series. That suggests the facility I saw was either under renovation or was later renovated, rather than being in the kind of disrepair that hurts a baseball heart.

It's unusual for a professional-level park in two ways – conventional seats along the first-base side but only bleachers on the third-base side, and a stone front that looks – pleasantly – like something out of the Middle Ages.

Empty of Minor League ball in 1972, Municipal hosted the second half of the Elmira Pioneers' home schedule after flooding at their Dunn Field.

Wichita, KS

Stadium name today: None (demolished)

Last stadium name while home to an affiliated team: Lawrence-Dumont Stadium

Organized Baseball teams: Wichita Indians, Western League, 1950-55; Wichita Braves, American Association, 1956-58; Wichita Aeros, American Association, 1970-84; Wichita Pilots, Texas League, 1987-88; Wichita Wranglers, Texas League, 1989-2007

How I got it: during my project, while passing through on a baseball vacation

The Class Double-A Wranglers left L-D for a new ballpark in Springdale, AR, for the 2008 season (see **Northwest Arkansas Naturals [CURRENT]**).

L-D hosted fifteen Triple-A seasons before the Wichita Aeros moved to Buffalo, NY (see **Buffalo Bisons [CURRENT]**), after the 1984 campaign. Long thought too historic to replace yet the reason Wichita lost affiliated ball, it was demolished after the 2018 season for a new facility for the Triple-A New Orleans Baby Cakes.

Opened in 1934, L-D gained fame with the National Baseball Congress World Series. The last College World Series outside Omaha, NE, was played here in 1949, but professional ball came in 1950.

During construction, the NBCWS was at Wichita State University's Eck Field. *The Wichita Eagle* reported in July 2019 some future Series games will continue at Eck. The new park is to house an NBC museum – although *Eagle* reporting has also cast doubt on that.

Epilogue: Is a Quantum Shift Coming?

As mentioned at the beginning of Chapter 8, **The Structure**, a troubling wind arose just as we started the production process for this book.

Minor League Baseball has been shrinking for decades – but not lately. During the 1940s "post-war baseball boom," the number of Affiliated Baseball clubs was well into the 400s. When I started my quest, it was 160. At some point, MiLB agreed to hold the number of teams at what it was at the time, with the exception of any necessitated by MLB expansion. That means, of course, there was some fluctuation in the slide from 400+ to 160. The expansion era, which began in 1960, took the number of big-league clubs from twenty-four to thirty – and each of the six new teams created a farm system of at least six teams.

I knew the Professional Baseball Agreement that codifies how MLB and MiLB work together in the hierarchy that has developed since 1903 was to expire at the end of the 2020 season. I had even discussed with a friend the possibility that the next agreement would shrink the four short-season levels from a total of forty teams to thirty to match the MLB complement. Actually, that 2018 conversation began in a much darker way, as I idly wondered if the Majors might dump the Minors in favor of the football/basketball model of letting the collegiate game develop young talent. My friend's instant rejection of that made me back off to taking out twenty-five percent of the short-season affiliated teams.

Also, the PBA is usually a quickly created formality. The last time it created any heat was 1990, when the Majors insisted on standards for ballparks in the Minors. Predictably, MiLB owners pleaded poverty. MLB owners insisted, pointing out that minors teams had become money-makers and that if they improved their facilities they would probably further improve their gates. As already discussed, this probably generated the wave of new ballparks that started in the early 1990s – and since that time the typical MiLB team's value has gone up considerably.

So, I decided I was worrying about nothing.

Then it became something. Something big. On the same 2019 off-season day, *Baseball America* and *The New York Times* reported that Major League Baseball had proposed to Minor League Baseball that the number be dropped to 120. That's *more than* twenty-five percent – not of the short-season affiliated teams but of Affiliated Baseball!

Why? While the number of fine stadiums in the Minors is very much up, a good many remain short of the 1990 standard; after thirty years, I can imagine MLB feels as if it's pulling teeth. When I worked in the Appalachian League one of our talking points said about fifteen percent of our players would play in the Majors; we meant that as a positive, to counter those saying none of our guys would play in the bigs, but crunching the dollar numbers suggests it isn't very cost-effective for the parent team paying the salary and expenses.

A couple of weeks after the original story broke, the *Times* fleshed it out. The number of vanishing teams was being variously reported as 40 or 42, and that turned out to be because MLB indeed wanted to contract 42 existing teams but pull two very nice stadiums in independent baseball and put affiliated teams in them. Those are reportedly in St. Paul, MN, and Sugar Land, TX – and given the constraints of geography, MLB protection zones, league footprints, etc., it appears to me St. Paul could only be the Minnesota Twins' Triple-A club and Sugar Land could only house the Houston Astros' Triple-A or Double-A team.

Class A-Short Season loses eleven of its twenty-two teams and Rookie-Advanced loses seventeen of its eighteen, with the survivors becoming full-season teams in what would be an entirely full-season system.

Initially, I thought this was as I characterized it earlier: a beginning proposal in a long negotiation. Two troubling quotes have changed that. 1) Several media outlets report MLB told MiLB something to the effect of "We're doing this with or without you, and if you don't agree we'll simply start our own minor leagues." 2) One minor-league team president says MLB told him this is just a first step, with a five-year goal of having only ninety teams in three levels: Class Triple-A, Class Double-A, and a single level of Class A (which currently has, as you know, three levels).

This initial proposal would see twenty-eight of the forty teams in the four short-season affiliated leagues disappear. The Appalachian League, New York-Penn League and Pioneer League would no longer exist. The other short-season circuit, the Northwest League, would be elevated to full-season in the new Class A – after jettisoning two of its teams. Nine of the New York-Penn League's fourteen teams would go, as would nine of the Appalachian League's ten clubs and all eight Pioneer League teams.

No one in Triple-A would fold, but the Pacific Coast League's Fresno Grizzlies would drop from Triple-A to the high-A California League. Four Double-A teams – the Binghamton Rumble Ponies, Erie SeaWoves, Chattanooga Lookouts, and Jackson Generals – would go. The same number of Class A-Advanced teams are on the block: the Daytona Tortugas, Florida Fire Frogs, Lancaster JetHawks, and Frederick Keys. Finally, six full-season Class A clubs would vanish: the Burlington Bees, Clinton LumberKings, Hagerstown Suns, Lexington Legends, West Virginia Power, and either the Beloit Snappers or the Quad Cities River Bandits – depending on whether the underway effort to build a new ballpark in Beloit succeeds or fails.

Triple-A wouldn't be completely unaffected. To reduce travel costs, the Pacific Coast League would lose four to six of its sixteen teams. All but Fresno would either go into a much-expanded International League or into one or the other of the IL or a new, third, Triple-A circuit.

It's called "the Houston plan," because Astros management developed and proposed it. Perhaps most troubling of all, Major League owners voted for this proposal 30-0.

One thing not being reported may be, in my opinion, quite significant. MLB teams are currently required to field at least one team in each full-season level, period. That is not a maximum, although no one currently has more than one. There is neither minimum nor maximum on short-season teams. Including the non-affiliated entry level, every MLB club has between two and six short-season teams – so a total of between six and **ten** farm teams. The proposal in play would not only eliminate affiliated short-season ball but also limit each MLB team to one farm team in each of the remaining five levels. This would limit every system to five teams and 150 minor-league players. Not only would this limit payrolls, it seems to me it would move MLB toward future parity.

If that's part of the Majors' true purpose, this is a zero-sum game and any team that regains its berth will bump another.

Minors owners are screaming bloody murder, of course. Some of their points are well taken. A couple of things, though: I'll bet we've heard every one of those points during every contraction while the Majors – whether or not by design – drew the Minors down from 400+ to 160.

The usual suspects from politics to the press are on the case, and almost no one but the thirty MLB owners seems to favor this. It's not a democracy, though. This is a business, and this piece of the business is funded by MLB owners who have every right to spend their money as they see fit.

If the model of 1903 no longer works to the benefit of both sides, things will change – and the side with the money will drive the changes. Whether exactly this way remains to be seen.